BERLIN AND THE COLD WAR

BAKER SERIES IN PEACE AND CONFLICT STUDIES

Edited by Ingo Trauschweizer

BERLIN
AND THE
COLD WAR

Edited by SETH GIVENS AND INGO TRAUSCHWEIZER

Foreword by Walter Momper

OHIO UNIVERSITY PRESS

ATHENS

Ohio University Press, Athens, Ohio 45701
ohioswallow.com
© 2024 by Ohio University Press

To obtain permission to quote, reprint, or otherwise reproduce or distribute material from
Ohio University Press publications, please contact our rights and permissions department
at (740) 593-1154 or (740) 593-4536 (fax).

Printed in the United States of America
Ohio University Press books are printed on acid-free paper ∞ ™

Library of Congress Cataloging-in-Publication Data
Names: Givens, Seth A., editor, author. | Trauschweizer, Ingo, editor, writer of introduction
| Momper, Walter, writer of preface.
Title: Berlin and the Cold war / edited by Seth Givens and Ingo Trauschweizer ; foreword
by Walter Momper.
Description: Athens : Ohio University Press, [2024] | Series: Baker series in peace and
conflict studies | Includes bibliographical references and index.
Identifiers: LCCN 2023046877 (print) | LCCN 2023046878 (ebook) | ISBN 9780821425343
(paperback) | ISBN 9780821425350 (pdf)
Subjects: LCSH: Berlin Wall, Berlin, Germany, 1961–1989. | Cold War. | World poli-
tics—1945–1989. | Berlin (Germany)—History—1945–1990. | BISAC: HISTORY /
Modern / 20th Century / Cold War | HISTORY / Europe / Germany
Classification: LCC DD881 .B4226 2024 (print) | LCC DD881 (ebook) | DDC
943/.10879—dc23/eng/20240227
LC record available at https://lccn.loc.gov/2023046877
LC ebook record available at https://lccn.loc.gov/2023046878

CONTENTS

Part II. Crisis, 1958–1971

Part III. Beyond the Cold War in Berlin, 1972–1990s

ILLUSTRATIONS

MAPS

PLATES

Following page 132

FOREWORD

If you ask someone to describe Berlin today as compared to Berlin thirty years ago, how do you think they would respond? The clear visual differences are striking: no wall dividing our city and people, no tense military presence near Checkpoint Charlie, no Trabant cars lining the streets of the east. Areas of Berlin that once clearly marked our separation through guard towers, barbed fences, and desolate landscapes are now bustling with business, life, and an incredibly diverse culture.

Today Berlin, the capital of a country once divided by war and strife, stands as a sign of unity. Here the remnants of the wall that once separated us stand as a stark reminder of how far we have come and how we can continue toward the future. Berlin remains and will always be a German city at heart, but much of its strength and allure around the world is in its openness. Here we see not just unity of East and West Berlin, but an ever-present and free-flowing diversity of people, industries, and knowledge, among so much more.

BERLIN: FALL OF WALL TO TODAY

Reunification was not easy. While many took immediate advantage of the newfound freedoms afforded by the fall of the wall, there was also confusion and immense uncertainty. Yes, now we were again one nation, but what did that mean? What did it look like? What were we, as once separate governments, now to do in order to bring our people together safely and efficiently?

After the initial elation following Günter Schabowski's announcement on November 9, 1989, it was unclear if reunification was an actionable and sustainable goal for Germany. As my predecessor Willy Brandt had said so eloquently in our joint appearance at Schöneberg Town Hall on

November 10: *"Jetzt wächst zusammen, was zusammen gehört"* (Now things that belong together grow together). We were unsure that night if this growth would mean unity, confederation—or a wilderness of two Germanys, growing apart and growing together, all at once. The voices within East Germany were speaking of different goals, and the SED, the East German Communist government, was still in power. It wasn't until Chancellor Helmut Kohl himself was in East Germany weeks later, seeing a sea of citizens chanting and carrying signs advocating for unification, that he saw it as a reality. It was no longer a small echo chamber rallying for freedom; it was the will of the people.

We had previously met Schabowski to discuss the easing of border crossing restrictions, and we entered November 1989 with plans to mitigate the potential influx of those from the GDR. It was the hope on both sides that while initial numbers under the new rules might be high, we could still find ways to mitigate the flurry of entrants. Of course, we could not have predicted how the events of that November 9 evening would actually transpire. Without those preparations, however, an already chaotic night could have shifted into something else entirely.

In our strategizing, plans were coordinated with police, public transport, and doctors, among others, that would see the immediate effects of changes to the previous wall crossing regulations. When it became clear that things were taking an unexpected turn, we all found we had to balance the pure jubilation that engulfed the city with hastily modified plans to allow for both safe passage and celebration.

Politicians in Berlin and across Germany had to work swiftly, and smartly toward official reunification. It was crucial to tout, not only to the country itself but to the world, the ability of Germany to successfully reunite. How could we show that we were ready to reunite, end the international occupation in Berlin, and run as a functioning and productive nation on our own?

While the international community played clear roles in the forced division of Berlin, it also greatly impacted our perception of the world, and vice versa. Not to be understated, however, is the influence, throughout the Cold War, of changing popular culture around the world.

Rock 'n' roll, for example, having reached international peaks outside the US and UK, evoked a certain type of attitude that particularly resonated with young people—quite a shift from the more traditional values both sides were attempting to enforce, a quintessential pillar of rock music being freedom of expression. Through dancing, clothing, music, art, and more, the common thread of this culture was to live freely and break down barriers.

Naturally, as it goes with this zeitgeist of rock 'n' roll, young people did not want to be told otherwise. Between the difference in rights of East and West citizens and the clear, physical threats of the East German secret police (Stasi) and Berlin Wall, they were surrounded by constant reminders of all the restrictions in their daily lives. For East Berliners this meant an inability to see family and friends in the West, as well as a mandated aversion to anti-Communist sentiments and popular culture. For the young adults seeking a different future, this was one of many justifications for fleeing.

While much of what transpired during and after the Cold War in Germany became increasingly geared toward the will of Germans, the progress to today would not have been possible without international support. Yes, we in Germany had the physical presence of Allied manpower throughout the country, but support through aid and education programs, and through garnering more allies in the international community, was invaluable to our continuing evolution.

US-GERMAN RELATIONSHIP BUILDING

As a nation, the US has continued to evolve and reinvent itself. It's a nation that is one of the largest melting pots in the world, as it has many dimensions of people to serve and focus on. No one should want to live in a monolith, nor should we ever. This American model, while not perfect, was vital to crafting a unified Germany as a coming together of different cultures from the East and West. Beyond the visible effort of American soldiers physically in Germany, there were a number of ways the US government also sought to extend its support within the Marshall Plan.

German feelings around the presence of US troops were also in some ways "reinvented" throughout the Cold War as well. After World War II, we were not sure how we could possibly build relations with militaries who were, until recently, the main forces against Germany. While the US was acting as a liberator in many ways, it would take more than its word, and ours, to reach the level of trust and understanding that we have today. But as American soldiers integrated more into German life, building friendships and romantic relationships with Germans, they showcased their consistent dedication to helping rebuild Germany, and that initial uncertainty slowly washed away. As well as the financial and other support provided by the US government, many of the soldiers who were in Berlin played pivotal roles in building this trust.

Even the young American soldiers who arrived in the 1970s and '80s and who did not physically fight in the war had this trust and admiration grandfathered into them. They came to Germany, defended the freedom of all its citizens, and, most important, stayed to see the recovery through. This was not, however, an entirely selfless act, as the US, along with France and the United Kingdom, wanted to stave off the spread of Communism by the USSR. It was, however, one that showed dedication to our much-needed rebuilding and sustainability efforts.

One of the earliest signs of the dedication and commitment of the US on a large-scale was the resolute response to Stalin's Berlin blockade. When West Berlin saw its first major isolation event of food, resources, and other necessities to live, there was a fear that this would finally be what drove the Americans away, leaving Germans to the fate of the Soviets. In a clear showing of their commitment, the US did not retreat or leave West Berliners to a surely untenable fate. Their government gathered allies and resources to come up with a plan to circumvent the isolation and ensure West Berlin had the food and supplies it desperately needed to survive. The success of this US-led effort was heavily doubted in the beginning. Many questioned how they could possibly strategize and support such a grand effort, which originally sought to transport over three thousand tons of goods a day. The Allies worried that West Berliners would desert them and start to buy their groceries in East Berlin. As there was no wall yet, crossing the border meant taking the subway or the S-Bahn. Berlin was a city divided on maps only. It was my predecessor, Ernst Reuter, mayor of Berlin, who united the West Berlin citizens to take on the struggle the Kremlin had brought upon the western part of Berlin.

When the airlift initially started, as with almost any quickly constructed plan of this capacity, there were quite a number of problems when it came to reaching transport goals. Even with people flying almost around the clock and ground crews attempting to swiftly coordinate it all, there was clearly room for improvement. And yet, even then, enthusiasm in West Berlin and Western Europe around these efforts was starting to boom. Once American

Maj. Gen. William Turner stepped in to revise the plan and increase productivity, there was no going back. Flight numbers soared, as did supply tonnage and efficiency across the board. Turner also opened the venue for Germans to work alongside the Allies in this effort. Serving as ground crews to help with unloading and repairmen for the airfield, the Germans very quickly helped increase the turnaround time of planes coming in and out of Berlin. An amazing showing of international collaboration, the Berlin Airlift included flight crews from Australia, Canada, New Zealand, and South Africa, who helped sustain this round-the-clock effort.

Perhaps the most famous story to come out of the airlift was Operation Little Vittles. Small chocolates have perhaps never held such power as when they were dropped by international pilots soaring over Tempelhof into the appreciative hands of West Berlin children. Not only did this ease the tensions of Germans toward their former wartime enemies, but it also showed the impact "small" actions can have to brighten even the darkest days. While this operation quickly became news around parts of Europe, it also became an opportunity for regular Americans to show support and solidarity.

As Germans softened to the presence of Allied forces occupying their country, so did many Americans and other skeptical international communities reconceptualize their views of Germans. During and immediately after World War II, there had been an understandable feeling of resentment toward Germany and its people. Incredibly, however, as both countries worked toward a communal goal, the Berlin Airlift and Operation Little Vittles provided a common ground for stymieing this animosity.

With Col. Gail Halverson as the bright, smiling face of Operation Little Vittles, Americans rallied to provide as much candy and handkerchief cloth as they could muster. Children and adults alike know the joy candy can bring, and quickly sought ways to support this effort. From average Americans donating chocolates and money, to large corporations like linen manufacturers and the Hershey Company donating in bulk, and a mostly volunteer-run headquarters for shipping in Massachusetts—this was truly a nationwide effort in America. Beyond the immense success of these undertakings, they were undoubtedly acts of citizen and international diplomacy that set a palpable line of trust between Germans and Americans.

* * *

As a nation that has seen much change over the past hundred years, Germany has faced a somewhat unparalleled question of how, and to what extent, this past should be acknowledged. To say nothing and try to evolve without any recognition of our past actions would be unconscionable. As new generations continue to grow up knowing only a unified and progressive Germany, it is important that they be aware and cognizant of the grave consequences of jingoism and isolationism in Germany and the world.

I want to extend a great thank-you you to the Ohio University Contemporary History Institute for putting on the symposium on which this volume is based, and Prof. Ingo Trauschweizer and Dr. Seth Givens for making it all happen. The transitions of Berlin and Germany from the Cold War to today are not just relevant to my country or Europe, but to the world. It is also crucial to have a grasp of the United States' role in this transformation as a basis for understanding our continued, strong allyship today. As we are still learning from our past and navigating our future, we hope some of the lessons we've learned can be universal. And those who don't retain or take these lessons to heart only serve as motivators and reasons for why we refuse to shadow the history of Germany. Or, as voiced by two renowned authors—one from America, one from East Germany—who echo each other in transatlantic unity:

The past is never dead. It's not even past. (William Faulkner)

Das Vergangene ist nicht tot; es ist nicht einmal vergangen. Wir trennen es von uns ab und stellen uns fremd. (Christa Wolf)

Walter Momper
Governing Mayor of Berlin, 1989–91

MAP 1. Occupation zones. Courtesy of the US Army Center of Military History

MAP 2. Occupied Berlin, 1945. Courtesy of the US Army Center of Military History

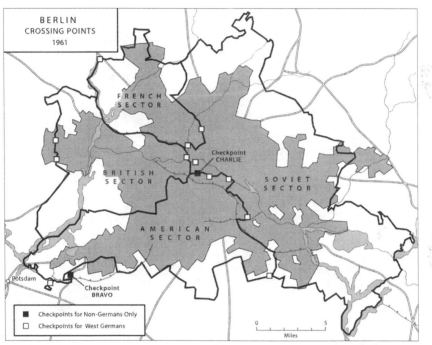

MAP 3. Berlin crossing points. Courtesy of the US Army Center of Military History

INTRODUCTION

INGO TRAUSCHWEIZER

The Cold War is back in the news. So is history, perceived as past geopolitical confrontations.[1] Such reflexive reactions lack nuance, of course, and
until the full-scale Russian invasion of Ukraine in February 2022, tended
to refer more to tensions between the US and China.[2] Neither is Russia's
aggressive war in Ukraine immediately part of a new cold war—though it
could certainly become one of its foundation pieces—nor should one define
history simply in terms of warfare and conflict. And yet, recent history has
great appeal in efforts to understand the dizzying and depressing events of
recent years. For example, correspondents and commentators have likened
the delivery of weapons systems, protective gear, and humanitarian aid to
a beleaguered Ukraine to the Berlin Airlift of 1948–49.[3] The question may
be to what extent relying on history as a guide has the potential to mislead
as much as to enlighten. Such issues were already on the horizon when we
met for an October 2021 symposium to discuss the history of the Cold War
through the lens of one of its most affected front-line cities and from the
perspective of Western and East German policy and strategy. Berlin, we
thought, could offer a host of questions, and maybe also a few lessons.[4]

There is no city that symbolizes the Cold War quite as much as Berlin.
When we think of it, we tend to emphasize the crises—the 1948–49 blockade and airlift, perhaps the 1953 East German workers' uprising, surely the

1

1958–61 crisis during which the Berlin Wall was built—and the climactic ending of the Cold War in Europe when the wall came down. We may conjure up iconic moments and tropes, from a statement attributed to Nikita Khrushchev in 1963 that Berlin was "the testicles of the West," where applying pressure hit home with greater pain, to John F. Kennedy's insistence that all free men had to be invested in the defense of Berlin and Ronald Reagan's insistence that "Mr. Gorbachev" ought to "tear down this wall."[5] For American presidents (or presidential hopefuls), Berlin and the Brandenburg Gate remained a powerful image even in the twenty-first century.[6] It is no coincidence that the great orators among US presidents since the end of the Second World War sought out the spot. Appearing there signals the strong leadership of the West, even though the proximate reasons why the West, as a political construct, emerged in the first place may be gone. In that sense, Berlin also stands for overcoming the past: first, West Berlin as the counterpoint not only to Eastern Communism but also to defeated fascism, and the new Berlin as the capital of a unified Germany and as a symbol that the West has won.

That latter proposition is hotly contested, of course. When a young State Department officer posited the notion, in 1989 as a question and in 1992 as an exclamation, that history itself had ended, he surely missed the mark (as Francis Fukuyama has since acknowledged himself).[7] He did, however, recognize a sea change: the end of the Cold War did appear to signify the end of a century shaped by a great power competition that had been enhanced in its brutality by powerful and destructive ideologies. The latter had been swept into the dustbin of history, but what about the former? And what—power or secular faith—had been the more important strain? Would great power competition reemerge, or had we entered an age in which nonstate actors and global networks provided the paradigm of the next enemy? As of the 2020s, the answer appears to be that both may yet be the case; while we cannot say for sure, we should continue to sharpen our sense of history, as a guide to the present and because there is much left to be discovered. *Berlin and the Cold War* provides fresh perspectives on the original Cold War that should help us engage with historical and contemporary questions.

The chapters in this volume chart a new path forward for the study of Cold War frontiers, aiming to balance the rising awareness of the conflict in and over the Global South with the need to keep a close eye on one of the hottest spots of the 1940s, 1950s, and 1960s, and the city that became a symbol for the Cold War's end in 1989.[8] Today's news often suggests that we're entering into a new cold war—maybe with China? Or with Russia? Or with regional actors such as North Korea and Iran? The details are uncertain, and it is unclear whether the comparison fits, but we believe that Berlin during the Cold War offers pointers for our contemporary world. Many of the challenges the West faces today are unresolved issues from the 1940s and 1950s, including the division of Korea, the status of Taiwan and questions of control in the South China Sea, and the sovereignty of countries that border Russia, particularly Ukraine. These areas, like Berlin during the Cold War, test Western resolve and unity, and there is an underlying sense of renewed conflict between liberal and authoritarian states. Berlin, as a case study for Cold War strategy of superpowers and their allies, for crisis management and diffusion, and for the policies that defined nearly five decades of the postwar period, thus could offer a window into past and present. Historian Sergey Radchenko, for example, makes the case that the standoff between Russia and NATO could be seen though the mirror of the 1961 Berlin Wall crisis, and he suggests that the crisis's long trajectory, from Nikita Khrushchev's 1958 ultimatum to solve the status of Berlin to the gradual de-escalation in late 1961 and 1962, may offer a way forward for Vladimir Putin and European and US leaders.[9] Sadly, the war that has since intensified makes this seem rather optimistic, though long-term conflict management could still offer a way to contain and even de-escalate warfare.

Complicating these challenges are questions of the durability of liberal democracies in Europe and the United States, a brazen Russia that meddles in Western polities and sends armed forces to rein in its neighbors (in Georgia and Transnistria and now also Ukraine), and the emergence of a mighty Communist Party–led China. There may be new frontiers, notably cyberspace: *Washington Post* national security correspondent David Ignatius argued in August 2021 that we are already in a cyberwar with Russia. But is it the same old enemies and dynamics that shaped the second half of the twentieth century?[10] This volume aims to inform present discussions of a "new cold war," consider what is yet to be learned from the Cold War in one of its most iconic locales, and point at the need to keep in mind that even as the Cold War became a global event that turned on a north–south axis, it also retained the East-West conflict dynamics that had led to renewed tensions, around geopolitics and ideologies, after 1945 in the first place. In so doing, we need to acknowledge that we still know much more about the actions and motivations of Western actors than of their Soviet and Eastern Bloc counterparts. The chapters that follow proceed to consider the Cold War in Berlin and its wider ramifications in three parts: the emergence of renewed conflict and the Berlin crises in the 1940s and 1950s; climactic crisis and greater stability in the middle decades of the Cold War; the way it ended and its implications for the contemporary world.

Samuel Miner places West Germany's relationship with Berlin, the former capital that was now technically not fully part of the new state, in the context of its integration in a Western economic, defense, and political sphere. This allows us to consider the nuances that lay between a Cold War policy of threatening retaliation against any government that recognized the new East German state and careful avoidance of any revanchist statements that could have echoed Germany's historical and recent drive to the east. Miner argues that the emerging de facto division of Berlin from summer 1945 served as an indicator for a wider separation of two German states that was then codified in 1949. He considers the status of Berlin and West German attitudes through both party-political and legal-constitutional lenses and concludes that attitudes of leading postwar politicians toward Berlin and the East rested on their experiences in the Weimar Republic, when political power in the city and its environs had been firmly held by Social Democrats. In the context of the evolving Cold War, local leaders in West Berlin managed to accomplish much the same as the West German government in Bonn, and their city became part of the Western economic system; and even though it could not be integrated into NATO structures, it was nevertheless supposed to be defended by American, British, and French armed forces. The Berlin question served both Christian Democrats, like Chancellor Konrad Adenauer, who could demonstrate tacit acceptance of the postwar division of Germany, and those Social Democrats, like Berlin mayors Ernst Reuter and Willy Brandt, who could show their commitment to West Germany's new transatlantic orientation, a policy initially challenged by SPD leaders in the late 1940s and early 1950s, who had clung to unification and to hopes of recovering what had once been their party's heartland.

The Western position in Berlin never seemed defensible by armed forces on the ground. And yet, the presence of American, British, and French soldiers was of more than merely symbolic importance. In chapter 2, Seth

Givens discusses how the US Army conceived of the nearly impossible task of defending Berlin in the early days of the Cold War era. He contends that we overlook critical developments if we strictly follow a periodization that considers the 1948–49 crisis resolved once the Soviet blockade of all land and water routes to the western sectors of Berlin had been lifted. Widening the lens to include the year that followed on blockade and airlift, Givens explores army plans that showed an increasing intertwining of political with operational and tactical considerations. It was in 1949–50 that American assets in Berlin came to be integrated under the office of the first US Commandant, Berlin (USCOB). Prior to late summer 1949, the commander of US Army forces in Berlin had held no direct sway over diplomacy or policy decisions. With General Maxwell Taylor's appointment in August, that changed. American officials also incorporated the western sectors into NATO plans, therefore making the defense of the city a matter of transatlantic security. That did not make Berlin any more defensible by scant American, British, and French armed forces in the city, but it increased the deterrent effect of their presence.

Christian Ostermann takes a fresh look at the June 1953 uprising in East Berlin and East Germany. He notes that a million people participated in the spontaneous protests, which were immediately perceived as a Cold War crisis by Soviet and German Democratic Republic (GDR) leadership. While Moscow had, in the wake of Joseph Stalin's death in early March, attempted to persuade the East German leader Walter Ulbricht to improve conditions for workers, Ulbricht had hardened his policies, which had derived from Stalin's own directives. The US, meanwhile, had spent several years building a capable intelligence network in Berlin, then still an open city that allowed Westerners access to East Berlin (and vice versa). Ostermann argues that organizations built or supported by the US government and the widely broadcast, American-funded Radio in the American Sector (RIAS) radio station were important actors in rallying protesters. RIAS, Ostermann shows, fueled the fire once the protests had begun, but Allied officials in Berlin and the Eisenhower administration in Washington feared that events could spiral out of control. Their caution became a first indicator that the aggressive 1952 campaign rhetoric of "rolling back Communism" quickly became a pragmatic and more defensive form of containment that was not so different from Harry Truman's policies in the late 1940s and early 1950s. At the same time, Dwight Eisenhower and Secretary of State John Foster

Dulles increased emphasis on psychological operations and active intelligence work in East Germany. The question for Washington was just how much one could poke the bear. For Moscow and for Ulbricht it was a matter of reasserting control in the wake of a heavily militarized suppression of the June 17 protests.

Susanne Muhle's chapter approaches the early Cold War from the perspective of the GDR and considers abductions from West Berlin by East German agents. Muhle demonstrates both the insecurity of the East German regime in the 1950s and the difficulties of protecting people in the western sectors of a still open city. We know, of course, that prior to the swelling stream of defectors that prompted East German officials to push for much harder borders, and eventually for the Berlin Wall, people who lived in East Berlin could visit the western sectors. We are less familiar with Stasi operations in the West and the fact that that these, albeit much more frequent in the 1950s, continued for years after the wall had gone up. By the mid-1960s, East German agents had managed to abduct four hundred people; twenty-four of them were tried and executed and ten more died in prison, while others remained imprisoned in East Germany for years, a few being released in intra-German exchange of Western funds for political prisoners. Those abducted included suspected intelligence operators as well as critics of the GDR regime. As the Stasi's focus from the mid-1950s shifted more and more toward internal dissenters, abductions slowed but did not stop after 1961. Considering that most of the abductees had once left East Germany introduces the additional element of a sense of betrayal and chasing defectors from within their own ranks was the primary reason for post-wall abductions. This was always governed by disproportionality: as Muhle notes, the threat posed by defectors who worked with Western intelligence or anti-Communist groups was far less than what East German agents and their leaders perceived.

Erin Mahan, in her chapter centered on the Berlin Wall crisis and the limits of NATO's ability to respond to crises within the Eastern bloc more generally, notes that we are better served thinking of Berlin and the first decade and a half of the Cold War as a perennial conflict rather than bookend our assessment with the 1948–49 and 1958–61 crises. In that respect, what happened in the Berlin blockade and Berlin crisis are punctuation points in an evolution—and after the wall went up and the Cuban Missile Crisis had passed in 1962, the trajectory turned toward lower-key confrontation for the remainder of the 1960s. Mahan considers in depth the Western response in 1961, when a young and untested US president (John F. Kennedy) and seasoned British and West German leaders (Harold Macmillan and Konrad Adenauer) had to find common ground and when French president Charles de Gaulle, still in the midst of a debilitating war in Algeria, served as a major obstacle to transatlantic unity. Yet even if the Allies had been more unified in their outlook and questions of a strategy shift—from Massive Retaliation to Flexible Response—and contentious calls by Washington that the alliance needed to greatly increase its conventional military strength weren't already on the horizon, NATO armed forces in summer 1961 were in no position to respond forcefully to further escalation of the crisis in Berlin, all contingency plans notwithstanding. What resolved the immediate crisis in summer 1961, then, was the wall itself, born from internal divisions in the Eastern bloc, a point explored by Hope Harrison in this volume. Yet, as Mahan shows, the divisions within the alliance and the increasingly tense Franco-American relationship made it more difficult to resolve perennial problems (burden sharing) or to convert American of French designs into plausible policies. If the wall eventually did signal weakness in the Eastern bloc, the Berlin crisis also demonstrated the challenges for NATO's deterrence strategy.

Hope Harrison reflects on the significance of the Berlin Wall from the initial crisis in 1958–61 to the present day. Looking at the crisis in Berlin, she shows just how much East Germany's leaders, most notably Walter Ulbricht, drove the agenda that led to the building of border fortifications in and around Berlin in summer 1961. There, the Berlin Wall took on immense material and visual importance—it became the embodiment of Cold War divides and frontlines. Over time, it became a symbol, exploited by presidents in the Cold War and thereafter. We are, Harrison implies, back in a time when the Cold War seems a useful guide, and she explores how Ukraine's president, Volodymyr Zelensky, used the Berlin Wall in his address of the German parliament to project a new divide, farther to the east, and to exhort German policymakers to greater exertions on behalf of a free and democratic Ukraine in its struggle for survival against a hostile invader. The memory of the wall and commemoration of those who died trying to cross the border from East into West Germany also served as a place of healing, and that has helped since 1989 to bring two halves of Berlin and of Germany closer together. That is not the entire story, however:

Harrison also notes that the role of the East German armed forces in a peaceful transition in 1989 has not been fully acknowledged, nor have the divides between East and West healed all that well. In Germany and across Europe, the Berlin Wall as a symbol could thus serve as a reminder that one should not take freedom and democracy for granted, but that they remain powerful and attainable.

Thomas Schwartz considers the decade after the wall went up from a political and strategic perspective. He notes that we tend to oversimplify: the immediate crisis may have ended in 1961 or, perhaps, 1962, if we assume that Berlin was one of the touchstones for the Cuban Missile Crisis, but long-standing conflict between East and West did not, and neither were tensions within the Western alliance resolved. For the administrations of Lyndon B. Johnson and Richard M. Nixon, both of whom sought forms of détente with the Soviet Union in the midst of a disastrous war in Vietnam as well as a costly nuclear arms race, Berlin was as much a problem as it was an opportunity. Yes, the West could still rally around it as a symbol of freedom, but that rhetoric and symbolism offered challenges to détente, and Berlin itself remained as vulnerable as ever. Even in the generally amicable relationship of the United States and West Germany, the question of Berlin's future loomed large, as did concerns in the Nixon White House that West Germany's newly defined openness to engagement with the Soviets and Eastern Europe (*Ostpolitik*) was at best naive and at worst foolish. Here, too, Berlin loomed large, since the architects of Ostpolitik, Chancellor Willy Brandt and his adviser Egon Bahr, had risen through the Social Democratic Party in that city and Brandt had been its lord mayor. Schwartz argues that the 1971 Quadripartite Agreement, which redefined the status of Berlin, was the most significant, yet often overlooked, aspect of the Cold War in central Europe after 1961. While the agreement was ostensibly an accord reached by the US, Soviet Union, France, and United Kingdom, Schwartz shows that it was the result of bilateral high-level negotiations between Moscow and Washington. He concludes that an agreement that seemed to enhance the Soviet position and weaken West German authority in Berlin stabilized an environment in which political resolve and economic prowess favored the West.

Stephan Kieninger picks up the story in the early 1970s. He argues that West German Ostpolitik became a centerpiece of the Cold War in Europe, and to the fate of Berlin, because commerce and economics rather than military or even nuclear questions came to be more crucial in the 1970s and 1980s. In all, he depicts a history of cooperation and calm, just as Cold War tensions were heating up again and the nuclear arms race seemed to be reignited. The most prominent example was the agreement to build the first of the natural gas pipelines from the Soviet Union to Western Europe that have taken on renewed controversy in 2022. Even though détente as a policy framework may have died, for the US, by the late 1970s, it persisted as pragmatic economic engagement in Europe, and West German chancellors from different political parties (Willy Brandt, Helmut Schmidt, and Helmut Kohl) all followed the same guiding principles. There was, for Western Europe at least, no "second cold war," even if the deployment of Pershing II intermediate-range missiles and nuclear warheads and the response of the West German antiwar movement or the nuclear war scare of fall 1983 that followed from NATO's Able Archer exercise may suggest otherwise. By looking at 1983 from a different angle, Kieninger shows progress in East-West relations at this seeming acme of Cold War tensions. Berlin, he argues, as a hub had become essential to that development, and the two German states, empowered by the Quadripartite Agreement, could negotiate cultural exchange without having to turn to the superpowers. Foreign affairs, and intra-German relations, had been normalized.

Peter Ridder interprets the end of the Cold War in Berlin as a moment when different visions for a reunited Europe emerged in Washington and Bonn and merged into one after the wall fell in November 1989. What started as an American New Atlanticism, driven by fear of losing influence, and West German proposals for a peace order for Europe led to a framework that tied a future unified Germany to the institutions of the Western alliance (NATO and the European Community) and led to the recognition by West German president Erich von Weizsäcker that sovereignty now rested in the alignment of the state to Western values and international organizations rather than the monopoly of violence. Ridder concludes that the joint German American vision, worked out primarily by Secretary of State James Baker and Foreign Minister Hans-Dietrich Genscher in 1990, also helped subdue alternative frameworks pursued by France (President Mitterrand's goal of a European confederation) and the Soviet Union (Mikhail Gorbachev's common European house). The resulting peace order, however, included eastward expansion of both the European Union, which soon emerged from the European Community, and NATO. That process was never free of tensions with Russia, and it has become one of the touchstones of Russia's aggression in Ukraine. Ridder suggests that the post–Cold War European order may now be at an end and the pressure on the Western alliance to restore peace in Europe is high.

Matt Cornish explores post-wall Berlin and shifts our focus onto the cultural realm. He discusses theater as a form of political activism in Berlin after the fall of the wall, as the city came to symbolize for many observers a major shift in German and world politics, one toward unity and a future defined by liberalism. Cornish finds that playwrights and artists instead emphasized fears and exposed darker pasts, reminding audiences of Prussian militarism and the brutality of the Nazi regime, strongly suggesting that the new Germany could be much like the old. Artists who had come of age in East and West Germany may have held different visions of past, present, or future, but they shared a sense that unification had to be more than a political act of removing borders and that Germans could not simply adopt an identity defined by the triumph of the West or by fraught national identity that predated the split of the second half of the twentieth century. Berlin, of course, had been a hotbed of political theater in the Weimar Republic, and the 1990s seemed to revive that tradition. As the process of unification appeared more like a Western takeover of a failed state, plays performed in Berlin grew sharper in their critique of elites. Theater, Cornish concludes, offers a vital function in society: it calls out the worst excesses and corruptions while offering the hope that the future can be different. He suggests that this can be transplanted onto the question of a new cold war, which Cornish deems unlikely.

These chapters buttress a general argument that current events should lead us to revisit and reinterpret subjects like the Cold War. When we talk of a "new cold war" we need to better understand the comparative point of reference, and looking at it through the lens of Berlin offers an opportunity to do so. The history of Berlin in the Cold War might have garnered a reputation as old and settled in the context of the war on terror and while Americans (and much of the world) were focusing on the Middle East and central Asia, but it is now once again highly relevant. Geography has not changed, nor have the key players: East-West confrontation, the purpose and resolve of the transatlantic alliance, and the role that the US and Germany play in questions of international security in Europe are at the forefront at the time of this writing as much as they were fifty or seventy years ago. This volume, because it covers five decades of history, offers readers a variety of analogues to today's pressing questions: operations short of war, superpower diplomacy, alliance politics, burden sharing, proxy war, crisis management, culture and cultural exchange, the power of symbolism, and conflict resolution. Our original intent was to show that Berlin offered more in Cold War studies than a case study in the crises, and it just so happened that current events made this a more immediately and viscerally present issue.

We owe sincere gratitude to sponsors who allowed us to host the symposium from which this book derived: Checkpoint Charlie Foundation (Berlin), the German foreign office and its consulate at Chicago, the Society for Military History, and at Ohio University the Baker Peace Studies Program and the Contemporary History Institute (CHI). Seth Givens thanks his employer, the US Marine Corps Histories Division, for allowing him to pour time and energy into this book. Ingo Trauschweizer thanks the students, staff, and faculty at CHI and in the History Department at Ohio University who have provided the creative environment necessary for projects such as this.

NOTES

1. The widely shared supposed *Time* cover of February 28, 2022, which proclaimed "the return of history," was a fake, but the sentiment itself seems to have hit the mark among Europeans and North Americans. Reuters Fact Check, "Fact Check—Time Magazine Cover Comparing Putin to Hitler Was Created by a Graphic Designer," Reuters, February 28, 2022. https:// www.reuters.com/article/factcheck-time-magazine-hitler-putin/fact-check -time-magazine-cover-comparing-putin-to-hitler-was-created-by-a-graphic -designer-idUSL1N2V32V3.

2. Hal Brands and John Lewis Gaddis, "The New Cold War: America, China, and the Echoes of History," *Foreign Affairs,* November/December 2021, https:// www.foreignaffairs.com/articles/united-states/2021-10-19/new-cold-war.

3. "Arming Ukraine: 17,000 Anti-Tank Weapons in 6 Days and a Clandestine Cybercorps," *New York Times,* March 6, 2022, https://www.nytimes.com/2022 /03/06/us/politics/us-ukraine-weapons.html.

4. Hal Brands, *The Twilight Struggle: What the Cold War Teaches Us about Great-Power Rivalry Today* (New Haven, CT: Yale University Press, 2022) applies a lessons-driven methodology to the global Cold War.

5. Andreas W. Daum, *Kennedy in Berlin* (Cambridge: Cambridge University Press, 2008); Ronald Reagan, "President Reagan's Address at the Brandenburg

Gate," Ronald Reagan Presidential Foundation and Institute, June 12, 1987, https://www.reaganfoundation.org/library-museum/permanent-exhibitions/berlin-wall/from-the-archives/president-reagans-address-at-the-brandenburg-gate/.

6. For two speeches Barack Obama gave in Berlin, in 2008 while in the Senate and seeking the presidency, and in 2013 as US president, see "Transcript: Obama's Speech in Berlin," *New York Times,* July 24, 2008, https://www.nytimes.com/2008/07/24/us/politics/24text-obama.html; and the White House, Office of the Press Secretary, "Remarks of President Obama at the Brandenburg Gate—Berlin, Germany," June 19, 2013, https://obamawhitehouse.archives.gov/the-press-office/2013/06/19/remarks-president-obama-brandenburg-gate-berlin-germany.

7. Francis Fukuyama, "The End of History?," *National Interest,* no. 16 (Summer 1989): 3–18; and *The End of History and the Last Man* (New York: Free Press, 1992).

8. For recent global histories of the Cold War, see Odd Arne Westad, *The Cold War: A World History* (New York: Basic Books, 2017); and Lorenz M. Lüthi, *Cold Wars: Asia, the Middle East, Europe* (Cambridge: Cambridge University Press, 2020).

9. Sergey Radchenko, "The Berlin Crisis, Ukraine, and the 5 Percent Problem," *War on the Rocks,* December 22, 2021, https://warontherocks.com/2021/12/the-berlin-crisis-ukraine-and-the-five-percent-problem/.

10. David Ignatius, "An Undeclared War Is Breaking Out in Cyberspace: The Biden Administration Is Fighting Back," *Washington Post,* August 10, 2021, https://www.washingtonpost.com/opinions/2021/08/10/an-undeclared-war-is-breaking-out-cyberspace-biden-administration-is-fighting-back/.

PART I

POSTWAR TO COLD WAR, 1945–1957

CHAPTER 1

Gone but Not Forgotten

The Status of Berlin and the Founding of the West German State,
1944–1952

SAMUEL MINER

The quote attributed to Konrad Adenauer, West Germany's first chancellor, that "Asia stands at the Elbe," reveals a great deal about West German political and legal attitudes toward Berlin in the 1950s. According to this dictum, Berlin, an oasis in Soviet-occupied territory, was about a hundred kilometers east of Adenauer's imagined East-West civilizational border.[1] West Germany—run by a government led by the Christian Democratic Union (CDU) in the first two decades of its existence—pursued a policy of Western integration with great haste, thereby abandoning the pretense of a near-term reunification of Germany. As West Germany in short order joined the European Coal and Steel Community (1951) and the Council of Europe (1951), following thereafter with an aborted attempt to join the European Defense Community (1952) and eventual accession into NATO (1955), the West German state further abandoned any immediate Eastern aspirations.[2]

The author would like to thank Felix Lieb and Jan Neubauer for their thorough comments on this chapter, and the anonymous readers for their responses.

Although not happy about the division of Germany and the loss of what was formerly Prussia east of the Oder-Neiße line, much less the division of Germany—after all, Adenauer and his cabinet pursued a policy of threatening any country that diplomatically recognized East Germany, called the "Hallstein Doctrine"—Adenauer did not make revanchist claims about the borders a central pillar of his policies.[3] This was a seismic shift for a leader of a German conservative party, and Adenauer was the right person to lead the change. From a Catholic Rhenish milieu, his antagonism toward Prussia and his federalist tendencies were clear enough; however, as the leader of a major German conservative party, abandoning nationalist revanchism was no easy feat, given that defeat and occupation were prime breeding grounds for nationalist sentiment. The "drive to the east" (*Drang nach Osten*) had been a cornerstone of the German nationalist policy held by most German conservatives since the nineteenth century.

Instead of Eastern aspirations, Adenauer focused on Western orientation and Western union, in the hopes that a united West would present the greatest bulwark against Soviet expansionism and secure a swift return of sovereignty and economic prosperity to postwar West Germany. Adenauer made every attempt to work with the Western Allies to regain German sovereignty and understood that nationalist saber-rattling would do little more than upset the Allies.[4]

This narrative of Western integration and a grudging acceptance of the division of Germany requires two addenda. First, the division did not begin with the founding of East and West Germany, but during the Second World War, and it was cemented by the founding of two states in 1949. The "Berlin question" must be analyzed, first and foremost, as a problem from the end of the Second World War until the return of sovereignty to the West German state and the rejection of Joseph Stalin's spurious offer to reunite the country based on neutrality in 1952.[5] That is to say, the "Berlin question" is a problem of the occupation period before Adenauer came to power. For German political parties of the immediate postwar, questions of federalism versus centralism animated legal-constitutional debates during West Germany's foundation. The federalism debate in Germany often centered around supposed "Prussian centralism" versus west-and-south German regionalism and federalism. Berlin, as the former capital, was the site of a fierce contest over the responsibility of "centralism" versus "federalism" as an explanatory paradigm for German Nazism. Second, while the country was ruled by the CDU after the 1949 elections, the Social Democratic Party (SPD) held a sizable minority and asserted substantial influence over the founding of the county. It maintained a critical opposition to Adenauer's policies toward Berlin as well as toward Western integration, for fear that it would forestall the reunification of Germany.

For the SPD, the loss of eastern Germany was an acute issue. Despite stereotypes about Prussian militarism, the eastern parts of Germany had been strongholds of Social Democratic political activism since the Wilhelmine era. The eastern state of Thuringia had been the founding location of one of the SPD's predecessor parties and a home to the mining labor unions of Germany. For the duration of the Weimar Republic, "Red Prussia" and its capital city of Berlin had been ruled almost without exception by the SPD.[6] The loss of these territories meant losing the electoral heart of the party. Kurt Schumacher, the SPD's first party leader after World War II, made German national unity a primary issue of the immediate postwar. After the signing of the Petersberg Agreements handing some sovereignty over to West Germany, Kurt Schumacher even labeled Konrad Adenauer the "Federal Chancellor of the Allies" in the West German parliament for not fighting hard enough for German national unity.[7] Given the long history of conservative nationalism in Germany, it was paradoxically the postwar SPD leadership who made the issue of national reunification a central pillar of early national politics. At the same time, the Berlin SPD, under the leadership of the mayors of Berlin Ernst Reuter and Willy Brandt, fought for an integration of West Germany and West Berlin into the Western economic and (eventually) military alliance.

In the chapter that follows, I will focus on West German attitudes toward Berlin in the immediate postwar, concentrating on the political debates among and between the two major parties of postwar West Germany (CDU and SPD) about the legal status of Berlin. I argue that while postwar mainstream West German conservatism turned toward the West and its political leaders fought against German nationalism by embracing a smaller, federalist, culturally more conservative West Germany as part of a European project, postwar West German social democracy fought for a unified West German state with the hope of a speedy reunification with (West) Berlin as the capital of a new struggle against Stalinism. Berlin as an "outpost of freedom" rather than the capital of a defeated Nazi state was born in the struggle between postwar social democracy and Stalinism over the city of

Berlin but had roots in a longer prewar history of shared left/liberal and social democratic activism in exile that sought to remake social democracy in the postwar.[8]

HISTORICAL BACKGROUND

Many of the leaders of postwar West Germany began their political lives in the Weimar Republic, so it provides a good starting point for a discussion of Berlin. In the chaos after the defeat of the First World War, the young mayor of Cologne Konrad Adenauer was first faced with a crisis about federalism and western Germany's relationship to Prussia. Under the banner of the predecessor party to the CDU—the Center Party—many Catholic politicians in the Rhineland supported the creation of a West German state carved out of the Prussian Rhine Province, which had been added to Prussia in the nineteenth century. The Prussian Rhine Province was under French occupation after the end of the First World War, and the independence movement and Adenauer's reaction to it show the complex interplay of domestic and foreign relations in twentieth-century German history.

Prime among the domestic fears of Adenauer and other conservatives was the possible victory of a Soviet-inspired Bolshevik movement in Berlin in 1919.[9] In the early months of 1919, the Spartacist uprising in Berlin rocked the country, as members of Germany's nascent Communist party did try to overthrow the socialist-led government of Friedrich Ebert. Even though Ebert and his coalition socialist government put down the Spartacist uprising with great force—thereby leading to an irrevocable split between German Communism and social democracy—German conservatives feared that a socialist coalition government was the first step toward a Bolshevik Germany.[10] This would become a recurring theme for many German conservatives. To them, Berlin was a place of cultural degeneracy and supposedly "foreign" political agitation. Among the radical right, Berlin became a main target for anti-Semitic propaganda, as the city's numerically larger Jewish population and its leftist politics were seen as prime examples of the domestic threat of "Judeo-Bolshevism," which would become a staple of Nazi propaganda.[11]

Adenauer never made such statements about Berlin, but he did confess his tepid support for a "Rhenish" state in a speech to the "Left Rhine Representatives to the Weimar National Assembly" in February 1919. For

Adenauer, the issue of creating a "West German republic" was of a dual nature: it was about securing the right foreign and domestic circumstances. Regarding foreign policy, Adenauer began his speech by laying out the possible situations for Germany's "hereditary enemy," France. France, according to Adenauer, could not forever rely on disarming Germany but instead required "real, worthwhile guarantees." None was more important than the creation of a "strategic border at the Rhine River." A "chauvinistic" French policy would make the Rhine a political border state, while a "moderate" French policy would make the Rhine a buffer state. It was up to the United States and the UK to convince France of the proper course to follow, as Germany was powerless in the negotiations. Adenauer believed the United States was in the grips of anti-German propaganda but was hopeful that the French-British entente would fall apart after the war over empire and the European balance of power. Regarding the Rhineland, Adenauer laid great hope at the feet of the British that they would hinder France's punitive claims.[12]

This brought Adenauer to the domestic situation behind the Rhineland independence movement. Here, Adenauer's aversion to Prussian power became more apparent: "A splitting of Prussia is in my opinion absolutely necessary and will happen." Without it, Prussia would become a "hegemonic state" that, absent a monarchy, would assert control over the Rhineland even though Prussia was "made up of very different economic areas and tribes (*Stämmen*)." Adenauer did not believe the independence movement in the Rhineland was an artificial creation, but rather "arose from the innermost essence of the *Volk* (*innersten Wesen des Volkes*)."[13] Independence from Prussia was not a political necessity but rather a reflection of the inherent differences between the Rhineland and easternmost Prussia. Adenauer did not expand on what "innermost essence" meant, though the context suggests that the religious and political differences were so great as to make continued union impossible.

Given these internal and external pressures, Adenauer called for a "*West German Republic in Union with a German Empire* [emphasis in original]" that would appeal to "Germany's enemies," who thought that "Prussia [was] the evil spirit of Europe, in their eyes the shelter of uncivilized, pugilistic militarism."[14] Adenauer was adamant that this was only the view of Germany held by its enemies, but he was equally adamant that only a splitting of Prussia would allow for a peaceful, internationally recognized solution to Germany's post–World War I problems.

In contrast to Konrad Adenauer, Kurt Schumacher—the first leader of the West German Social Democrats after World War II—was thoroughly socialized in Prussian politics. Born in Kulm, West Prussia (modern day Chełmno, Poland), Schumacher, so severely wounded in the First World War that he lost an arm, completed his legal studies in Berlin at the end of the war and joined the Berlin SPD during the heady days of the November Revolution.[15] Other future leading members of the SPD were also engaged with Berlin at this point. Ernst Reuter, the future mayor of Berlin during the Berlin blockade, was in fact a member of the German Communist party and at that point fought for the overthrow of the Weimar Republic before he had a decisive break with the party in the early 1920s.[16] Louise Schröder, the Social Democratic mayor of Berlin before Ernst Reuter, also moved to Berlin from Hamburg and taught at a labor welfare school and a university, while maintaining her mandate in the Reichstag from Hamburg Altona; she held these posts until she received a "professional ban" after the Nazi seizure of power.[17]

Such biographies were typical for Social Democratic politicians in the Weimar Republic. As the heart of political activity in the Republic, Berlin also attracted the interest of the Nazi Party in the latter half of the 1920s. As leader of the Berlin section of the Nazi Party, future propaganda minister Joseph Goebbels battled throughout the 1920s to build support for National Socialism in the traditionally leftist city of Berlin. Through a combination of violent street brawling begun by Nazi paramilitary SA men and seizing on the crisis of liberal democracy and capitalism caused by the Great Depression in 1929, the Nazi Party went from 1.4 percent of the Berlin electorate in 1928 to 12.8 percent of the vote in 1930 (still well under their national electoral average of 18.3 percent).[18] Although other parts of Germany showed decidedly more support for National Socialism, and Prussia remained a Social Democratic state, the "breakthrough election" of 1930 also brought the Berlin Nazi Party into the center of the Berlin political arena.

After the Nazi seizure of power in 1933, Adolf Hitler bestowed on Munich the honorary title of "capital city of the movement," consolation for the fact that Berlin would be the capital of the new "Third Reich." Throughout the Nazi dictatorship, Berlin embodied the heart of National Socialism. The large boulevards of the government district became crowded with discrete Nazi ministries, each of which would vie for more power with the expansion of the German empire. The decision-making heart of the

Nazis' war of aggression and genocide of Europe's Jews was found alongside the large government buildings of the Wilhelmstraße with the SS, Gestapo, and Reichssicherheitshauptamt (RSHA) buildings on the adjacent Prinz-Albrecht-Straße. Tiergartenstraße 4 on the southern side of the Tiergarten park would become the namesake and headquarters of the T4 Program of medical murder of the mentally handicapped. The RSHA security apparatus of the Nazi state chose the leafy suburb of Wannsee to host the conference that coordinated all government ministries into the European-wide dimensions of the Holocaust. During the bombing campaign against Germany, the British Bomber Command placed great importance on the psychological effect of bombing the German capital and striking at the Nazi leadership and their offices. All told, the Western Allies conducted more than three hundred bombing raids on Berlin, often timed to coincide with events led by high-ranking Nazis.

After the Second World War turned against the Nazis, Berlin became the great prize for the Allied powers: whichever power could reach Berlin first could claim to have destroyed the heart of the Nazi empire. That honor went to the Soviet army after the Battle for Berlin. The fanatical defense of the Nazi capital showed just how much the city had become a symbol of Nazism. The Battle for Berlin cost both sides together 120,000 military killed in action and over 500,000 casualties. More than 20,000 civilians were also killed in the battle.[19]

Looking at Berlin from the perspective of the Allies in May 1945, it is very difficult to imagine that only three years later both the Western Allies and the Soviets would be fighting a propaganda war over which part of the German city better represented their respective systems. It was during the occupation and the early days of the Cold War that Berlin went from being the city of fanatic Nazi resistance to the centerpiece of Cold War drama. While it is true that the city would come to develop a Cold War meaning for the erstwhile Allied powers, its place in German politics also had a great deal to do with the Nazi past.

BERLIN IN THE POSTWAR

In the immediate postwar, Germans did not control the fate of Berlin. Rather, it was the Allies who had already decided on many of the important points. In Tehran the Big Three agreed to create the European Advisory

Commission, which worked in 1944 to create the borders of the Allied occupation zones. It was the Soviets who suggested a tripartite division of Berlin,
which the Anglo-Americans agreed to in fall 1944. At the Yalta Conference
in 1945, Stalin agreed to give the French a zone of occupation in the West
and in Berlin (out of the US and British sectors) and the leaders of the three
countries ratified the divisions of Germany and the capital city of Berlin.[20]

When the Western Allies allowed for the re-creation of parties in their
zones during the summer and fall of 1945, the old disagreements about the
city of Berlin reemerged with the added dimension of the Nazi past. Much of
the party/political divergence between the Social Democrats and the Christian Democrats in attitudes toward Berlin can be explained by different
causal explanations for the rise of National Socialism and the supposed role
of Berlin in that process, set against the backdrop of earlier federalist and
regionalist sentiments. Party leadership is again illustrative in this regard. In
March 1946, Konrad Adenauer gave one of his first speeches as the leader
of the CDU in the British Zone of Occupation, in front of students in
Cologne. In that speech, Adenauer tried to explain how National Socialism
"found in broad segments of the population a poison seed." To Adenauer,
"the German Volk suffered on all strata from a false understanding of the
state, of power, and of the position of the individual." Historically, this
flawed conviction "spread from Prussia after the Wars of Liberation [1813–14
against Napoleon]. Then it conquered the whole of Germany after the victorious war of 1870/1871."[21] Prussia's victory was a victory for a mentality of
state worship.

The victory of Prussia also enabled the victory of a "materialistic worldview," according to Adenauer. The rapid industrialization of the country
only possible under Prussian tutelage brought an "associated up-rootedness
of the people [that] made the path free for the rampant devastation of the
materialistic worldview in the German people." Adenauer's next sentences
are worth quoting in length, because they reveal something about how he
connected National Socialism to Marxism, and how he would make the
jump from a "materialistic worldview" to a condemnation of Berlin:

> The materialistic worldview of Marxism contributed to this develop-
> ment to a very large extent. Whoever strives for a centralization of
> political and economic power with the state or with a class, is an en-
> emy of the freedom of the individual. He inevitably prepares the way

of dictatorship in the feeling and thinking of his followers, if finally, it is another who also treads the already-prepared path of dictatorship. That this development is inevitable is shown by the history of such states in which Karl Marx is the Messiah and his teachings are the gospel.

National Socialism was nothing else than a consequence of the worship of power and disregard, even contempt, for the value of the individual, which resulted from the materialistic world-view and which was pushed to the point of criminality. In a people thus prepared spiritually and mentally first by the Prussian exaggerated conception of the state, its essence, its power, the unconditional obedience owed to it, then by the materialistic world view, a doctrine could prevail relatively quickly, favored by the poor material situation of wide circles of the people. This was a doctrine according to which one's own race is the master race and one's own people the master people, and the other peoples are inferior, in part worthy of destruction, but according to which the political opponent in one's own race and in one's own people must be destroyed at all costs.[22]

Adenauer's adopted theory of totalitarianism held that Marxism and National Socialism shared a godless materialism that made state-worshipping citizens ready to accept a dictatorship. This totalitarian theory also accepted a peculiar version of the German "special path" to modernity, which held that Germany's supposed areligious nature made the German catastrophe possible, that "National Socialism found its strongest resistance in the Catholic and Protestant parts of Germany and the least in those which succumbed to the teachings of Karl Marx and socialism," and that only through Christianity and Christian democracy could a democratic reconstruction of Germany happen.

The problem facing Germany was that "Germany is one of the most irreligious and unchristian people of Europe. This was already true before 1914. Despite the fact that the Berliners had some valuable qualities, I always had the feeling of being in a heathen city back then."[23] Adenauer did not continue to describe Berlin as a "foreign" much less "Jewish" city, but he did ascribe a morally degenerate quality to the city that matched the rhetoric of other conservatives of the day. The juxtaposition of a reconstructed, Christian Germany and a heathen, Marxist Berlin in the center of militarist

Prussia was certainly a political calculation tailored against the SPD, but it also expressed Adenauer's pre–World War II belief in a more conservative and Christian West Germany.

A biographer of Adenauer, Hans-Peter Schwarz, described the immediate postwar period in Adenauer's life as his "Prussian-critical phase," which Schwarz attributed to Adenauer's attempt to tie western Germany closer to the Western Allies by distancing Western Allied–occupied West Germany from Soviet-occupied East Germany (including much of former Prussia). This desire to foster rapprochement with the Allies also combined with "the alarming realization that Communist Russia now stood in the heartland of Germany and could advance to the west."[24] To this observation it must be added that Adenauer considered Berlin to be a "heathen" city at the heart of a "materialist" movement in opposition to the necessary Christian democratic values which would reconstruct a new Germany. The old anti-Communism of the German right which viewed Berlin as a leftist threat to Germany lived on in the postwar.

Adenauer's view of the Prussian east could not be more different from that of the SPD leader Kurt Schumacher. In a speech to party leadership in Munich in the first months of 1947, Schumacher surveyed the situation for the SPD with dismay about the question of Germany's future national unity. "The Social Democratic Party is the only party that is living under emergency laws," and only the SPD was facing a "full ban in the Eastern Zone. Which practically means the party is only breathing in one lung. The East of Germany, which can give us an absolute primacy is closed out to us."[25] Schumacher understood that the eastern parts of Germany were where the SPD had its greatest strength, so he feared the loss of the East would mean that the party would be hobbled in any national elections.

Schumacher tied the issue of Berlin to the German unification question, and in doing so he again distanced himself from Konrad Adenauer, who had called for Frankfurt am Main to become the capital of united Germany, which Schumacher called a "bias in a particularistic world of ideas." As Berlin was the seat of seat of the central Allied administrative apparatus, it only made sense for it to be the seat of any future German government. Frankfurt was the seat of the US Military Government, and Schumacher worried that locating the capital there would assure German disunity. Schumacher's insult that Adenauer was "Chancellor of the Allies" had deep roots.

In his speech at the Party Meeting of the SPD later in 1947, Schumacher made his Eastern policy clear: "Europe is possible with Russia, at its best Europe is possible with Russia, but Europe and Germany cannot be Russian."[26] Schumacher, unlike Adenauer, wanted to keep a door open to the east, with the clear goal of reuniting Germany. Schumacher was not naive about East Germany or the Soviet Union. In 1946 the SPD in East Germany had been forced into a popular front party with the Communist party. The *Zwangsvereinigung* (forced unification) had resulted in the banning of Social Democratic political activities and the arrest of dozens of Social Democratic political activists.

Schumacher blamed politicians with a "particularistic" view of Germany for "promoting a politics which in truth has very centralistic tendencies in its purview and who denies all subordinates freedoms and does now want to grant them to any superiors."[27] The "particularism" about which Schumacher was speaking was the decentralized and federalist tendencies of the CDU and its sister party in Bavaria, the Christian Social Union, who already by 1947 was calling for a weak to nonexistent central government and increased autonomy to the states, which would make up a loose federation.

Kurt Schumacher came up with the "magnet theory" in 1946 and 1947, which held that a breakneck economic reconstruction tied to a democratization of society in the western zones would inevitably create the conditions for a reunification of the country. This policy of economic reconstruction carried out through nationalization of heavy industry and massive price controls ran against the wishes of the conservative parties wanting a small central government. As such, Schumacher saw the particularism of these parties as a central hindrance to German unity.

Kurt Schumacher had frosty relationships with some other members of the SPD. Schumacher and his close confident Erich Ollenhauer formed the core of the "Hannover Circle" within the SPD. At least two other major regional SPD groups formed after the war had different ideas from Schumacher about the "German question," western integration, and a more positive attitude toward the Western Allies. One group in Hessen was built around the very electorally successful Hessian SPD, which eschewed some of the fierier rhetoric for which Schumacher was so famous. The other group, crucial to the history of the postwar West German state, was the Berlin SPD. As representatives during the writing of the constitution, they lobbied for Berlin's interests, which often ran against those of Kurt Schumacher and the party leadership.

BERLIN AND THE FOUNDING OF THE FEDERAL REPUBLIC

Political events proceeded at such a pace in Berlin between 1946 and 1949 that the nascent West German political elite were forced to react to the emerging Cold War conflict. As already mentioned, in spring 1946 the East German Communist party, under pressure from the Soviet occupiers, forced a merger between the Social Democrats and the Communist Party—creating the Socialist Unity Party (SED) in the Soviet Zone of Occupation. Despite their proximity to the Soviet zone, members of the West Berlin SPD, led by Berlin regional chair Franz Neumann, overwhelmingly rejected integration into the SED. The forced unification of the two parties was crucial in consolidating single-party rule in what would become East Germany.[28]

This split was reflected in the 1946 city assembly election—the last Berlin-wide free elections until 1989. The SPD won almost 50 percent of the vote, decisively showing the third-placed SED and their Soviet backers that free elections in Berlin would not bring the SED to power. The SPD candidate for mayor, Otto Ostrowski, had signaled a willingness to work with the Soviets. The winter of 1946–47 was called the "hunger winter" in Germany, and Ostrowski believed cooperation with the Soviets was the only way to secure food and provisions for the city of Berlin. He had nominated several SED members to his municipal authority, which angered prominent members of the West Berlin SPD to such an extent that they organized a vote of no confidence.

The clear candidate to replace Ostrowski was the recently remigrated politician Ernst Reuter. Despite his securing the necessary votes from the city assembly, in June 1947 the Soviet Kommandatura exercised veto power to prevent Reuter from taking office. The officially given reason for the rejection of Reuter was that during his exile in Turkey he had gone to the office of the German ambassador to Turkey, Franz von Papen, to renew his passport, which suggested a supposedly intolerable level of collaboration with the Nazi regime. This fictional outrage masked the fact that in the eyes of the Soviets Reuter had committed a deadly sin: in the early 1920s he had risen to high ranks in the Communist Party, even traveling to the Soviet Union to govern the Volga Soviet Republic, then had turned his back on the USSR and Communism. As an American intelligence report from June 1947 stated: "Behind . . . [Soviet] official objections, however, lies the fact that Reuter committed the unpardonable offense of being taken into the Communist party, having been smiled upon by the greatest Communist leaders, rose to a position of authority within the party, and then repudiated it and went back to the SPD."[29]

Weimar political biographies followed Reuter the same way they did for Konrad Adenauer and Kurt Schumacher. Due to the veto against Reuter, Louise Schröder would serve as acting mayor for more than a year. Reuter would not serve as mayor until the Berlin blockade of 1948–49 cemented divisions among the erstwhile Allies.

The immediate catalyst for the Berlin blockade and ensuing airlift was the currency reform of the Anglo-American Bizone in mid-1948; however, the months prior had also seen a sharp deterioration in American-Soviet relations. In February 1948, the Czech coup ousted the last semblance of democratic government there. Furthermore, in early 1948 the US had announced the final details of the Marshall Plan, which the Soviet satellite states were forced to reject.

The Berlin blockade would make Ernst Reuter world famous. Several months into the blockade, standing in front of the Reichstag and a crowd of three hundred thousand people, Ernst Reuter gave his famous "people of the world" speech. Reuter refused to see Berlin handed over to the Soviets as a political bargaining chip. He appealed to the West to continue sending planes but also "to stand firmly and unbreakably with the people of Berlin and their shared ideals."[30] Reuter's speech did not just offer comforting messages of Western unity and solidarity. In the same speech, Reuter declared that once the Battle for Berlin was won: "We will bring our values back to Helmstedt, Munich, to Frankfurt, Dresden, Leipzig, *and eventually they will go to Breslau and to Stettin* [emphasis added]."[31] Reuter was declaring that the Eastern demarcation of Germany's borders was not a settled matter. Although Reuter would be one of social democracy's firm advocates for placing Germany within the Western alliance, he too brought the "Eastern question" to the front of his speech.

Despite the fiery rhetoric of politicians like Ernst Reuter, the issue of a divided Berlin was not central to the writing of the West German Basic Law, because the Allies made clear that the military governors would veto any revision of borders in the constitution. The constituent assembly included symbolic nonvoting members from Berlin to show their support for the city, but the divided and uncertain status of isolated Berlin made the city's future a matter for high diplomatic debate among the Allies.

The plans to create a German state emerged out of the meeting of the Four Power Council of Foreign Ministers in spring of 1947, and the disagreements from that conference set the stage for German division. American,

British, French, and Soviet delegates met in Moscow and debated every aspect of state building: the occupation of the Saarland, the control of the Ruhr industrial region, denazification, reparations, and the organizational structure of the government—all were discussed in the meetings. Especially contentious among the delegates was the constitution. The United States delegation, led by George Marshall, called for immediate elections, followed by a provisional constitution enacted by the Allied Control Council in Germany; this last was to be replaced by a German constitution created on democratic grounds "when the deliberative processes of an elected constitutional assembly lead to final ratification by the people."[32] This proposal was rejected by the French and Soviets, who wanted a provisional constitution with oversight by the Allied Control Council, followed by elections with no reference to a permanent constitution.

Disagreements between the Americans and British on the one hand, and the French and Soviets on the other, were generally over the issue of centralization of government. While the Soviets argued for a strong centralized state, the American delegation and the especially wary French delegation were in favor of federalization. The French delegation, fearing a revanchist Germany, wanted an almost nonexistent central government, while the US delegation wanted to copy ideas of federalism present in the US constitution.

The United States and the Soviet Union could not agree about the degree of centralization in any future German state. In a radio address to the American public, George Marshall said that "agreement was made impossible at Moscow because, in our view, the Soviet Union insisted upon proposals which would have established in Germany centralized government" resulting "only in a deteriorating economic life in Germany and Europe and the inevitable emergence of dictatorship and strife."[33] Disagreement about the structure of the German state would soon be eclipsed by the Soviet attempt to starve the city of Berlin; however, some of the groundwork for the break in US-Soviet relations also lay in very different views on the future German state.

Western Allied diplomacy played a decisive role in the creation of the West German state through the London Six Power Conference of May 1948; this time the three occupying powers of West Germany and the Benelux countries met without the Soviet Union. The German framers of the constitution were never made privy to the minutes of the Six Power Conference.

Instead, they were handed a series of decrees, known as the "Frankfurt Documents," given to the minister-presidents of the eleven states in the Western Occupation Zone in July 1948. The first document was the only document to deal with the process of drafting a constitution.[34] On the content of the constitution, the first document said the Germans would have to "draft a democratic constitution," which would establish "a government structure of the federal type" "and contain guarantees of individual rights and freedoms."[35]

Much of what happened at the Six Power Conference influenced the course of the work of the Parliamentary Council before it had even been created. The two-month-long diplomatic meetings, which took place between the United States, Great Britain, France, and the Benelux countries, were designed to control how the new state would be organized. When questioned by the French delegation as to whether the military governor of Germany, Lucius Clay, would be able to control the course of events, Clay responded that the military governors of the states would follow the activities of the drafting committees closely, and when necessary they would "make known agreed principles which they (the Germans) would be required to follow." Clay was not worried, as he was sure "a high degree of German cooperation is likely as long as [the] Red Army is across the Elbe."[36] Influence over key issues—such as the status of Berlin—was assured by the fear of a Soviet invasion.

When, on June 7, 1948, the three military governors finally met with the eleven minister-presidents of the German states, they reiterated the message of the Six Power Conference, noting that while "there are several means of which a democratic, decentralized but federal government can be obtained," they believed there were certain "desirable governmental structures" that the three governments had in mind. Those were a bicameral legislative system, a greatly weakened executive, and "an independent judiciary empowered to review federal legislation, protect the civil rights of the individual, and adjudicate conflicts of jurisdiction between federal and state authorities."[37]

Within the operating framework of the Frankfurt Documents and three meetings with the military governors, the minister-presidents began to set up the process by which the Basic Law would be drafted. Against the wishes of the American occupation authorities, the minister-presidents called for local parliaments to elect population-proportionate representatives to serve in a Parliamentary Council starting September 1, 1948.[38] At

the July meeting of the minister-presidents in Koblenz only two weeks into
the Berlin blockade, the West German delegates invited former mayor of
Berlin Louise Schröder to give the honorary opening speech to talk about
the plight of Berlin.

What was needed in the German constitution, according to Louise
Schröder, was "a new house," a house in which the door was large, so that
"the states of the German east can move into this new German house."[39]
Their job was to "lay the groundwork for a constructive reconstruction of
all of Germany, a Germany in which Berlin can once again take the position
which it had in its glorious past, a position in which ideally it can take part
in the incorporation of all the countries of Europe for a better future."[40]

Schröder and all the attendees of the conference understood that
this would be the "groundwork" for a future incorporation of Berlin, but
the "house" that Schröder mentioned was a reference to the federalism/
centralism debate, which the SPD members in the meeting all understood
to mean that the future German state had to be centralized enough to someday incorporate the Eastern territories. It was at this meeting that the ministers decided that because the document was created under the auspices of
Allied occupation, the German constitution would be called a *Grundgesetz*
(basic law) rather than a *Verfassung* (constitution).[41]

Several days after Schröder gave her speech in Koblenz, Ernst Reuter
arrived from Berlin to again represent the wishes of the encircled Berliners
to another meeting of German delegates in the town of Niederwald. He too
focused on the desire for a provisional constitution that would be replaced
when Germany was reunited. Unlike the party leadership of the SPD in
West Germany, Reuter called for an immediate integration of any form of
West German state with the Western powers: "We believe that the political
and economic consolidation of the West is an elementary prerequisite for
the recovery of our conditions as well and for the return of the East to
the common motherland."[42] In his statements in Koblenz, Reuter expressed
a tension in the SPD between prioritizing German unity versus Western
integration.

The party leadership around Kurt Schumacher, Erich Ollenhauer,
Walter Menzel, and the Berlin party chairman Franz Neumann believed
western integration would forestall reunification. Meanwhile the Berlin
SPD around Ernst Reuter, the future chancellor Willy Brandt and other
parts of the SPD in the west believed that western integration best served

Berlin's interests.[43] Both the Hannover Circle and Berlin SPD wanted to see a national reunification but fundamentally disagreed on the technical-constitutional mechanisms for achieving that process. Schumacher wanted a barebones temporary constitution that allowed for the nationalization of industry with strict rules against Allied interference in German affairs to keep reunification possible, and Reuter and segments of the Berlin SPD wanted a more thorough constitution, with the promise of western integration. Broadly speaking, this was a struggle between the old Social Democratic Party of the Weimar Republic represented by Kurt Schumacher and the younger SPD, which would eventually coalesce around future West Berlin mayor Willy Brandt.

In August, before the council began, the minister-presidents convened a gathering of constitutional experts from the parties to begin working on proposals for the Parliamentary Council. The experts met on an island in a Bavarian lake at the Herrenchiemsee Palace. Kurt Schumacher's influence on the drafting of the constitution was limited by his deteriorating health condition, which had resulted in the amputation of his left leg likely due to mistreatment at the hands of the Nazis during his twelve years in concentration camps.

While Louise Schröder and Ernst Reuter had represented Berlin at the earlier conferences, Otto Suhr was the honorary representative from Berlin at the Herrenchiemsee Conference. Before the conference began, he met with the leaders of the SPD at the conference: Hermann Brill, Carlo Schmid, and Fritz Baade. Hermann Brill—himself a member of the East German SPD who had fled Soviet persecution—left a documentary record of the meeting which shows how the Allies shaped matters:

> The alleged change of front in Berlin politics between Ko-
> blenz and Niederwald, i.e. between Louise Schröder and
> Ernst Reuter, is, according to Suhr, due to a poorly under-
> stood conception of the Koblenz speech by Louise Schröder.
> Louise Schröder had merely said in Koblenz that she wished
> to be regarded as a guest so that Berlin's unity could be pre-
> served vis-à-vis the Allies. This was also Reuter's point of view
> and his own point of view. In Niederwald, Reuter had merely
> emphasized how strongly it was in the interest of all of Berlin
> in the development of a glacis in the West.[44]

The "glacis" Reuter was referring to was a western military boundary against any further advances by the Soviets. Reuter was giving the same message he would famously give in his "people of the world speech" in Berlin about a month later. Still, Schröder's comments about being an honorary guest were enough for Schröder (whose health was at the time failing) to be replaced by Ernst Reuter in the next meeting.

The SPD representatives didn't want Berlin to come into the debates of the Parliamentary Council. All four present at that meeting believed that the Allies would decide the fate of Berlin. According to Brill "the Parliamentary Council should not let itself get caught up in Berlin— instead it must address every single state of the Soviet Occupation Zone through the current parliamentary presidents."[45] They wanted the constitution to be a temporary document that left the door open for a reunification.

The Basic Law that resulted from the Parliamentary Council was not drafted under Allied edict. Rather, the outer limits of acceptable conduct were policed by the Western Allies, who used the fear of the Soviet Union to assure compliance. Few matters were more crucial to Allied diplomatic policy than assuring that border disputes did not lead to conflict with the Soviets. The Basic Law as adopted in May 1949 was adopted along party-political lines, with the CDU, SPD, and FDP (Liberals) voting for the constitution and the Bavarian Christian Social Union (CSU) and Communist Party of Germany (KPD) voting against it. The CSU's justification for voting against the constitution was that it was overly centralistic. Konrad Adenauer's leadership role in the Parliamentary Council assured that he would become the first chancellor after the success of the CDU in the parliamentary elections of 1949, after which, as chancellor, he led a flurry of diplomatic activity to normalize West Germany's relations with other countries around the world and integrate the West German economy with the rest of Western Europe's.

From within the CDU, the main opposition to Adenauer's policy of Western integration came from the former leadership of the East German branch of the party: especially from the former head of the CDU in East Germany, Jakob Kaiser. Kaiser—himself a resistance fighter against the Nazis actively implicated in the July plot—came from the "left wing" of the CDU and was always closely integrated with the Christian labor union movement. Kaiser belonged to the founding group of the "Advisory Board Indivisible Germany" made up of intraparty representatives who campaigned for the unity of Germany and a return to the 1937 borders of Germany—that is, for the return of Silesia, Pomerania, East Brandenburg, and East Prussia to Germany.[46] Adenauer remained distant from this organization for fear it would jeopardize his policy of integration.

It should not be surprising that it was former East German CDU members in exile who wanted a reunification, but it is important to note that the opposition to Adenauer's policy most vocally came from the *left,* both within his own party and from parts of the SPD. They were fighting a rearguard action against a military and diplomatic integration of West Germany into Western alliance systems for fear that it would forestall reunification. In 1952 Kurt Schumacher died, after several years of bad health. International events also changed political discourse and public opinion about a Western alliance and eventual West German rearmament: no event did more in this regard than the Soviet-backed North Korean invasion of South Korea.[47] Schumacher's death, West Germany joining the European Coal and Steel Community, the Korean War, and Konrad Adenauer's thorough rejection of the Stalin note all made clear by 1952 that West Germany was on a solid path to integration into Western military and defense alliances.

* * *

When Willy Brandt began his campaign to become chancellor, his adviser Egon Bahr coined the term "change through rapprochement" (*Wandel durch Annäherung*) to describe Brandt's *Ostpolitik* in 1963. Bahr saw this policy to be an extension of Dwight Eisenhower's and then JFK's "politics of peace," that is, a way to promote peaceful relations between East and West to avoid the risk of nuclear annihilation.[48] Bahr's speech fit well with a non-state-centered model of international relations, which saw the possibility for a "peaceful coexistence" rather than the looming threat of nuclear war.

Most important, perhaps, "change through rapprochement" was a question first and foremost of German-German relations. It emerged out of Berlin's second crisis, in which a wall was built between a Germany both Egon Bahr and Willy Brandt wanted to see reunited. Inasmuch as Brandt and Bahr's rapprochement called for trade between states, the rapprochement was to ease the situation of East Berliners and East Germans in the hope that it would someday lead to unification. Whether or not this policy sped up reunification is beyond the scope of this essay, but Ostpolitik emerged out of the issues of German division and multiple crises in Berlin. Willy Brandt, Ernst Reuter, and other Western-oriented Social Democrats had been early proponents of western integration against the wishes of some of their party leaders, including Kurt Schumacher and Franz Neumann. Brandt believed that Ostpolitik could be combined with western integration.

During a 1948 meeting of the SPD in Hamburg, Willy Brandt wrote that "the Berlin party . . . has become very unique in German Social Democracy. Not because the people who live there are any better than the people in other parts of Germany, but because since 1945 they have been shaped by conditions and dragged into another conflict." This conflict, according to him "had awakened them to political realities quicker than other people in our organization."[49] Unlike in the rest of West Germany, immediate confrontation with the Soviet Union was a very real possibility in Berlin, and it shaped the unique position of the SPD in West Berlin.

A militant democratic spirit imbibed Reuter, Schröder, Brandt, and many other non-Communist leftists' earlier engagement in Berlin. For them, the struggle against Stalinism and the decrepit authoritarianism of the Soviet state was not the abstraction of lost Eastern territories, but rather an intensely personal struggle. Very early in the Cold War, a generation of non-Communist German leftists fresh from the experience of combating fascism confronted Stalinist oppression head-on in Berlin. That confrontation would deeply shape social democracy as it emerged after the untimely death of the SPD's first leader, Kurt Schumacher, in 1952.

As for the CDU variant of German conservatism, the great change of the postwar period was the turn to Western-oriented organizations and pan-European projects rather than the old habits of national chauvinism and revanchist border claims. Adenauer famously declared that there could be no party to the right of the Christian Democrats. The CDU would be the standard-bearer of German conservativism, and it pursued a policy of integration with the West befitting of a post–National Socialist conservative party. Adenauer was the right person for this task. He had already, in the Weimar Republic, supported a vision of a smaller Germany. The Rhenish Catholic federalism of Adenauer was well matched by the independent-mindedness of the CDU's Bavarian sister party, the Christian Social Union. Given the external pressures of occupation and territorial dismemberment, however, it is still a remarkable feat that the CDU did not drift into nationalist revanchism.

Konrad Adenauer and the Christian Democrats never celebrated the loss of Berlin and the Eastern territories, but following Adenauer's lead, West German conservatives were equally happy to lay the blame for National Socialism, militarism, and aggressive warfare at the feet of a Prussia (including Berlin) that was—at least for the time being—lost to Soviet occupation under the auspices of the Cold War conflict. Politically, during the early days of the Federal Republic, both the left and the right could gain political advantages out of the division of Germany. Adenauer could promote the image of jack-booted Prussians as those truly responsible for National Socialism, and Schumacher could claim that the SPD was creating a nationally conscious social democracy—rebuffing the timeless charges that the Social Democratic Party was somehow aligned with Communism by touting the party's resistance to division and persecution in East Germany. Schumacher's younger successors in the SPD changed the course of the party in the 1950s, themselves eventually embracing a model of western integration and a broader appeal as a *Volkspartei* (majority party). Neither party could control the outcomes of Allied deliberation around the fate of Berlin, but both parties could develop a modus vivendi about that division.

NOTES

1. There are many variations of this quote; however, this version is the one that survived in writing. Quoted in Patrick Thaddeus Jackson, *Civilizing the Enemy: German Reconstruction and the Invention of the West* (Ann Arbor: University of Michigan Press, 2006), vi. Other Adenauer quotes from before the "Third Reich" include Adenauer saying that "the Asian Steppe begins at Braunschweig," that he would close his train curtains when he arrived in Magdeburg, and that he spat when crossing the Elbe. For some of these anecdotes, see Holger Löttel, "Konrad Adenauer und Preußen," Konrad Adenauer website, accessed July 5, 2022, https://www.konrad-adenauer.de/seite/konrad-adenauer-und-preussen/.

2. One of the most convincing arguments in support of this comes from Joseph Foschepoth, "Westintegration statt Wiedervereinigung: Adenauers Deutschlandpolitik 1949–1955," in *Adenauer und die Deutsche Frage,* ed. Joseph Foschepoth (Göttingen: Vandenhoeck & Ruprecht, 1998), 29–61.

3. For Adenauer's opposition to the Oder-Neiße Line, see Axel Frohn, "Adenauer und die deutschen Ostgebiete in den fünfziger Jahren," in *Vierteljahrshefte für Zeitgeschichte* 44, no. 4 (1996): 485–525.

4. Hope Harrison, "Berlin and the Cold War Struggle over Germany," in *The Routledge Handbook of the Cold War,* ed. Artemy M. Kalinovsky and Craig Daigle (London: Routledge, 2016), 56–70.

5. On the "Stalin Note," see Jürgen Zarusky, ed., *Die Stalin-Note vom 10. März 1952: Neue Quellen und Analysen,* Schriftenreihe der Vierteljahrshefte für Zeitgeschichte 84 (Munich: R. Oldenbourg Verlag, 2002).

6. Dietrich Orlow, *Weimar Prussia: The Unlikely Rock of Democracy* (Pittsburgh: University of Pittsburgh Press, 1986).

7. Michael Feldkamp, "Der Zwischenruf 'der Bundeskanzler der Alliierten!' und die parlamentarische Beilegung des Konfliktes zwischen Konrad Adenauer und Kurt Schumacher im Herbst 1949," in *Von Freiheit, Solidarität und Subsidiarität—Staat und Gesellschaft der Moderne in Theorie und Praxis: Festschrift für Karsten Ruppert zum 65. Geburstag,* ed. Von Markus Raasch und Tobias Hirschmüller (Berlin: Decker & Humboldt, 2013), 665–708.

8. For a much deeper look at this topic, see Scott Krause, *Bringing Cold War Democracy to West Berlin: A Shared German-American Project, 1940–1972* (London: Routledge, 2019).

9. Hans-Peter Schwarz, *Adenauer, Der Aufstieg: 1876–1952* (Stuttgart: Deutsche Verlags-Anstalt, 1986), 213.

10. For two new histories of the German revolution and its consequences, see Mark Jones, *Founding Weimar: Violence and the German Revolution of 1918–1919* (Cambridge: Cambridge University Press, 2016); and Robert Gerwarth, *November 1918: The German Revolution* (Oxford: Oxford University Press, 2022).

11. On the idea of "Judeo-Bolshevism," see Paul Hanebrink, *A Specter Haunting Europe: The Myth of Judeo-Bolshevism* (Cambridge, MA: Harvard University Press, 2018).

12. Konrad Adenauer, "Ansprache vor einer Versammlung der linksrheinischen Abgeordneten zur Nationalversammlung der linksrheinischen Abgeordneten zur prueßischen Landesversammlung und der Oberbürgermeister des besetzten rheinischen Städte im Kölner Hansasaal," in *Konrad Adenauer Reden 1917–1967: Eine Auswahl* (Stuttgart: Deutsche Verlags-Anstalt, 1975), 28–30.

13. Adenauer, 31.

14. Adenauer, 32.

15. For Kurt Schumacher's biography, see Peter Merseburger, *Kurt Schumacher: Patriot, Volkstribun, Sozialdemokrat* (Munich: Pantheon, 2010).

16. David E. Barklay, *Schaut auf diese Stadt: Der unbekannte Ernst Reuter* (Berlin: Siedler, 2000).

17. Antje Dertinger, *Frauen der ersten Stunde: Aus den Gründerjahren der Bundesrepublik* (Bonn: J Latka Verlag, 1989).

18. "Weimar Republic 1918–1933 Reichstagwahlen Wahlkreis Stadt Berlin," Wahlen in Deutschland, accessed September 6, 2022, https://www.wahlen-in-deutschland.de/wrtwberlin.htm.

19. David Glantz and Jonathan House, *When Titans Clashed: How the Red Army Stopped Hitler* (Lawrence: University Press of Kansas, 2015), 399 (Table Q).

20. For details on the planning, see William Stivers and Donald A. Carter, *The City Becomes a Symbol: The U.S. Army in the Occupation of Berlin* (Washington, DC: U.S. Army Center of Military History, 2017), 18–22.

21. Konrad Adenauer, "Grundsatzrede des. 1 Vorsitzenden der Christlich-Demokratischen Union für die Britische Zone in der Aula der Kölner Universität, March 24, 1946," in *Reden*, 85.

22. "Grundsatzrede," 86–87.

23. "Grundsatzrede," 88.

24. Schwarz, *Adenauer der Aufstieg*, 449.

25. Kurt Schumacher, "11.1.19947 Stellungnahmen Schumachers zu Deutschlandfrage, zu einer Wiederzulassung der SPD in der Ostzone und zur Rolle der Gewerkschaften in einer Sitzung des Parteiausschusses in München," in *Kurt Schumacher Reden-Schriften-Korrespondenzen 1945–1952* (Bonn: Verlag J. H. W. Dietz, 1985), 479–80.

26. Kurt Schumacher, "Deutschland und Europa," in *Protokoll der Verhandlungen des Parteitages der Sozialdemokratischen Partei Deutschlands vom 29 Juni bis 2 Juli 1947 in Nürnberg* (Hamburg: Verlag und Druck, 1947), 39.

27. Schumacher, 40.

28. Even the term "forced unification" has faced criticism, but the author thinks the historiography has shown that the occupying Soviets exerted enormous pressure on the KPD. For a classic account, see Dierk Hoffmann, *Otto Grotewohl (1894–1964): Eine politische Biographie* (Munich: Oldenbourg Verlag, 2009), 195–258.

29. Office of Military Government Berlin Sector (OMGUS Berlin), Special Report of Civil Administration and Political Affairs Branch, "Analysis of Current Situation in Berlin Administration and Political Affairs" (June 25, 1947) NACP RG 59, Central Decimal File 1945–1949, 740.00119 box 3709 Control (Germany)/7–347, 6.

30. Ernst Reuter, "Ernst Reuters Rede am 9 September 1948 vor dem Reichstag," May 15, 2023. https://www.berlin.de/berlin-im-ueberblick/geschichte/artikel.453082.php.

31. Ernst Reuter, "Ernst Reuters Rede am 9. September 1948."

32. "Summary of CFM Agreements and Disagreements on Germany," box 364, Records of the Control Office, Records of the Executive office, OMGUS U.S., RG 260, NARA CP, 70.

33. "George Marshall Statement on Moscow Conference" April 29, 1947. box 234, The Governmental Structures Branch, CAD, OMGUS (US), RG 260, NARA CP, 8.

34. The other two dealt with the occupation of the Ruhr and the continuance of the occupation statute.

35. "Frankfurt Documents," Office of Military Government for Germany (US). *Documents on the Creation of the German Federal Constitution* (Berlin: Civil Administration Division, 1949), 54.

36. "Outgoing Telegrams," May 20, 1948, box 237, The Governmental Structures Branch, CAD, OMGUS (US), RG 260, NARA CP.

37. "Proposed Oral Comments for Use in Meeting with the Minister-Presidents," Folder Minister-Presidents Notes on Meeting RE LTR to MP, June 7, 1948, box 2, General Records, 1947–1952, Office of the Executive Secretary, RG 466 HICOG, NARA CP.

38. "Parliamentary Council Documents: Introductory Notes," Office of Military Government for Germany (US). *Documents on the Creation of the German Federal Constitution* (Berlin: Civil Administration Division, 1949), 50.

39. Document nr. 6 "Konferenz der Ministerpräsidenten der westdeutschen Besatzungszonen Koblenz (Rittersturz) 8–10 July 1948," in *Der Parliamentarische Rat 1948–1949: Akten und Protokolle Band 1 Vorgeschichte,* ed. Johannes Volker Wagner (Boppard: Harald Boldt Verlag, 1975), 63.

40. Document nr. 6, 63.

41. Document nr. 6, 76–80.

42. Document nr. 11 "Konferenz der Ministerpräsidenten der westdeutschen Besatzungszonen Jagdschloß Niederwald, 21–22 Juli 1948," in *Der Parliamentarische Rat 1948–1949: Akten und Protokolle Band 1,* 192.

43. Krause, *Bringing Cold War Democracy to West Berlin,* 112–13. The other oppositional group to Schumacher was based in Hessen, where the SPD first achieved an electoral majority in 1946. Under Minister-President Karl Geiler, and then Christian Stock, a cabinet including Georg August Zinn and Hermann Brill created another center for reform-minded pro–western integration Social Democracy.

44. Hermann Brill, "Chiemseer Tagebuch," 1, Nachlass 1086/383, Bundesarchiv Koblenz.

45. Brill, 2.

46. Werner Conze, *Jakob Kaiser: Politiker zwischen Ost und West 1945–1949* (Stuttgart: Kohlhammer, 1969).

47. David Clay Large, *Germans to the Front: West German Rearmament in the Adenauer Era* (Chapel Hill: University of North Carolina Press, 1995).

48. Egon Bahr, "Wandel durch Annäherung," speech, July 15, 1963, 100(0) Schlüssel Dokumente zur deutschen Geschichte im 20. Jahrhundert, accessed December 12, 2023, https://www.1000dokumente.de/index.html?c=dokument_de&dokument=0091_bah&l=de.

49. Harold Hurwitz, *Demokratie und Antikommunismus in Berlin nach 1945 Band 1: Die Politische Kultur der Bevölkerung und der Neubeginn konservativer Politik* (Cologne: Verlag Wissenschaft und Politik, 1983), 8.

CHAPTER 2

The First Crisis

US Army Planning and the Defense of Berlin, 1945–1950

SETH GIVENS

At the dawn of the Cold War, the United States, Britain, and France struggled to solve the problem of defending Berlin.[1] Marooned 110 miles inside the Soviet occupation zone, the Allies' sectors in the western half of the city were the result of wartime debates and agreements.[2] Beginning in 1947, the US Army, charged with defending the American position, debated potential responses to Red Army provocations and the likelihood of a general war. These discussions occurred between headquarters and offices in Berlin, Frankfurt, and Washington at the theater commander, service chief, and secretary levels.

The debate about defending Berlin was a component of a larger discussion about Western Europe. The army did not view Berlin and Western Europe defense as separate issues.[3] The linkage meant that the army did not comprehend the political nature of Berlin and struggled to devise military

---

The opinions expressed in this chapter are the author's own and do not reflect the views of the United States Marine Corps History Division, the United States Marine Corps, or the United States government.

solutions to the Soviet blockade of rail and ground access to the Western sectors in June 1948. This chapter examines the US Army's planning process for Berlin and the role of the city in the defense of Europe. It focuses on the discussions that occurred between the various echelons of the army—from US Army Europe (USAREUR) headquarters to the Pentagon—and seeks to show the evolution of how the service viewed and talked about defending an undefendable city. Moreover, the story of the US Army and Berlin is illustrative of the intertwining nature of politico-military considerations in the Cold War and how, in the years following World War II, American national strategy transformed from continentalism to a globalized defense.[4]

Works that examine the first Berlin crisis begin in 1945 and stop with the diplomatic solution for the blockade in May 1949.[5] Much of these military history studies are restricted to the airlift.[6] This chapter argues that bracketing the first crisis between June 1948 and May 1949 skews our understanding of the period toward diplomacy and crisis management. Extending analysis of Berlin during the first crisis to the summer and fall of 1950 reveals how the West attempted to solve the dilemma of defending the city. By then, the Western Allies had created the North Atlantic Treaty Organization (NATO), an alliance based on the premise of collective defense and deterrence. American officials insisted on incorporating the Western sectors of Berlin into NATO territory, merging the city and European security. This, in part, was a solution to the problem that the army never could solve. It did not, however, end tension over Berlin, as we will see in subsequent chapters of this volume.

POSTWAR TO COLD WAR, 1945–48

The first elements of the US Army arrived in Berlin on July 1, 1945.[7] The trophy of the Four Powers was undeniably a city of rubble. British and American bomber crews had launched 363 air raids on the German capital over the course of the war and had dropped 75,000 tons of bombs.[8] The Battle of Berlin in April 1945, fought between 85,000 German defenders and 1.5 million Soviet troops, had begun with unrelenting Red Army artillery and rocket shelling and had ended with vicious street fighting that shattered the capital block by block.[9]

The division of Berlin was a microcosm of Germany's occupation zones, with the city split in half between East and West sectors. The US Army

element in the city, called US Headquarters, Berlin District, and number-
ing around 26,000 troops, took over administration of six boroughs in the
southwest.[10] The British sector was located to the west, the French eventually received a sector in the north, and the Soviets controlled the eight
boroughs in the eastern half of the city. From summer 1945 to spring 1947,
the military governments in the sectors generally cooperated, but they did
spar on everything from mail delivery to Berliners' daily caloric intake.[11]

The US Army's initial combat power in Berlin was a modest force
composed of the 2nd Armored Division, 702nd Tank Destroyer Battalion,
and 195th Airborne Antiaircraft Battalion (Automatic Weapons).[12] Assorted
combat-service support troops totaled 7,763. Sundry other units of military
police, counterintelligence, finance, and the like constituted another 1,314
soldiers.[13] These forces and all army operational units in Europe reported
to US Forces, European Theater (USFET), at Frankfurt am Main, under
the command of Gen. Dwight D. Eisenhower. With the emphasis on de-
mobilizing in the months after the end of the war, army units redeployed
and deactivated, and individual soldiers returned home on a points system,
hollowing out veteran combat units that then became occupation forces.[14]
The Joint Strategic Survey Committee, the senior policy advisory group
to the Joint Chiefs of Staff (JCS), assumed that only 400,000 American
soldiers and airmen would be necessary in Europe by May 1946.[15]

The Pentagon did not consider the Soviet Union an immediate threat
when it planned for the postwar. Technological advances in strategic weapons and long-range delivery systems during World War II had made the national security establishment anxious that the American mainland was now
vulnerable. The Soviet Union possessed a massive land force but no strategic
air power or blue-water navy and therefore posed no immediate danger. It
was not until after World War II, when the US military considered how politics and economics influenced a competitor's intentions, that the Pentagon
changed its outlook from solely national defense to maintaining stability
and the balance of power in Europe.[16] Senior military leaders estimated in
late 1946 that the Soviet Union would pursue a general war to advance its
strategic interests, but not until 1950.[17]

In spring 1947, various echelons of the US Army on both sides of the
Atlantic began contemplating what a Red Army invasion of Europe would
look like. There were three unified or US Army headquarters and offices
that studied the problem below the level of the Joint Chiefs. Two under the

leadership of Lt. Gen. Lucius D. Clay were located in Germany. Clay became the theater commander for US forces in Europe and the US military governor for Germany in March 1947. He took over the reconstituted USFET, a unified command called European Command (EUCOM) with US Army, Air Force, and Navy components. EUCOM had two elements: the Office of Military Government, United States (OMGUS), and Headquarters, EUCOM. OMGUS was located in Berlin and formed policies for administering the American occupation zone and sector. It also controlled American forces in the city, which redesignated as Berlin Command in October 1946. Headquarters, EUCOM, was located in Frankfurt am Main and was responsible for the security of all US personnel, organizations, and units in the occupation. Lt. Gen. Clarence B. Huebner was triple-hatted, serving as deputy commander in chief and chief of staff of EUCOM as well as the commanding general of USAREUR. Huebner had operational control of US forces in Europe and was responsible for general staff functions, including the formulation of EUCOM plans.[18] In Washington, Army General Staff–level planning occurred within the Plans and Operations Division, located at the Pentagon under the direction of Maj. Gen. Lauris Norstad. The division was responsible for developing strategic and operational plans and providing recommendations to Secretary of the Army Kenneth C. Royall on joint service planning.

In June 1947, the same month that the United States unveiled the Marshall Plan, Clay's office in Berlin began forming plans in conjunction with EUCOM and Plans and Operations Division.[19] EUCOM took the lead initially and assumed that, in the event of war, the Red Army would attack the British and Americans simultaneously. Clay hoped for such a scenario, as he was more worried about the consequences of the Soviets focusing on only one power at a time. If that occurred, the political and legal time involved in one ally aiding the other could amount to several days, crippling US and British forces' ability to absorb the Soviet attack and remain on continental soil. Crucially, all army planning assumptions were based on Allied forces withdrawing from Europe.[20]

The most glaring issue for the US military in Europe was a lack of combat power. In the immediate postwar years, the United States struggled to balance the necessity of demobilization with the maintenance of military capabilities. Five million service personnel were discharged between May 1945 and January 1946, leading the army to report to Congress that further drawdowns would put into question the service's ability to accomplish its overseas missions.[21] There were sixty-one US Army divisions in Europe at the end of World War II, but only one of them remained by 1946. Augmenting the division were three constabulary regiments conducting a gendarmerie mission.[22] In Berlin, rotations and redeployments reduced US security forces in the city from one division at the beginning of 1946 to one battalion by the end of the year.[23] US intelligence analysts believed that, by contrast to available Allied forces, the Soviets enjoyed preponderant military power in Europe despite their own drawdown. In July 1946 the Red Army reportedly had forty-two divisions in Germany alone.[24] The imbalance was little changed a year later. Scholars have argued that American intelligence officials tended to overestimate Soviet military power in Europe, but it is difficult to imagine how a more accurate appraisal would have changed US leaders' nuclear calculus.[25] By 1947, US Army units were organized for occupation duty, were dispersed, and lacked tactical training and combat readiness.[26] Adding to the army's issues, the service was also suffering from a degradation of capabilities and culture.[27]

An increase in political upheaval on the peripheries of the Soviet sphere made US officials view Moscow as a threat to American strategic and economic interests in 1947.[28] In December the lack of military readiness and the contentious political situation in Germany spurred a change in thinking within Plans and Operations Division, now under the direction of Maj. Gen. Alfred C. Wedemeyer.[29] EUCOM had acted on the June 1947 discussions and drafted plans for the possibility of a Soviet surprise attack. When Wedemeyer's office reviewed the EUCOM plans, it concluded that an Allied defense was unlikely to succeed, given the disparity in strength.[30] The army spent much of December contemplating a withdrawal from the European continent in detail. In a best-case scenario, US and British units would have to fight a delaying action at the Rhine River while dependents evacuated to Dunkirk, France. Le Havre, France, and Bremerhaven, Germany, were also rallying points and were to have military and civilian ships waiting to ferry the remnants of the Western units across the English Channel. Even abandoning the European continent presented considerable risk, however. Soviet airborne troops could seize crossings at the Rhine and the Channel ports with little warning. Army staff planners recommended to EUCOM that units and soldiers' dependents withdraw on assigned routes.[31]

The US Army viewed Berlin and Vienna similarly in the event of a Soviet invasion. Both capitals were co-administered among the Four Powers and located within Soviet occupation zones. If the Red Army invaded Western Europe, the Allied garrisons would be behind enemy lines. EUCOM therefore planned for those garrisons to capitulate. The outright surrender would leave 18,588 US and Allied civilian and military personnel, along with two battalions of the 16th Infantry Regiment, to fend for themselves.[32]

Therein was the paradox of Berlin for the US Army. The city was the Western powers' most vulnerable position in Europe, but it was also the Allies' best hope for detecting a Soviet invasion. Since the Red Army would likely reckon with Berlin first, military leaders believed there would be some warning in the city before a full-scale Soviet attack on the Allies' main forces, providing an opportunity to withdraw from the Continent.[33] This was why, at the end of 1947, the US Army became hypersensitive to Soviet behavior in Berlin. Any technical or administrative difficulties in the city could be more than just harassment; they could be the opening sequence in an invasion of Western Europe.

Clay expected a showdown with the Soviet Union, but he did not believe that it would escalate to war. "The penetration of Communism," he wrote to Wedemeyer on December 27, "has been checked, if not stopped, by the thin American and British screen through the middle of Germany and the middle of Austria." Clay discounted the possibility of war, but the specter of Pearl Harbor made him vigilant.[34] If war came, he predicted that the Red Army could sweep aside his ground forces and march to the Pyrenees. He trusted, however, that the American atomic monopoly ensured the Soviets paid a high price if they attempted to take Europe. With this calculus in mind, he acted with confidence in Berlin.[35]

Despite Clay's faith in the atomic monopoly, army planners at EUCOM and the Pentagon planned for conventional operations only. By contrast, JCS planners began creating contingencies in spring 1946 that relied upon an atomic air offensive from the US Air Force's Strategic Air Command. The planners, developing their ideas in the absence of high-level policy guidance, assumed that the Soviet objective was world domination but that Moscow would not resort to war in the short term to achieve it. If war did come before the Soviets were ready, it would be because of a miscalculation. In the opening stage of a war, the Red Army could seize all of Western Europe, the northern coast of the Mediterranean, and much of the Middle East.[36] The planners' reliance on an air offensive was optimistic, given that America's atomic monopoly amounted to all of thirteen bombs in July 1947, none of them assembled.[37] Moreover, the United States lacked a coherent doctrine, strategy, application, and even consensus on the use of atomic weapons.[38]

Berlin planning shifted from Germany to Washington in January 1948, when Secretary Royall ordered Wedemeyer to study the courses of action if the Soviets attempted to push the Western Allies from the city. Planners estimated that Moscow had two options: direct military force or disruption of city administration to the extent that the Allies would abandon Berlin. Direct military force was unlikely, given the possibility of triggering a general war for what was a relatively limited goal of expulsion. The Pentagon and Clay both believed administrative interference was probable, and they concluded that any plan beyond retreat would mean maintaining at least a token force in the city. Even one battalion, the logic went, would make it risky for the Soviets to attempt armed intervention, lest they increase the chances of war.[39]

The consideration of politico-military issues was an important distinction between the levels of planning bodies. EUCOM concerned itself with the technical problem of defending Berlin. The Pentagon, by contrast, appreciated the politico-military nature of the Cold War. The Office of the Secretary of the Army therefore agreed with EUCOM that the Soviets were likely to restrict road, rail, and water access to Berlin, but it also believed that such obstructionism was not a first step toward general war. This put the Pentagon in agreement with Clay, who often made decisions based on his perspective as military governor, not as theater commander. Clay's keen sense for the political characteristics of the competition in Germany, however, meant he sometimes made military suggestions that alarmed even the army. Clay's continued confidence in the American atomic monopoly led him to argue at the end of 1947 that an armed convoy was the best way to defeat a potential Soviet blockade of Berlin.[40]

Clay had been involved with the issue of Western access to Berlin since June 29, 1945, when he was the American representative in discussions regarding the movement of troops to the Western sectors. The Americans and British requested two highways, three rail lines, and two air corridors from Berlin to Frankfurt and Hamburg. The Soviets countered with one highway—the Berlin-Magdeburg-Hanover Autobahn—one rail line, and one air corridor, reasoning that Red Army troops would be clogging the other roads into the city during their withdrawal.[41] Clay agreed but stipulated that discussion of access rights should resume once all garrisons were operational. This reevaluation never occurred, nor did a written agreement guaranteeing ground access. Clay did not expect future troubles and later dismissed the notion that the Soviets would not have blocked access in 1948 had there been an agreement. He instead attributed Moscow's aggression to a miscalculation of American interest in Europe after they watched US forces on the Continent shrink to a division and a half within the first year of the occupation.[42] Clay's proposals for an armored convoy were therefore a result of his background with the access issue and his belief that Soviet actions were merely harassment in the early stages of the blockade. For this reason, Clay viewed a combat team passing through the Soviet occupation zone to the Western sectors in Berlin as a political rather a military act, an Allied declaration of access rights rather than a provocation.[43]

The Pentagon was never willing to wager that the Soviets would understand such distinctions, but it did agree with Clay that the United States should show resolve in the face of administrative difficulties. They did so because they foresaw two negative outcomes of withdrawing from Berlin. First, the Western Allies would be abandoning over two million Berliners to Communism, a move that would damage American prestige. Second, they would be laying the groundwork for the dissolution of the Allied Control Council, all but finalizing the division of Germany into East and West blocs.[44]

The Plans and Operations staff study on Berlin made its way through the halls of the Pentagon throughout January 1948. Secretary of Defense James V. Forrestal received a copy from Royall on January 19. Both Forrestal and Secretary of State George C. Marshall concurred with the army's conclusions. The study was not, however, sent to the National Security Council (NSC) for referral, as Royall argued that the army, navy, and the State Department already agreed in principle. Six months before the Berlin blockade, then, there was a consensus in the Pentagon: leaders believed the Soviets would attempt administrative difficulties and that the United States should stand firm. Crucially, however, there was no plan on how to do the latter.[45]

This lack of planning was laid bare in early spring 1948, when a war scare swept over Washington. The scare was the product of a March 5 cable that Clay had sent to the US Army's director of intelligence, Lt. Gen. J. Stephen Chamberlin, indicating a change in Soviet attitudes in Berlin and the potential for a conflict exploding in Europe without warning. The cable was Clay and Chamberlin's designed attempt to alarm Congress into passing a pending military appropriations bill for fiscal year 1949.[46] The impetus was the February 17–25 Communist coup in Czechoslovakia. The suspected murder of the Czech foreign minister, Jan Masaryk, sparked yet more public concern about Soviet encroachment in Germany, convincing Americans of the need for further US engagement in Europe.[47]

The Truman administration was still convinced that war was unlikely in the near term, but the "war warning" cable, as the Defense Department began calling it, nonetheless achieved Clay and Chamberlin's intended effect. The new army chief of staff, Gen. Omar N. Bradley, ordered OMGUS and Gen. Douglas MacArthur's occupation headquarters in Japan to survey emergency plans and ensure their execution if needed.[48] The Joint Chiefs expedited an emergency war plan on March 13 that called for atomic-equipped US Air Force bombers and carrier-based, conventionally armed US Navy aircraft to degrade Soviet war-making capacity.[49] On March 17 Truman addressed Congress and requested an increase to the military appropriations bills for fiscal year 1949.[50] In the weeks afterward, the services seized on the opportunity to increase their respective budgets. When Congress passed a defense budget, it authorized $13.9 billon, a billion more dollars than Truman had requested.[51] The sum of the March war scare was an alignment between civilian leadership in Washington and the US Army in Germany concerning the importance of preparing for a war, even if one was not imminent.

It was in this environment of heightened sensitivities to Moscow's intentions that the Soviet military government announced on March 30, 1948, new identification and inspection protocols for Allied trains transiting between the Western zones and Berlin.[52] Red Army soldiers stopped four trains entering Berlin the next day. The restrictions were in retaliation for the London Six Power Conference, which resulted in British, French, American, and Benelux recommendations to integrate the three Western occupation zones into the Marshall Plan and establish a provisional federal German government.[53] The "April crisis" was relatively minor—the British and Americans launched a small-scale airlift to move personnel and supplies between the zones and sectors—but it was significant for three reasons. First, it forced the Allies to find solutions to the question that the Pentagon had identified months before of how the American garrison could withstand Soviet pressure. Until then, the army was proactive and planned for the worst, studying how to evacuate 10,790 American civilians from Berlin.

Second, the discussions about those solutions formed the basis for emergency planning in June, when the Soviets blocked rail and ground access to Berlin. Third, the episode made Bradley contemplate the possibility that Soviet interference could begin small but then lead to a choice between leaving an untenable position or remaining and risking war.[54]

In Bradley's and army leaders' review of existing contingencies, they concluded that Clay's armed convoy, which he lobbied for once again, was out of the question. The Allies were outnumbered, and it was foolhardy to consider a strictly military option for a politico-military issue.[55] The army's discussion of responses in Berlin concerned the State Department that fighting for the city could affect other US objectives, including the Marshall Plan. If the United States took measures against the Soviets, there were myriad ways Moscow could counter, including placing restrictions on strategic materials, such as manganese and chrome, that the Soviet Union provided to the United States.[56] The State Department preferred taking planning out of the Pentagon's hands, and it volunteered to draft a long-term program for retaliatory Allied measures in case of future Soviet harassment. Many of their early suggestions were asymmetric responses and centered on harassing Soviet shipping around the globe. London, however, rejected the plans, particularly disrupting shipping through the Suez Canal.[57] Berlin, therefore, presented a unique problem: defending it with military means was unthinkable, but it was too risky to apply pressure on the Soviets elsewhere to guarantee its safety.

CRISIS, 1948–49

While Washington debated, Clay's subordinate commands prepared ways to withstand or counter Soviet pressure on Berlin. On March 25, the director of the Office of Military Government, Berlin Sector, Col. Frank Howley, directed his staff to draw up contingency plans for the short-term survival of the Western sectors on the assumption that the Soviets would split their sector from the other three, denying the Western boroughs supplies that came from the Soviet sector and zone. Dubbed Operation Counterpunch, the idea was to buy time, not outlast a Soviet blockade.[58] Howley's staff calculated how much food and coal would be required for a month, and they planned for a temporary, Western-only city administration to maintain general day-to-day needs of the sectors.[59]

Shortly afterward, Lt. Gen. Curtis E. LeMay, commander of US Air Force, Europe (USAFE), made his own contingency plans. LeMay worried about EUCOM running out of supplies, as the command's lifeline stretched to Bremerhaven, 250 miles north of where most US forces were stationed.[60] On April 1 he reported to Washington that the Soviets could overrun the US position within eight hours, making current EUCOM plans insufficient. The Allies could not rely on air supremacy, given that one fighter group could not provide sufficient air cover for the army's plan to retreat to the Rhine.[61] With the limited aircraft on hand, LeMay knew that it would be "stupid to get mixed up in anything bigger than a cat-fight at a pet show."[62] Until there was combined planning, USAFE and EUCOM could not ensure a defense at the Rhine, let alone an orderly withdrawal from Europe.

The March war scare had stiffened EUCOM and OMGUS's resolve, but it made officials in Washington warier. The April crisis only added to that difference of opinion. Clay was confident that he and his staff were correctly interpreting the Soviet moves, while the Pentagon and State Department began to plan for the worst. The first stage would be evacuating dependents from Berlin, either to Frankfurt or London. For the first time, Congress even weighed in when members began asking Royall and Bradley why American civilians were not out of harm's way.[63] The lack of an airlift for noncrucial personnel was not because the military had overlooked one. Since late 1947, army staff contingencies for Berlin had called for the evacuation of dependents upon Soviet pressure in the city. After March 1948, Wedemeyer and his planners were in immediate contact with Clay and Huebner about such operations.[64] Planners found that only half of EUCOM's 130 C-47s were ready to fly. With a capacity of only thirty people and a roundtrip to Rhein-Main Air Base of four hours, it would take considerable time to evacuate the 10,790 US civilians in Berlin.[65]

For Clay, the evacuation debate was not if they could do it but if they should. He worried that removing dependents would be both politically disastrous and harmful to the military situation. Since he believed the Soviet objective was to pressure the West into withdrawing, he reasoned that an American evacuation of any size would communicate to the Soviets that their eviction plan was working. In a test of will, an evacuation could also create hysteria among Berliners, accompanied by a "rush of Germans to communism for safety."[66] There was also the possibility of the Soviets using an evacuation for propaganda, arguing that the West was preparing for war.

Clay reasoned that American citizens were not at risk in Berlin, because the Soviets were not prepared to threaten war to achieve their objectives. The dependents were already, in effect, hostages, and it was paradoxically riskier if they left than if they stayed.[67]

The episode was illustrative of how differently EUCOM and Washington saw the potential outcomes for remaining in Berlin. Clay did not see Berlin and a Western stand in it as existing in a vacuum, and it appeared to him that that point was lost on Washington. Clay believed that the cost of an evacuation of Berlin would be American prestige and likely larger negative effects for Europe.[68] Spring 1948 appeared to him as a shift in Moscow's favor, especially with Italy and France flirting with Communism. If Berlin fell and Communist groups consolidated their gains in Western Europe, it could spell disaster for a free and independent Germany. The logic for defending the city, therefore, could never be proven militarily because Berlin was of supreme political importance. Clay, responsible for both OMGUS and EUCOM, understood this and did not divide the problems he faced into military and political categories. "If we mean that we are to hold Europe against communism," he wrote Bradley, "we must not budge." The "future of democracy requires us to stay here until forced out."[69]

More than the war of nerves with the Soviet Union, there was also a strategic component to an American stand. A Western evacuation of Berlin would roll back democracy's outpost, making the Western zones in Germany the new frontier. In a marked departure from his thoughts in March of not expanding forces in the city, Clay asked Bradley on April 12 for the Allies to supply one division to each of their garrisons.[70] If the Soviets allowed the transit of reinforcements across their zone, the West would deliver a blow to Moscow's attempts to control access. If the Soviets blocked entry by force, however, it would precipitate war. Clay viewed this likelihood as remote, but the West would not be at fault if it did, and forces might be better used in a fight for Berlin than in trying to defend the open territory of the zones. Clay's request for reinforcements capped off his growing belief that Western Europe needed American backbone and a defensive complement to the Marshall Plan's economic power to contain the expansion of Communism. Bradley, however, did not see the situation the same way, and he rejected the plan.[71]

Clay was unique within the army in his views on Berlin's politico-military importance, and internal conversations continued to focus on withdrawing. Six days before the Soviet Union blockaded Berlin, staff planners prepared a study on the situation, modifying their position from the beginning of the year. They highlighted Joseph Stalin's relative freedom of action. If the Soviets were indeed determined to force a withdrawal, they could do so by means and methods short of war or by risking war.[72] There was no guarantee, however, that the Americans could control the situation if Stalin risked the latter. The study still recognized that Berlin's greatest strength was its psychological advantage in the Cold War, but planners recommended that maintaining the advantage was not worth all costs. If the Soviets did block land access, the Americans would be unable to supply the civilian population with food and coal. The Pentagon planners argued that the Allies should withdraw to prevent Berliners from becoming victims of a Cold War battle.[73]

The United States did not have answers to any of these questions when the Soviet Union blocked rail traffic on the night of June 23, 1948, in retaliation for the Western powers' inclusion of Berlin's western sectors in zonal currency reform. The literature suggests that the blockade caught decision makers off guard.[74] The volume of US Army discussions about Berlin contingencies for more than one year suggests that the opposite is true. The issue was a lack of guidance and policy at the JCS and White House level before the blockade, which meant there was nothing to implement when the crisis occurred. It is well established that State and Defense Department officials attempted to brief Truman on three courses of action and advocated for withdrawing from the city.[75] Truman's decision on June 28, 1948, to state unequivocally that the United States would maintain its rights to remain in Berlin was a declaration of American resolve and created a position that no subsequent presidents in the Cold War could contradict. Truman offered no guidance on the issue of how to remain in the city. He did realize the importance of a show of force in Europe, and he approved the deployment of three Boeing B-29 Stratofortress bomb groups to the United Kingdom and Germany.[76]

With Truman's decision that US forces would remain in Berlin, Army Headquarters had to find ways in July 1948 to maintain the Allied position while preparing for a potential rout. Planners formed contingencies that aligned with Truman's order but also advocated for the evacuation of nonessential personnel and reducing the size of the garrison to a tactical force. Now understanding the political components of Berlin planning, they made the recommendations with the caveat that they were offering courses of action rather than any statement of policy.[77] On June 24 Clay directed Huebner and the commanding general of the 1st Constabulary Brigade, Brig. Gen. Arthur G. Trudeau, to form a task force of 6,000 troops.[78] The plan, however, found little support in the Pentagon or White House.[79] Bradley and Royall ordered Clay to take no actions that could lead to an escalation, which is why they—once again—attacked Clay's suggestion to utilize an armed convoy.[80]

The resistance within the Department of the Army to plan for a military defense of Berlin was because of the understanding that a conflict without employing atomic weapons was sure to be lopsided. Despite the short-term measures taken at the national level to improve preparedness, army combat forces in Germany and Austria were both still too few and under strength. They consisted of the 1st Infantry Division, which could boast only 12,180 troops, with one of its battalions garrisoned in Berlin. The US Constabulary was a highly mobile force of 15,776 troops, but the six regiments were lightly armed. For all of Austria, the army had only the 350th Infantry Regiment, outfitted with old equipment and possessing an estimated combat efficiency of 50 percent. British and French forces added another 178,426 troops, split between five divisions, three brigades, five regimental combat teams, and four independent infantry battalions. These forces had to counter 348,000 Red Army troops divided between twenty-three divisions. In Berlin alone, there were only five Allied battalions against four Soviet divisions within a twenty-five-mile radius of the city.[81]

With no obvious military solution to the defense of Berlin, Truman and his advisers concluded that an airlift was a nonprovocative, short-term solution until the Allies crafted a more concrete policy and a diplomatic initiative. In the absence of the latter, the former became the policy.[82] There was not a consensus among US leaders about how successful an airlift would be. The April airlift had not convinced the Pentagon that the concept was workable in the short term, as it failed to make even minimum requirements for the sector by one-third.[83] The deficiency was due to the ad hoc nature of planning between air bases and the British and Americans conducting airlifts independent of one another.[84] Mostly, though, it was because of an inadequate number of aircraft. LeMay had already requested fifty additional C-54s to increase the daily Allied tonnage to three thousand, a plan that Clay endorsed in his communications with Bradley.[85] The chief of staff was skeptical that an airlift could work, but he recommended eighty-five more C-54s be sent to Germany, all that the airports could handle.[86] The airlift decision was not without potential dangers to a defense of Europe. An airlift operation with an indeterminate end date had implications for USAFE's ability to carry out other missions and compromised emergency war plans, since meeting the daily tonnage requirements to sustain Berlin reduced by 25 percent the number of aircraft available for an evacuation of Europe.[87]

The Allied airlift nonetheless succeeded after some initial difficulty in the herculean task of supplying the western sectors of Berlin in summer 1948.[88] Doing so offered leaders the ability to manage the crisis day to day, rather than choosing between withdrawal and war.[89] In the meantime, the Western Allies discussed negotiation strategies. There was relative agreement between the Americans, British, and French about the implementation of an airlift, but there was spirited debate about fundamental questions regarding Berlin's administration and place in a solution to the German question. From July to September, the military governors and foreign ministers alike failed to come to a consensus with their Soviet counterparts, leading to the issue going before the United Nations Security Council in October for mediation.[90]

The lack of diplomatic settlement into fall 1948 and the approach of winter led the military to anticipate a perpetual standoff in Berlin. On October 16, Wedemeyer tasked his Pentagon planners with studying the military impact of stalemate. His personal view was that the West was at a political and military disadvantage to the Soviets, who were better adept at waging operations short of war. Expanding on the findings of the study, he pushed for the United States to withdraw from Berlin and redeploy forces in Western Europe to the Frankfurt area, "to be prepared for active Soviet agression [sic] at any time in the future."[91] By December 7, discussion of perpetual blockade rose to the level of the War Council, composed of the secretary of defense, secretary of the army, secretary of the navy, secretary of the air force, chief of naval operations, chief of staff of the United States Army, and chief of staff of the United States Air Force.[92] Within one month, however, tentative negotiations between diplomats renewed, and after five months of earnest talks, the Four Powers announced an end to the blockade on May 5.[93]

Most studies of Berlin during this crisis period end any analysis of military action after the conclusion of the blockade. This misses a key point: surviving the blockade did not bring clarity to the Western powers' position in Berlin.[94] The Western Allies had succeeded in transforming Berlin into a symbol of resolve in the face of Communist aggression, but they were still responsible for 2.2 million West Berliners in a city that had minimal

economic output and Red Army divisions surrounding it.[95] Five days after
Stalin lifted the blockade, the NSC met in the White House to discuss
possible courses of action if Moscow resumed access restrictions, a question decision makers were still struggling to answer.[96] Despite discussion
of using military force in the future, the NSC concluded in the resulting
policy paper, NSC 24/1, that the only option available to them was an airlift
and avoiding any ground access probe.[97]

GLOBAL COLD WAR, 1950

It was not until summer 1950 that American discussions on how to defend
the city moved beyond the considerations of 1947–48. These came as a result
of pivotal Cold War structures that were put into place between April 1949
and June 1950. The founding of NATO on April 4, 1949, bound together the
West in a collective security agreement against the Soviet Union, encouraging European political integration. The founding of the Federal Republic
of Germany (FRG) out of the Western occupation zones on May 23, 1949,
and the German Democratic Republic (GDR) out of the Soviet occupation
zone on October 7, 1949, delayed a solution to the German question and
therefore one for Berlin. The drafting of NSC 68 on April 7, 1950, created a
US national security framework that stressed containment and the buildup
of political, economic, and military strength.[98] The largest effect of these
structures on US strategy was that US officials viewed Berlin as a global
issue rather than a regional one.

This new outlook on Berlin was demonstrated on June 25, 1950, when
90,000 North Korean soldiers crossed the Thirty-Eighth Parallel and invaded the Republic of Korea. Prior to June 1950, US officials had relied
on a strategy of withstanding Soviet harassment to contain Communism,
built on the belief that Moscow would not escalate pressure to the point of
war. US officials had thought the same was true in Korea, where there was
also a planned temporary division of the country, but they instead found
themselves involved in a shooting war far from where they had anticipated
a Communist strike would come.[99] The Korean War confirmed for army
leaders in Washington, Frankfurt am Main, and Berlin that the Soviets were
shifting their expansionist strategy from direct confrontation with the West
to operating through proxies. In Berlin, this meant Moscow could use East
Germany to attack the Western position in the city.[100]

That supposition led the United States to seek new solutions to the problem of Berlin's defense. The primary architect in the post-blockade period was Maj. Gen. Maxwell D. Taylor, who was US Commander, Berlin. Like other army leaders, Taylor viewed East Germany as a proxy for the Soviet Union. He identified the newly created paramilitary force, the Volkspolizei Bereitschaften, as the primary threat to the western sectors.[101] A police force in name only, the unit was 90,000 strong in summer 1950.[102] It was nominally an anti-riot and anti-insurgency force, but its disposition, organization, and equipment made it the East German army six years before the GDR established one. The Bereitschaften was composed of five groups that were housed in barracks across the country and, most worrying to US officials, had one tank and one motorized division each.[103]

Taylor defined these problems and proposed courses of action in an August 10, 1950, study that he sent to both EUCOM and Clay's civilian successor, US high commissioner for Germany John J. McCloy. The paper served as the basis for Allied discussion about Berlin policy. In it, Taylor concluded that the Allies could not defend Berlin, but he saw propaganda value in an economically prosperous and politically free West Berlin.[104] He predicted that GDR officials would claim sovereignty after the October 1950 general election, giving them control of Berlin access. The East Germans would then declare the Allies were in the city illegally, demand an evacuation they knew would not happen, and then impose a blockade.[105] Taylor's solution was to replicate the Bereitschaften, and he recommended expanding the Berlin police to create a paramilitary and home-guard force.[106] The suggestion fed into a larger debate about German rearmament, which had created a number of disagreements between Bonn and Washington. Ultimately, a West German self-defense force was stillborn, but Taylor's study did set the conditions for a militarization of police inside Berlin along the lines of, as he perceived it, the US National Guard.[107] Allied officials, including the Joint Chiefs, agreed with Taylor's plans. Within months the Berlin police rearmed, its ranks grew by three thousand men, and it added a volunteer reserve force of six thousand.[108]

Taylor's augmentation of Western military power with local forces was a positive step toward integrating Berliners into plans for their own defense. That did not offer a structural solution to the problem, however, which required decisions at the national level. A concerted Allied effort to connect Berlin to the broader defense of Europe occurred at the New York

Foreign Ministers meeting in mid-September 1950. The conference was not originally intended to focus on Germany and Berlin, but interdepartmental conversations throughout August and McCloy's prompting steered the proposed topics of discussion in that direction.[109] At the meeting, the three Western powers discussed a section of Taylor's August 10 paper, on how to maintain the Allied position in Berlin against potential East German military force. Taylor stressed the need for the Allies to state their unequivocal intention to maintain their rights in the city at the risk of war. He argued that a declaration would be the "most potent single force for the protection of West Berlin," and would make clear that no "action of the Korean pattern will be tolerated in Germany."[110]

The Western Allies made such a declaration on September 19, 1950. Within a communiqué on Germany, they declared that they would treat any attack against the Federal Republic or Berlin as an attack upon themselves.[111] In a separate agreement on Berlin security, they restated their warning and also explicitly warned Moscow that the Soviet Union would be held responsible for an East German attack. If there was an attack, the West vowed to defend the city by force and invoke NATO's Article 5 mutual-defense clause.[112] In making the western sectors of Berlin NATO's frontier outpost, the Allies bought time for the fledgling alliance. As a deterrent, the agreement protected Western Europe as much as it did Berlin, fitting into NATO's conventional force posture. The United States, Britain, and France were still responsible for administering the western sectors of Berlin, but the city's defense theoretically fell to NATO. There would be troubles later about NATO's authority in western Berlin compared to the three powers, but the alliance proved remarkably resilient in those occasions.[113]

* * *

Every war plan must identify a political objective, lest planners rely on military policy for setting objectives.[114] The US Army's initial plans for a war in Europe lacked an attainable political goal by emphasizing retreating from central and northwestern Europe with whatever forces they could withdraw and using either the English Channel or Pyrenees as a defensive barrier. In that arrangement, Berlin would have to be sacrificed. When Truman declared that the United States would remain in the city because of access rights earned during World War II, Berlin transitioned from the first area to be ceded in the event of war to the first to be defended. Truman, however, never identified a political objective, which accounts for why the army struggled to find military means to achieve an unclear political end without initiating the war that planners had been arguing for two years that the United States would lose.

Tying the city into a transatlantic, politico-military defense arrangement solved the army's problem of defending an indefensible position because it integrated Berlin into the West's deterrence strategy. That did not alter geography, to be sure, but it did lower a shield over Berlin, thereby deterring Soviet or East German aggression by raising the specter of general war. This would create other problems at the end of the 1950s and not avoid another crisis eight years later, as other chapters in this volume will discuss. Crucially, however, the solution created more military options for leaders later, when Berlin became a flashpoint of the Cold War yet again.

NOTES

1. Kori Schake, "The Berlin Crises of 1948–49 and 1958–62," in *Securing Peace in Europe, 1945–62: Thoughts for the Post–Cold War Era,* ed. Beatrice Heuser and Robert O'Neill (New York: St. Martin's Press, 1992), 65–70.

2. Daniel J. Nelson, *Wartime Origins of the Berlin Dilemma* (Tuscaloosa: University of Alabama Press, 1978), 155–70; Carolyn Eisenberg, *Drawing the Line: The American Decision to Divide Germany, 1944–1949* (New York: Cambridge University Press, 1996), 14–70.

3. William Stivers and Donald A. Carter, *The City Becomes a Symbol: The U.S. Army in the Occupation of Berlin, 1945–1949* (Washington, DC: Center of Military History, 2017), 47.

4. Ingo Trauschweizer, *The Cold War U.S. Army: Building Deterrence for Limited War* (Lawrence: University Press of Kansas, 2008), 24–27. For the beginning of this shift, see Mark A. Stoler, "From Continentalism to Globalism: General Stanley D. Embick, the Joint Strategic Survey Committee, and the Military View of American National Policy during the Second World War," *Diplomatic History* 6, no. 3 (Summer 1982): 303–21.

5. W. Philips Davison, *Berlin Blockade: A Study in Cold War Politics* (Princeton, NJ: Princeton University Press, 1958); Avi Shlaim, *The United States and the Berlin Blockade, 1948–1949: A Study in Crisis Decision-Making* (Berkeley: University of California Press, 1989); Daniel Harrington, *Berlin on the Brink: The Blockade, the Airlift, and the Early Cold War* (Lexington: University Press of Kentucky, 2012).

6. For example, John Tusa and Ann Tusa, *The Berlin Airlift* (New York: Atheneum, 1988); Thomas Parrish, *Berlin in the Balance: The Blockade, the Airlift, the First Major Battle of the Cold War* (Boston: Addison-Wesley, 1998); Richard Reeves, *Daring Young Men: The Heroism and Triumph of the Berlin Airlift, June 1948–May 1949* (New York: Simon & Schuster, 2011); Barry Turner, *The Berlin Airlift: A New History of the Cold War's Decisive Relief Operation* (London: Icon Books, 2018).

7. Henrik Bering, *Outpost Berlin: The History of the American Military Forces in Berlin, 1945–1994* (Chicago: Edition Q, 1995), 1–10.

8. Cornelius Ryan, *The Last Battle* (New York: Simon and Schuster, 1966), 420; David Clay Large, *Berlin* (New York: Basic Books, 2000), 371; Ann Tusa, *The Last Division: A History of Berlin, 1945–1989* (New York: Perseus Books, 1997), 11.

9. Public Relations, Statistical and Historical Branch Office of Military Government, "A Four Year Report: Office of Military Government, U.S. Sector, Berlin," box 1, Papers of Frank L. Howley, U.S. Army Heritage and Education Center, Carlisle, PA (hereafter AHEC); Large, *Berlin*, 371; Tusa, *The Last Division*, 11.

10. Stivers and Carter, *City Becomes a Symbol*, 47.

11. Frank L. Howley, *Berlin Command* (New York: GP Putnam's Sons, 1950), 77–134.

12. The 82nd Airborne Division relieved the 2nd Armored Division after only one month.

13. Stivers and Carter, *City Becomes a Symbol*, 47.

14. John C. Sparrow, *History of the Personnel Demobilization in the United States Army* (Washington, DC: Office of the Chief of Military History, US Army, 1951), 257–59.

15. James F. Schnabel, *History of the Joint Chiefs of Staff*, vol. 1, *The Joint Chiefs of Staff and National Policy, 1945–1947* (Washington, DC: Office of the Chairman of the JCS, 1996), 93.

16. Michael S. Sherry, *Preparing for the Next War: American Plans for Postwar Defense, 1941–45* (New Haven, CT: Yale University Press, 1977), 198–238.

17. Steven T. Ross, *American War Plans, 1945–1950* (London: Frank Cass, 1996), 6–7.

18. Oliver J. Frederiksen, *The American Military Occupation of Germany, 1945–1953* (Frankfurt: United States Army, Europe, 1953), 32–41.

19. Clay had offices in both Frankfurt am Main, where OMGUS was headquartered, and Berlin, where the four military governors of the victorious powers met as the senior policy-making committee, the Allied Control Council.

20. Planning Paper, P&O Division, "Course of Action of U.S. Forces in Europe in Event the Soviets Attacks either the U.S. or UK Forces in Europe without Immediately Molesting the Other," July 31, 1947, folder: P&O 381 TS (Section V-A) (Part I) (Case 88 Only) (Sub-Nos. 1–34), box 102, Plans & Operations

Division Decimal File, 1946–48, RG 319, National Archives at College Park, College Park, MD (hereafter NACP).

21. Schnabel, *Joint Chiefs of Staff and National Policy,* 102–3.

22. Ross, *American War Plans,* 11.

23. Stivers and Carter, *City Becomes a Symbol,* 135–36.

24. Ross, *American War Plans,* 9.

25. Phillip A. Karber and Jerald A. Combs, "The United States, NATO, and the Soviet Threat to Western Europe: Military Estimates and Policy Options, 1945–1963," *Diplomatic History* 22, no. 3 (Summer 1998) 399–429; Ernest R. May, John D. Steinbruner, and Thomas W. Wolfe, *History of the Strategic Arms Competition, 1945–1972,* part I (Washington, DC: Office of the Secretary of Defense Historical Office, 1981), 1–103.

26. Donald A. Carter, *Forging the Shield: The U.S. Army in the Cold War, 1951–1962* (Washington, DC: U.S. Army Center of Military History, 2015), 8.

27. Brian McAllister Linn, *Elvis's Army: Cold War GIs and the Atomic Battlefield* (Cambridge, MA: Harvard University Press, 2016), 10–35.

28. Melvyn P. Leffler, "The American Conception of National Security and the Beginnings of the Cold War, 1945–48," *American Historical Review* 89, no. 2 (April 1984): 349.

29. Wedemeyer replaced Norstad as director of the Plans and Operations Division on October 31, 1947. Norstad became the deputy chief of staff of operations for the air force.

30. Briefing Paper for Wedemeyer, "Brief of EUCOM Plan for Joint Operations in Event of Soviet Aggression," December 12, 1947, folder: P&O 381 TS (Section V-A) (Part I) (Case 88 Only) (Sub-Nos. 1–34), box 102, Plans & Operations Division Decimal File, 1946–48, RG 319, NACP.

31. Memorandum for Wedemeyer, "EUCOM Plan for Joint Operations in Event of Soviet Aggression," December 12, 1947, folder: P&O 381 TS (Section V-A) (Part I) (Case 88 Only) (Sub-Nos. 1–34), box 102, Plans & Operations Division Decimal File, 1946–48, RG 319, NACP. Memorandum for Schulyer, "EuCom Plan for Joint Operations in Event of Soviet Aggression," December 22, 1947, folder: P&O 381 TS (Section V–A) (Case 88 Only) (Part VI) (Sub-Nos. 131–), box 103, Plans & Operations Division Decimal File, 1946–48, RG 319, NACP.

32. EUCOM planning paper, "Joint Operations Plan for Operations in Event of Hostilities with the USSR," September 30, 1947, folder: P&O 381 TS (Section V–A) (Part I) (Case 88 Only) (Sub-Nos. 1–34), box 102, Plans & Operations Division Decimal File, 1946–48, RG 319, NACP.

33. Memorandum, Porter for Wedemeyer, "Plan for Joint Operations in Event of Soviet Aggression," December 22, 1947, folder: P&O 381 TS (Section V-A) (Part I) (Case 88 Only) (Sub-Nos. 1–34), box 102, Plans & Operations Division Decimal File, 1946–48, RG 319, NACP.

34. William Harris, "March Crisis 1948, Act I," *Studies in Intelligence* 10, no. 4 (Fall 1966): 4.

35. Harris, "March Crisis 1948, Act I," 8.

36. Ross, *American War Plans,* 8–20.

37. David Alan Rosenberg, "The Origins of Overkill: Nuclear Weapons and American Strategy, 1945–1960," *International Security* 7, no. 4 (Spring 1983): 14.

38. John M. Curatola, *Bigger Bombs for a Brighter Tomorrow: The Strategic Air Command and American War Plans at the Dawn of the Atomic Age, 1945–1950* (Jefferson, NC: McFarland, 2016), 15.

39. Memorandum, Wedemeyer to Royall, "Memorandum for the Secretary of the Army," January 2, 1948, folder: P&O 381 TS (Section V–A) (Part I) (Case 88 Only) (Sub-Nos. 1–34), box 102, Plans & Operations Division Decimal File, 1946–1948, RG 319, NACP.

40. It is generally perceived that Clay's armed convoy proposal originated in March 1948, but he told a historian at the Historical Office, Office of the Secretary of Defense, that he first proposed it in December 1947. See Harris, "March Crisis 1948, Act I," 4. The telegram appears in Walter Millis, ed., *The Forrestal Diaries* (New York: Viking, 1951), 460. For discussion of the telegram, see Harrington, *Berlin on the Brink,* 136–37.

41. Lucius D. Clay, interview by Jean Edward Smith, February 11, 1971, in New York City, transcript, Columbia University Oral History Research Office, 591.

42. Notes of Conference, Clay, Weeks, Parks, June 29, 1945, *Foreign Relations of the United States: Diplomatic Papers, 1945, European Advisory Commission, Austria, Germany,* vol. 3, ed. William Slany et al. (Washington, DC: Government Printing Office, 1969), Document 298; Earl F. Ziemke, *U.S. Army in the Occupation of Germany, 1944–1946* (Washington, DC: U.S. Army Center of Military History, 1990), 300–301; Robert Murphy, *Diplomat among Warriors: The Unique World of a Foreign Service Expert* (New York: Doubleday, 1964), 262; Lucius D. Clay, *Decision in Germany* (New York: Doubleday, 1950), 24–27. Clay interview transcript, 598.

43. Clay interview transcript, 729.

44. Memorandum, Royall to Forrestal, "U.S. Course of Action in the Event the Soviets Attempt to Force Us Out of Berlin," January 19, 1948, folder: P&O 381 TS (Section V–A) (Part I) (Case 88 Only) (Sub-Nos. 1–34), box 102, Plans & Operations Division Decimal File, 1946–48, RG 319, NACP.

45. Royall to Forrestal, "U.S. Course of Action in the Event the Soviets Attempt to Force Us Out of Berlin."

46. Jean Edward Smith, ed., *The Papers of General Lucius D. Clay, Germany 1945–1949,* vol. 2 (Bloomington: Indiana University Press, 1974), 568; hereafter *Clay Papers.*

47. Peter Svik, "The Czechoslovak Factor in Western Alliance Building, 1945–1948," *Journal of Cold War Studies* 18, no. 1 (Winter 2016): 158–59.

48. Omar Bradley and Clay Blair, *A General's Life* (New York: Simon and Schuster, 1983), 477. See also author's note, *Clay Papers,* 569.

49. Steven L. Rearden, *Council of War: A History of the Joint Chiefs of Staff, 1942–1991* (Washington, DC: Joint History Office, 2012), 75.

50. Special Message to the Congress on the Threat to the Freedom of Europe, March 17, 1948, *Public Papers of Harry S. Truman,* vol. 4 (Washington, DC: US Government Printing Office, 1964), 184.

51. Michael J. Hogan, *A Cross of Iron: Harry S. Truman and the Origins of the National Security State, 1945–1954* (New York: Cambridge University Press, 1998), 103, 113.

52. Report on the Exchange of Letters between General Dratvin and General Gailey regarding Soviet Interference with Allied Access to Berlin, March 30–31, 1948, in *Documents on Berlin, 1943–1963* (Munich: R. Oldenbourg, 1963), 56; Harrington, *Berlin on the Brink,* 47.

53. Marc Trachtenberg, *A Constructed Peace: The Making of the European Settlement* (Princeton, NJ: Princeton University Press, 1999), 78–79.

54. Memorandum to Wedemeyer, "Data on Airlift, Civilians in Berlin and Maps of the Area," March 31, 1948, folder: P&O 381 TS (Section V–A) (Part I) (Case 88 Only) (Sub-Nos. 1–34), box 102, Plans & Operations Division Decimal File, 1946–1948, RG 319, NACP.

55. Cable, Clay to Bradley, April 1, 1948, *Clay Papers,* 608.

56. Memorandum, P&O Division, "Transit through Soviet Zone—Berlin," April 5, 1948, folder: P&O 381 TS (Section V–A) (Part I) (Case 88 Only) (Sub-Nos. 1–34), box 102, Plans & Operations Division Decimal File, 1946–48, RG 319, NACP. See also Memorandum, Marshall to Sawyer, July 9, 1948, *Foreign Relations of the United States: 1948, Eastern Europe; The Soviet Union,* vol. 4, ed. Rogers P. Churchill, William Slany, and Herbert A. Fine (Washington, DC: Government Printing Office, 1974), Document 350.

57. Teleconference, Clay, Royall, Bradley, April 2, 1948, folder: Berlin Crisis, box 150, President's Secretary File, Subject File, Harry S. Truman Presidential Library, Independence, MO (hereafter HSTL); Cable, Clay to Bradley, April 1, 1948, *Clay Papers,* 607.

58. Howley, *Berlin Command,* 201.

59. Howley, 201–2.

60. Curtis E. LeMay, *Mission with LeMay: My Story* (Garden City, NY: Doubleday, 1965), 411.

61. Memorandum, Mayo to Wedemeyer, "Brief of AF Telecon with CG USAFE 1 April 1948," April 2, 1948, folder: P&O 381 TS (Section V–A) (Part I) (Case 88 Only) (Sub-Nos. 1–34), box 102, Plans & Operations Division Decimal File, 1946–48, RG 319, NACP.

62. LeMay, *Mission with LeMay,* 411.

63. Memorandum of Conversation, April 2, 1948, folder: Berlin Crisis, box 150, President's Secretary File, Subject File, HSTL.

64. Cable 98817, Mayo to EUCOM, April 1, 1948, folder: P&O 901 Germany TS (Section I) (Cases 1–), box 13, P&O TS Decimal File, RG 319, NACP; Cable 71866, Wedemeyer to Clay and Huebner, April 1, 1948, folder: P&O 370.05 TS (Section I) (Cases 2–12), box 84, P&O TS Decimal File, RG 319, NACP.

65. Memorandum, Mayo to Wedemeyer, March 31, 1948, folder: P&O 381 TS (Section V–A) (Part I) (Case 88 Only) (Sub-Nos. 1–34), box 102, Plans & Operations Division Decimal File, 1946–48, RG 319, NACP.

66. Teleconference, Clay with Bradley, April 10, 1948, *Clay Papers,* 623.

67. Teleconference Clay with Collins, Chamberlin, March 17, 1948, *Clay Papers,* 580.

68. Teleconference, Clay with Bradley, April 10, 1948, *Clay Papers,* 623.

69. Teleconference, Clay with Bradley, April 10, 1948, *Clay Papers,* 623.

70. Teleconference, Clay, Bradley, and Wedemeyer, March 31, 1948, *Clay Papers,* 606.

71. Memorandum, P&O Division, April 14, 1948, folder: P&O 381 TS (Section V–A) (Part I) (Case 88 Only) (Sub-Nos. 1–34), box 102, Plans & Operations Division Decimal File, 1946–48, RG 319, NACP. See also John H. Backer, *Winds of History: The German Years of Lucius DuBignon Clay* (New York: Van Nostrand Reinhold, 1983), 236–39.

72. Deborah Welch Larson, "Truman and the Berlin Blockade: The Role of Intuition and Experience in Good Foreign Policy Judgment," in *Good Judgment in Foreign Policy: Theory and Application,* ed. Stanley A. Renshon and Deborah Welch Larson (Lanham, MD: Rowman & Littlefield, 2003), 131.

73. Deborah Welch Larson, "The Origins of Commitment: Truman and West Berlin," *Journal of Cold War Studies* 13, no. 1 (Winter 2011): 131.

74. Wilson D. Miscamble, "Harry S. Truman, the Berlin Blockade, and the 1948 Election," *Presidential Studies Quarterly* 10, no. 3 (Summer 1980): 307; Charles E. Bohlen, *Witness to History, 1929–1969* (New York: W. W. Norton & Co., 1973), 276; Stivers and Carter, *City Becomes a Symbol,* 230.

75. For accounts of the meeting, see Bradley and Blair, *A General's Life,* 479; Millis, *Forrestal Diaries,* 453. For analysis, see Shlaim, *United States and the Berlin Blockade,* 220–24; Larson, "Origins of Commitment," 195–97; Harrington, *Berlin on the Brink,* 88–90.

76. Millis, *Forrestal Diaries,* 455; Cable from Clay to Draper, June 27, 1948, *Clay Papers,* 707–8; Roger G. Miller, *To Save a City: The Berlin Airlift, 1948–1949* (College Station: Texas A&M University Press, 2000), 45–48.

77. Memorandum, Timberman to Schuyler, "Notes on the Berlin Situation (Army View)," June 30, 1948, folder: P&O 381 TS (Section V–A) (Case 88 Only) (Part VI) (Sub-Nos. 131–), box 103, Plans & Operations Division Decimal File, 1946–48, RG 319, NACP.

78. Stivers and Carter, *City Becomes a Symbol,* 226.

79. Memorandum for the President, July 23, 1948, folder: Memo for the President: Meeting Discussions (1948), box 186, President's Secretary File, HSTL; Millis, *Forrestal Diaries,* 460; Harrington, *Berlin on the Brink,* 136–37.

80. Bradley and Blair, *A General's Life,* 479–80; Teleconference TT-9667, June 25, 1948, in Smith, *Clay Papers,* 699. P&O Division memorandum, "Transit through Soviet Zone—Berlin."

81. Memorandum, Plans and Operations to Bradley, "Military Situation in Berlin," July 17, 1948, folder: P&O 381 TS (Section V–A) (Case 88 Only) (Part VI) (Sub-Nos. 131–), box 103, Plans & Operations Division Decimal File, 1946–48, RG 319, NACP.

82. Harrington makes a convincing argument that counters the narrative about US leaders steadfastly choosing to break the blockade through an airlift. Harrington, *Berlin on the Brink,* 102–3.

83. Memorandum for the Secretary of Defense, "US Military Courses of Action with Respect to the Situation in Berlin," July 17, 1948, "P&O 381 TS (Section V-A) (Case 88 Only) (Part II) (Sub-Nos 35–80)" folder, box 103, Plans & Operations Division Decimal File, 1946–1948, RG 319, NARA.

84. They would eventually merge in October 1948. Harrington, *Berlin on the Brink,* 296.

85. Cable Clay to Bradley, July 10, 1948, *Clay Papers,* 730.

86. Harrington, *Berlin on the Brink,* 130.

87. Memorandum to Bradley, "Military Implications of Continued Supply of Berlin by Air," July 18, 1948, folder: P&O 381 TS (Section V-A) (Case 88 Only) (Part VI) (Sub-Nos. 131–), box 103, Plans & Operations Division Decimal File, 1946–48, RG 319, NACP.

88. See Miller, *To Save a City.* For a counter to the triumphant narrative, see William Stivers, "The Incomplete Blockade: Soviet Zone Supply of West Berlin, 1948–49," *Diplomatic History* 21, no. 4 (Fall 1997): 569–602.

89. Harrington, *Berlin on the Brink,* 140.

90. Philip C. Jessup, "The Berlin Blockade and the Use of the United Nations," *Foreign Affairs* 50, no. 1 (Oct. 1971): 163–73; Philip C. Jessup, "Park Avenue Diplomacy—Ending the Berlin Blockade," *Political Science Quarterly* 87, no. 3 (September 1972): 377–400.

91. Memorandum for the Director of Plans and Operations, "The Military Situation in Germany," October 16, 1948, "P&O 381 TS (Section V-A) (Case 88 Only) (Part VI) (Sub-Nos 131–)" folder, box 103, Plans & Operations Division Decimal File, 1946–48, RG 319, NARA.

92. Memorandum, Secretary Royall to Secretary Forrestal, "Support of Berlin Throughout an Indefinite Period of Blockade," December 7, 1948, "P&O 381 TS (Section V-A) (Case 88 Only) (Part VI) (Sub-Nos 131–)" folder, box 103, Plans & Operations Division Decimal File, 1946–48, RG 319, NARA.

93. Bohlen, *Witness to History,* 283; Dean Acheson, *Present at the Creation: My Years in the State Department* (New York: W. W. Norton, 1969), 267; Condit, *Joint Chiefs of Staff and National Policy,* 81.

94. W. Philips Davison, *Berlin Blockade: A Study in Cold War Politics* (Princeton, NJ: Princeton University Press, 1958); Avi Shlaim, *The United States and the Berlin Blockade, 1948–1949: A Study in Crisis Decision-Making* (Berkeley: University of California Press, 1989); Giles Martin, *Checkmate in Berlin: The Cold War Showdown That Shaped the Modern World* (New York: Henry Holt, 2021).

95. US Bureau of the Census, *Population of the Federal Republic of Germany and West Berlin: International Population Statistics Reports, Series P-90, no. 1* (Washington, DC: US Government Printing Office, 1952), 50–51.

96. Summary of Discussion of NSC Meeting, May 17, 1949, folder: NSC Meeting 40, box 178, NSC Meetings File, Subject File, President's Secretary File, HSTL.

97. NSC 24/2, "Possible U.S. Courses of Action in the Event the USSR Reimposes the Berlin Blockade," June 1, 1949, folder: NSC 24/2, box 3, Policy Papers, Records of the NSC, Entry 1, RG 273, NACP.

98. Norman Friedman, *The Fifty-Year War: Conflict and Strategy in the Cold War* (Annapolis, MD: Naval Institute Press, 2000), 137; Hogan, *Cross of Iron,* 265–314.

99. William J. Webb, *The Korean War: The Outbreak, 27 June–15 September 1950* (Washington, DC: Center of Military History, 1995), 9–11.

100. For Morgan's expanded analysis, which was intended to brief McCloy on Korea's effect on Germany, see "Appraisal of Next Soviet Moves in Germany," July 10, 1950, folder: Page Hold, box 5, Miscellaneous Files Relating to Berlin, Office of the Executive Secretary, RG 466, NACP.

101. Memorandum, Taylor to HICOG and EUCOM, "A Review of Berlin Situation," August 10, 1950, folder: Page Hold, box 5, Miscellaneous Files Relating to Berlin, Office of the Executive Secretary, RG 466, NACP.

102. Cable 762B.00/8–1550, "SovZone Report no. 19," August 15, 1950, folder 2, box 3906, Central Decimal Files, 1950–54, RG 59, NACP; Memorandum, HICOG, "A Review of the Berlin Situation," August 24, 1950, folder: HICOG-EUCOM Meeting, August 28, 1950, box 3, Office of the Executive Director, General Hay's Files, 1949–1951, RG 466, NACP.

103. Cable, McCloy to Byroade, August 18, 1950, folder: August 1950 Top Secret Documents McCloy Project TS (50) 65 to TS (50) 100, box 2, Top Secret General Records, Records of the High Commissioner RG 466, NACP.

104. Ingo Trauschweizer, *Maxwell Taylor's Cold War: From Berlin to Vietnam* (Lexington: University Press of Kentucky, 2019), 38.

105. Taylor, "A Review of Berlin Situation."

106. Speech, Maxwell Taylor, "Method Used in Berlin to suppress Communist activities in West Sect.," September 20, 1950, folder: Maxwell D. Taylor—Speeches,

Public Pronouncements, Briefings—2 Sept. 49–19 Jan. 51, box 3, Taylor Papers, National Defense University Special Collections, Archives, and History, Washington.

107. See David Clay Large, *Germans to the Front: West German Rearmament in the Adenauer Era* (Chapel Hill: University of North Carolina Press, 1996), 31–81.

108. Cable, Taylor to HICOG, October 7, 1950, *Foreign Relations of the United States: 1950, Central and Eastern Europe; The Soviet Union,* vol. 4, ed. William Z. Slany, Charles S. Sampson, and Rogers P. Churchill (Washington, DC: Government Printing Office, 1980), Document 467. See also Minutes, Joint Allied High Commission-Berlin Commandants Meeting, November 9, 1950, folder: Berlin Papers Re: Unified Defense, box 2, General Hay's Files, Office of the Executive Director, RG 466, NACP.

109. Cable (963), McCloy to Acheson, August 3, 1950, folder: August 1950 Top Secret Documents McCloy Project TS (50) 65 to TS (50) 100, box 2, Top Secret General Records, Records of the High Commissioner, RG 466, NACP.

110. Taylor, "A Review of Berlin Situation."

111. Communiqué on Germany, Foreign Ministers of the United States, Britain, and France, September 19, 1950, *Foreign Relations of the United States: 1950, Western Europe,* vol. 3, ed. David H. Stauffer et al. (Washington, DC: Government Printing Office, 1977), Document 589.

112. Western Foreign Ministers Decision, "Allied Agreement on Berlin Security," September 19, 1950, *Foreign Relations of the United States, 1950,* Document 589.

113. Bruno Thoss, "Information, Persuasion, or Consultation? The Western Powers and NATO during the Berlin Crisis, 1958–1962," in *Transatlantic Relations at Stake: Aspects of NATO, 1956–1972,* ed. Christian Nuenlist and Anna Locher (Zurich: Center for Security Studies, 2006), 73–94. See also Ingo Trauschweizer, "Adapt and Survive: NATO in the Cold War," in *Grand Strategy and Military Alliances,* ed. Peter R. Mansoor and Williamson Murray (New York: Cambridge University Press, 2016), 166–95.

114. David Kaiser, "US Objectives and Plans for War with the Soviet Union, 1945–54," in *The Fog of Peace and War Planning: Military and Strategic War Planning under Uncertainty,* ed. Talbot C. Imlay and Monica Duffy Toft (New York: Routledge, 2006), 205–23.

CHAPTER 3

The United States, Berlin, and the 1953 Uprising

CHRISTIAN F. OSTERMANN

Seventy years later, the United States' role in the events surrounding the June 1953 uprising in East Berlin and East Germany has remained a subject of public controversy. For example, in her 2023 book, *Beyond the Wall: East Germany, 1949–1990,* German-British journalist and historian Katja Hoyer argued—referencing some of my early work on the subject—that there was "some truth to the idea" that the uprising was an "attempted fascist coup" instigated and coordinated by Western agents in Germany. Hoyer argued that the uprising—while a "spontaneous event born out of the frustration over workload and pay"—was "stoked by the West." Her reading of the events—and of my work—in turn provoked critical reviews in a variety of outlets, including one by Franziska Kuschel in the prominent German weekly *Der Spiegel.* The following chapter will revisit the American involvement in the events of 1953, based in part on my research for my 2021 book, *Between Containment and Rollback: The United States and the Cold War in Germany.*[1]

This chapter highlights two aspects of a larger, proactive US rollback strategy vis-à-vis East Germany that dates back to the Harry S. Truman administration and sought to destabilize the GDR: covert US sponsorship of anti-Communist rollback groups in Berlin and the role of the US-controlled

Radio in the American Sector. Only in recent years has the declassification of relevant sources allowed historians to appreciate the extent of this sustained (if altogether limited) "psychological cold warfare" against the GDR. It was the darker, lesser-known corollary to US containment strategy that prioritized the integration of the Federal Republic of Germany with the West to bolster Western European recovery, prosperity, and defenses. The Truman administration had launched, and the Eisenhower administration had readily continued and expanded, a broad counteroffensive to keep alive the spirit of resistance behind the Iron Curtain, raising expectations among East Germans (and others in the Soviet orbit) that the West would come to their aid in opposing the Communist government. Neither the sponsorship of rollback groups nor RIAS broadcasts were specifically aimed at instigating an uprising in East Germany, and US officials were almost incredulous when news of the unrest first broke. Yet these activities—however one may judge them—no doubt contributed to fostering a sense of—and at times acts of—opposition on the part of the population and a sense of siege on the part of the Communist regime.

For the Truman administration, Germany's division and the establishment of two competing states in 1949 brought on a new sensation of vulnerability vis-à-vis the East. The way the founding of the GDR had been staged as a response to alleged Western "separatism" was only one reason for the profound sense of uncertainty besetting the US High Commission in Germany. Fears that, with the Communist-run state in Germany, Soviet leader Joseph V. Stalin had acquired a new instrument for pursuing his larger goals in this most important of Cold War battlegrounds fed increasingly gloomy assessments of the "worldwide correlation of forces" that to many seemed to be shifting in favor of the USSR by 1950. American officials therefore believed that beyond building a politically and economically vibrant West Germany that would exert a "magnet effect" on the GDR, the West needed to actively prevent being "rolled up" by Eastern unity propaganda: by persistently denying the second German state international legitimacy through nonrecognition, by wresting the initiative in the discourse over German unity, and by developing psychological warfare apparatus and programs that could counter Communist efforts. The American counteroffensive entailed a massive program of overt and covert measures that went well beyond inoculating the Federal Republic politically against similar measures from the East. The US High Commission in Germany began to develop and implement psychological warfare plans that, envisioning an active roll-back of Communist control, aimed to keep alive the spirit of resistance in the East. As it sought to shore up support for a West German defense contribution within a European Defense Community, the Truman administration also worked with more hard-line elements in the West German government and supported a network of anti-Communist (sometimes far right wing) groups operating out of West Berlin and the Federal Republic to counter East German initiatives. Declassified US documents make clear that the program was not confined to planning papers in Washington and Berlin. Soviet and East German archival materials also help to demonstrate the extent to which this program affected the "hearts and minds" of the Communist leadership and the East German population. This American counteroffensive in Germany (and Eastern Europe) was part of a larger Cold War context in which the events in June 1953 unfolded.

Historians now estimate that close to one million people took to the streets in East Berlin and in some seven hundred communities throughout East Germany to protest dismal working and living conditions and demand greater freedoms and national unity.[2] The uprising was rooted in Stalin's industrialization, collectivization, and militarization drive in 1951–52 and the mass terror and repression in the late Stalin period that had brought the Soviet empire in Eastern Europe to the brink of collapse. Despite the many differences and intense jockeying for supremacy among his cronies following Stalin's death on March 5, the new Soviet leaders had agreed on the need for putting the brakes on Stalinist overdrive and implementing far-reaching political and economic liberalization. Among Moscow's East European satellites, the crisis brewing in East Germany became a priority. The "forced construction of socialism" under SED strongman Walter Ulbricht, announced in July 1952, had caused an exodus of refugees from East Germany to the West, moving through the open border in Berlin. By the spring of 1953, refugee numbers were swelling to alarming heights, since Ulbricht, instead of easing Stalinist policies, had hardened his course after Stalin's death. By early June, the increasingly alarmed Soviet leaders had settled on a set of political and economic reforms for the GDR; they ordered a German Communist leadership delegation to Moscow and warned it of an impending catastrophe unless it corrected course, prescribing down to the wording the announcement of a "New Course," which was to be implemented immediately. The German Communist leadership's stunning retreat from the harsher Stalinist course backfired: the party's rank and file were shocked, confused, and demoralized, and large numbers of the workers sensed confusion and weakness on the part of the regime. In the days after the New Course announcement on June 11, workers demanded a reduction of excessive industrial work norms, which had been excluded from the new policy. Once those had been rescinded, on June 16 the workers were joined by protesters from all walks of life in demanding more far-reaching political changes. Strikes and demonstrations on June 16 and 17 quickly gripped the entire state. Only a massive display of Soviet military might in the Soviet sector of Berlin and other cities throughout the GDR—the largest Soviet military operation in Europe since World War II—prevented an overthrow of the Communist government. At least fifty-five people died in the ensuing unrest.[3]

"ACTION POINT" BERLIN

On July 23, shortly after the 1953 uprising, President Eisenhower wrote to Chancellor Konrad Adenauer that he was "quite certain that future historians, in their analysis of the causes which will have brought about the disintegration of the Communist empire, will single out those brave East Germans who dared to rise against the cannons of tyranny with nothing but their bare hands and their stout hearts, as a root cause." Eisenhower began his letter, publicized three days later, by denying the "fantastic explanation put out by Moscow that the uprising was caused by American provocateurs."[4] Eisenhower was correct, but the very fact that he had to make this point suggests that the narrative spun by Soviet and East German officials that somehow the Americans had been involved in the uprising had gained some traction. The day after the June 17 protests, Eisenhower's staunchly anti-Communist secretary of state, John Foster Dulles, identified more than anyone else with the liberation rhetoric that became a hallmark of Eisenhower's foreign policy agenda, had to assure the assembled National Security Council in Washington that "the United States had nothing whatsoever to do with inciting these riots, and that our reaction thus far had been to confine ourselves, in broadcasts which were not attributable, to expressions of sympathy and admiration, with an admixture of references to the great traditions of 1848."[5] There was, in fact, considerable uncertainty what had happened on the ground in Berlin and the GDR in the hours and days after the protests had begun. Much of this uncertainty related to the role that German anti-Communist rollback groups—fully or partly sponsored but never fully controlled by the United States—had had in the uprising.

Since the beginning of the Truman administration began, West Berlin had played an important role as an American base for psychological and economic warfare against the fledgling East German state. As early as 1947/48, US officials realized that the joint Allied occupation of Berlin had provided them with a forward base deep inside the emerging Soviet sphere of influence. With its open borders, Berlin offered an extraordinary opportunity for the United States to make Western influence felt far behind the Iron Curtain at a time when Moscow sought to shut out the West from its buffer zone of satellite states in Eastern Europe. As put by Robert D. Murphy, who was America's top diplomat in occupied Germany and political adviser to the US occupation government, Berlin was an "action point far inside Soviet-held territory from which to observe developments and to support and influence resistance to Communism in a vital area."[6] During the 1948 blockade crisis, US officials fretted over the loss of those strategic advantages that Berlin afforded the United States. Then, in June 1948, the CIA informed Truman that, contrary to public perceptions, the main detrimental effect of Soviet access restrictions was not the interference with transport and supply. Instead, the tightened Soviet security measures that had accompanied the closing of the zonal borders had "impaired Berlin's usefulness as a center of a U.S. intelligence network" spanning the city, the Soviet zone, and Eastern Europe. Increased police controls in and around Berlin had also made "access to Soviet deserters and anti-communist Germans more difficult." And the CIA advised the president that restrictions on the free movement by West Germans in the Soviet zone threatened American "support [for] anti-Communism within the Soviet Zone" and dissemination of "pro-West" publications.[7]

Multiple US agencies in Berlin were engaged in intelligence operations in East Berlin. In their efforts, they employed anti-Communist groups, which had shot up in western Berlin in the shadow of the blockade. Since the merger of the Soviet zone SPD with the KPD in April 1946, the western SPD's East Bureau, for example, utilized its links with former party members in the zone, to engage in espionage and black propaganda, claiming, according to CIA documents, some two thousand agents or informants in the East. Many of these groups started out as charitable organizations that provided services to families searching for information on family members detained by Soviet security services in the Soviet zone. Their databases soon became of interest to Western Allied agencies.

The most prominent of these groups was the Fighting Group against Inhumanity (Kampfgruppe gegen Unmenschlichkeit, known by its acronym, KgU). Its driving force was Rainer Hildebrandt, who announced the establishment of the KgU at a public rally, the Rally against Tyranny, in October 1948. During the rally, Hildebrandt decried the Soviet zone as "one big concentration camp" and called Nazi methods "children's play" compared to the Stalinist practices of the Soviet secret police, promising that his organization would systematically investigate such crimes by Soviet zone authorities. Hildebrandt did not shy away from accusing the Western powers of complacency in the face of developments across the zonal border. In a series of speeches and campaigns in the following months, Hildebrandt effectively called for a cold war against the Soviet zone.[8]

The Fighting Group started building a registry for informers and Communist officials in the Soviet zone. In late 1948 Severin F. Wallach, head of the Berlin office of the US Army's CIC (Counter Intelligence Corps), began to draw on the KgU for intelligence purposes. In return, he provided financial support. After it was licensed by the Allied Kommandatura as a political organization in April 1949, the KgU developed multiple links to the US intelligence community in Berlin, including the Military Intelligence Division and, later, the CIA's Office for Policy Coordination. Under American tutelage, the KgU, from its Berlin base, turned increasingly toward active opposition to the Soviet zone authorities.

By 1949, the CIA's Office of Policy Coordination had "taken command" of supporting anti-Communist groups in West Germany and West Berlin, extending US financial aid to a growing network of individuals and organizations. American officials found that "a great deal" could be accomplished by "stimulating" these German private organizations to increase their independent propaganda activities and sponsor American-inspired projects. The American High Commission's public affairs chief, Alfred "Mickey" Boerner, a key node for many of the overt and "grey" activities in Berlin in 1951–53, felt that such an approach scored "successes all out of proportion to our investment in time and money."[9]

A favorite among the groups supported by CIA's Office of Policy Coordination (OPC) was the Untersuchungsausschuss freiheitlicher Juristen

(Investigating Committee of Free Lawyers, or UFJ), founded in October 1949 by Horst Erdmann (alias Dr. Theo Friedenau). The UFJ tracked illegal acts by the SED regime and collected evidence that could lead to criminal indictments in a reunited and democratic Germany, considered by many Germans still a reasonably likely prospect. In addition, the UFJ provided counseling in West Berlin for East Germans seeking legal advice. The group took advantage of the large corpus of basic rights proclaimed by the first GDR constitution of 1949. It also produced informational and propaganda materials with a particular focus on legal issues. The organization's reach into East Germany expanded rapidly, and by the end of 1950 it had been visited by twenty thousand people from all over the GDR. Some two hundred people a day knocked on the UFJ's doors. While it did receive support from other West German agencies, the CIA's Berlin station became the UFJ's main sponsor. The CIA's interest went beyond "hand[ing] Erdmann an occasional assignment or debrie[fing] him along lines of interest to [the CIA]"; the agency also decided to involve the UFJ in its planning of clandestine paramilitary "stay-behind operations" that would be activated behind the lines in case of "Day X"—a Soviet invasion—to maintain contact and keep radio equipment, arms, and explosives. When Erdmann's second-in-command and head of the group's Economics Department, Dr. Walter Linse, was kidnapped by GDR state security in July 1952, CIA deputy director Frank Wisner pressed the State Department to unleash a full set of reprisal measures—a measure of the CIA's appreciation of the UFJ's efforts.[10]

The UFJ never condoned violent acts of resistance. In that respect it differed from the KgU. Under Ernst Tillich, Hildebrandt's deputy and 1951 successor, the KgU's activities across the Iron Curtain grew increasingly more militant.[11] The CIA's Berlin Operations Base (BOB) regarded the group as an asset in its espionage and psychological warfare efforts. Though Tillich had spoken out against industrial sabotage as too dangerous and pointless unless it contributed to a "well-organized, general and decisive effort," the KgU engaged in increasingly hard-hitting "rollback" operations against the Communist regime in the East. These ranged from removing or disfiguring Communist posters and exploding handbill rockets to sabotaging projects involving arson, explosions, and assassinations. KgU agents launched balloons carrying propaganda material across the zonal border, blackmailed SED officials, exposed Soviet and Soviet zone security personnel, and carried out acts of sabotage against East German government structures and vehicles.

The CIA's OPC took over funding the group in 1949, and by 1950 the KgU had become a "principal project" for OPC Berlin, with the CIA covering about half of the organization's budget. Under OPC tutelage, the KgU's covert activities in the GDR grew not only more professional and conspiratorial, but also ever more militant and expansive. Covertly, Henry Heckscher, the deputy chief of the CIA's Berlin Operations Base, provided hands-on direction—yet even CIA officials could at no time assert full control over the myriad propaganda and sabotage activities the KgU carried out. In the fall of 1950, the KgU stepped up its operations in East Germany, including terror attacks and assassination plots. For the CIA, the KgU constituted a "flexible instrument for conducting a full range of covert operations against the East German regime." Clearly believing it had the Americans' license to do so, the Fighting Group's activities grew more radical and riskier. In 1951–52 alone, Soviet and GDR authorities arrested hundreds of people in the GDR in (alleged) connection with KgU operations, and many of those arrests resulted in death sentences and long labor camp penalties. Altogether, Soviet services carried out more than 130 death sentences against people accused of collaborating with the KgU.[12]

It is highly likely—though difficult to trace in the surviving documents—that in June 1953 most of these anti-Communist groups became involved in the unrest. They did not instigate the uprising—many seem in fact surprised by its timing and scope—but with their contacts in the East, they were likely attuned to the increasing volatility and explosiveness of the situation in East Berlin and the GDR and sought to both further and take advantage of the protests. At the time, US officials were uncertain about the extent to which anti-Communist groups sponsored by OPC had joined the unrest. In early July, the US High Commission's top GDR watcher in Berlin confessed that the degree and nature of Western encouragement was "not completely known." Circumstantial evidence suggested to him that it might be possible that the KgU "took an active hand in affairs in East Berlin on June 17." British officials, too, noted the role of anti-Communist groups in the American sector, "where the propagandists do not always seem to be under control."[13]

RIAS

With leading US officials out of pocket during the height of the uprising on June 16–17, it fell to the staff of Radio in the American Sector to react to the evolving protests. RIAS had launched in February 1946, initially as a wired broadcast station, to offer an alternative to the Soviet-controlled Radio Berlin as hopes in the immediate postwar period for a quadripartite radio operation for all of Berlin dissipated. Run by German Communists, Radio Berlin had resumed broadcasts within days of the German capitulation in May 1945, and for the first three years it dominated the airwaves in the city. With Cold War tensions increasingly undercutting quadripartite rule in Berlin, Clay launched "Operation Talkback," in which US-controlled media took on increasingly anti-Communist positions they had previously eschewed. And by late 1948 RIAS, until then second in popularity to the Soviet-controlled Radio Berlin, had, with its improved equipment and personnel, been transformed into a dedicated anti-Communist propaganda station that had become the most-listened-to radio station in Berlin, with a deep reach into the Soviet zone. According to opinion surveys, by 1949 some 90 percent of Berliners identified RIAS as their favorite station. RIAS, as the first US high commissioner, John J. McCloy, had put it in stark terms in 1950, constituted "the spiritual and psychological center of resistance in a Communist-dominated, blacked-out area" and "poison to the Communists."[14]

Throughout the spring of 1953, labor dissatisfaction had been a central theme in RIAS broadcasts. The station no doubt contributed to forging "an atmosphere of protest and dissatisfaction" in the GDR. Earlier than other Western stations, on the afternoon of June 15, RIAS began reporting on strike activity at the Stalinallee construction site. Broadcast in the evening and then again in the early morning of June 16, when reception throughout the GDR peaked, these reports were at first met with disbelief within the American establishment in Berlin: "They had thought we'd gone off the deep end," the station's political director, Gordon Ewing, later recalled.[15]

RIAS's pioneering reports on the strike plans gave early visibility to the workers' demands beyond Berlin, which proved critical for transforming local actions into a country-wide uprising. By noon of June 16, the station had confirmed the ongoing demonstrations at the Stalinallee and Friedrichshain construction sites, in part by monitoring the East Berlin police radio system. After a short announcement of the news at 1 p.m., it was on the 4 p.m. news that RIAS broadcast a lengthier account of the day's events transpiring across the Soviet sector, providing vivid accounts of the shift in the demonstrators' demands from rescission of the higher work quotas to political change expressed in shouts of "We want free elections."[16]

While RIAS did not drive the "radicalization of the protests," its broadcasts echoed and increasingly championed the rapid escalation of the demonstrators' concerns beyond labor issues. Not surprisingly, then, it was RIAS to which a delegation of East Berlin workers turned on the afternoon of June 16 with requests to air their call for a general strike the next day. RIAS officials recognized that the rebelling workers expected the radio station to become their mouthpiece and central coordinating point, since only RIAS could effectively establish a link between strikers and the general population. The delegates, one of the RIAS officials later recalled, counted on RIAS's full support for their strike, followed by a Western Allied invasion to reestablish order. Caught between neutral reporting and taking on a direct role in stoking and steering the mass demonstrations, local RIAS staff decided on a cautious response. Mindful of the warning that night from Charles Hulick, the US High Commission's Eastern Affairs Element chief—"I hope you know what you are doing. You could start a war this way"—RIAS director Ewing decided that the station could not directly act as a mouthpiece for the workers. Instead, it would factually and fully disseminate information about the demonstrations.[17]

But this policy decision, soon confirmed in Washington, was easier stated than carried out. RIAS evening broadcasts saw "factual reporting" of the day's news give way to unvarnished encouragement of the protests in editorial comments. In his nightly commentary, Eberhard Schütz, RIAS's program director, called the regime's reversal on the norm question on the sixteenth "a victory, which our Ostberliners share with the entire working population of the Soviet Zone." The regime would have never reacted as fast as it did, Schütz argued, if the workers had not manifested their opposition in discussions, passive resistance, and strikes throughout the zone. The East Berlin workers had not limited their demands to the question of work quotas but had indeed called for the resignation of the SED regime and the introduction of Western-style liberties. "We would be unworldly and would not deserve the confidence of our listeners if we could not acknowledge the justification of the demands. . . . What the population of East Berlin and the Soviet Zone demands today and what it views as feasible is nothing less than the end to the totalitarian rule of the Kremlin's German satellites." Emphasizing that "everyone had to know himself how far he could go," Schütz encouraged his listeners to support the demonstrators. "It is your task today to show the Soviet and German rulers that we do not accept 'mistakes' anymore as mistakes, that we and you expect a change of mind which is not limited to a rescission of the 10 percent increase in work norms but which creates conditions for free decisions which go way beyond the so-called 'voluntary norm increases.' We," Schütz concluded, "would be happy to be able to report more such victories in the next days."[18]

Throughout the night, RIAS broadcasts regularly repeated the workers' demand to continue the strike the next day, calling specifically for all East Berliners to participate in a demonstration at 7 a.m. on June 17 at the centrally located Strausberger Platz. In the early morning hours, West Berlin labor leader Ernst Scharnowski (in a statement cleared with the Americans) reassured the demonstrators on air that West German unions stood behind their colleagues and called upon the population for support: "Don't leave them alone. They are fighting not only for the social rights of labor but for the human rights of everyone in the East Zone. Join the movement of East Berlin construction workers, of East Berlin tram and rail employees! Every town has its Strausberger Platz!"[19]

The authority RIAS broadcasts enjoyed during the uprising was reflected, at least implicitly, by Soviet High Commissioner Vladimir Semenov, who told the East German leaders in the midst of the crisis on June 17 that according to RIAS reports "a government no longer existed in the GDR." As an aside, he acknowledged to a Soviet colleague: "Well, it is almost true." After the uprising, an internal CIA report stated that "competent observers feel that the RIAS broadcasts of the first unrest in East Berlin acted as a signal for the additional uprisings in the other German communities."[20]

THE US REACTION TO THE JUNE UPRISING

Washington was taken by surprise by the unrest in the GDR. American observers had come to believe that the Communist government was in firm control of events, at the moment they started to unravel. Some US observers had considered the vastly increased refugees numbers to be weakening the ferment of unrest in the GDR. Earlier in the year, the US mission in Berlin had reported to Washington that, even if called upon to do so, the East Germans would not be capable of carrying out a revolution, or be willing to do so, unless such a call coincided with a declaration of war and/ or assurance of Western military support. Once the unrest broke out, the Western Allied commandants agreed—even before the Soviet declaration of martial law shut down the Soviet sector midday on June 17—that their primary duty was "to maintain law and order in their sectors." West Berliners and GDR residents in the surrounding suburbs, they decided, "should if possible be dissuaded from mixing in East Berlin demonstrations where serious possibility of bloodshed existed." Western Allied authorities were also concerned that "many demonstrators in border areas have been under the influence of alcohol," and they pondered closing liquor stores and cafés in the border areas. Concerned about an escalation of the crisis in the wake of the Soviet military intervention in the eastern half of the city, the US commandant reportedly pulled US forces back from the sector border; by 5 p.m. on June 17, all US troops had been confined to their quarters. Not until the next day, June 18, did the Western commandants issue a formal letter to the Soviet commandant, Maj. Gen. Sergei Alexeyevich Dengin, protesting Soviet military actions in East Berlin.[21]

In Washington the uprising was greeted by some within the Eisenhower administration as a welcome opportunity to push a more offensive agenda. Eisenhower's special assistant for Cold War matters, C. D. Jackson, thought the Soviet military's brutal suppression of the uprising afforded Washington an "excellent propaganda opportunity." This was the moment, Mallory Browne, a member of the advisory Psychological Strategy Board (PSB) staff, argued, "to hit hard through C.I.A. to make all possible trouble covertly." Others thought it might be helpful to prevent the Soviets from sealing off the Soviet sector if the East Germans could "be persuaded to 'blur' the border." As they learned of the first casualties, PSB members urged "immediately to martyrize" the victims. "With very fundamental issues . . . involved," the PSB agreed on June 17 that all possible moral support should be given to the "East Berliners," both to help them achieve improvements and "to stimulate further Soviet repression," which would provide "ammunition" for the future.[22]

Such thinking was well ahead of the president's and that of his senior advisers. They lacked solid and timely intelligence on the uprising even after it started. With the Soviet sector "hermetically sealed off" by the Soviet military, American espionage agencies, including the US-sponsored Gehlen Organization, which had hundreds of informers in the GDR, experienced an almost complete collapse of information flow from the East. Early CIA reports thus speculated about the possibility of the unrest being a "controlled demonstration" by the regime, which had "flared up into near revolt." Meeting on June 17, the PSB members decided to launch a "special fact-finding operation" through its own channels "to determine first exactly what transpired in East Berlin . . . what its effects are likely to be, and what lay behind the whole affair." As late as June 18, the Western Berlin commandants apparently had "no precise information on hand" on the status of the strikes in East Berlin. Later that day the US High Commission's Berlin office did pass on "unconfirmed reports [of] unrest and strikes" in major GDR cities, but the scarcity of intelligence made it "impossible [to] evaluate [the] extent" of the disturbances. Blaming "drastically reduced information" on events in East Berlin and GDR under conditions of martial law, the US High Commission was still "unable" on June 19 to "estimate degree of unrest and strikes." By June 26 the CIA's Office of Current Intelligence was still transmitting unsubstantiated information from German sources claiming that the demonstrations had been the subject of "elaborate prior planning."[23]

Discussions at the National Security Council in Washington on June 18 therefore took a much more sober tone than had the initial PSB discussions. The unrest in East Germany was a "sign of real promise," but it also "posed a very tough problem for the United States to know how to handle." C. D. Jackson posed the "64-dollar question" of how far the administration was prepared to go "if this thing really gets cracking." Asked by Eisenhower "whether Mr. Jackson meant that we should intervene to prevent the slaughter by the Soviet forces," Jackson replied: "Not only that, but it is now quite possible that some of the satellite regimes are now prepared to follow the road Tito [has] taken." Indeed, he added, "this could be the bell pealing the disintegration of the Soviet empire. Do we stand idly by, or do we help the disintegration? And how much responsibility are we willing to take for the results of helping?"[24]

Eisenhower took a far more cautious approach. For him the decision to intervene "depended on how wide-spread the uprising became. Would the riots spread to China, or even possibly to the USSR itself? If this should happen, we would probably never have a better chance to act, and we would be well-advised, for example to supply arms." As to whether "we should ship arms to the East Berliners," Eisenhower reasoned that "if to do so was just inviting a slaughter of these people, you certainly didn't supply the arms. If, on the contrary, there was a real chance of success, you might well do so. Our problem was to weigh the prospects of success." In his opinion, the president added, the revolts had to be more serious and widespread than at this moment before they promised real success and indicated the desirability of US intervention. Jackson pressed on, asking whether US actions could "help [to] make this movement more serious and more widespread." But Eisenhower thought such ideas premature. To him, it was "very important that the unrest spread to China, because while the USSR would have no great difficulty in crushing uprisings in Europe alone, they would find it tough to deal with trouble both in Europe and in the Far East." For the moment, Eisenhower concluded, "The time to 'roll them out for keeps'" had not "quite" arrived. The NSC policy directive guiding the US response to the uprising, NSC 158, adopted by the NSC at its meeting on June 25, explicitly precluded a call for mass rebellion. In approving PSB D-45, Eisenhower (and Secretary of State Dulles) asked specifically that, when it came to stimulating opposition to the regime, "more emphasis be placed on passive resistance."[25]

Eisenhower found his choices in responding to the unrest in East Germany limited. Aside from avoiding a potential massacre should the United States equip the protesters with weapons in the face of overwhelming Soviet firepower, he could not risk an escalation of the crisis into a superpower conflict with potentially devastating global consequences. He was also constrained by the reactions of his European allies. British premier Winston Churchill, who prior to the uprising had initiated preparations for a summit with the post-Stalin leadership, was eager to return to business as usual in Berlin as quickly as possible. The British prime minister hence reacted violently to the West Berlin commandants' June 18 statement that criticized the Soviet's "irresponsible recourse to military force." Citing diplomatic reports that characterized Soviet behavior as markedly restrained, he harshly reprimanded the commandants' action, arguing that the Soviet government had the right to declare martial law in order to prevent anarchy. "We shall," Churchill concluded, "not find our way out of our many difficulties by making for purposes of local propaganda statements which are not in accordance with the facts." The French government, too, favored a "policy of watchful waiting." Both the British and French governments were adamantly opposed to any active Western intervention.[26]

The American attitude—in both Washington and Berlin—in fact soon grew tougher, for several reasons. First, US intelligence was beginning to get a clearer picture of the scope of demonstrations and strikes as they spread throughout East Germany. The extent of the unrest gave the administration grounds for greater confidence. A second reason was political in nature: Eisenhower and Dulles were sensitive to the gap between the markedly restrained actions of the United States during the first days of the uprising and the rhetoric of "liberation" on which they had campaigned and on which the expectations of many East Germans rested. At the same time, the uprising threatened to upset the larger US agenda for Germany. While Washington had hoped to keep attention focused on the Federal Republic's entry into the Western alliance, the New Course announcement and the ensuing unrest had thrust the issue of German reunification to the forefront, both on the international scene and in the West German election campaign, prompting a groundswell of calls for Four Power talks. "In addition to bringing back in increased strength the feeling that something must be done to unify Germany," the US high commissioner in Bonn reported, the riots had also "created the new feeling that something can be done."[27] Sensing a broader shift in Cold War correlations of forces, many East Germans apparently expected the United States and the West Europeans to begin providing active support.[28]

Failing to meet widespread expectations of American support for the protests had the potential to upset the administration's larger goal of West Germany's integration with the West. Already public criticism of Western inaction, particularly of West German chancellor Adenauer's reserved response to the turmoil in East Germany, was on the rise. "Unless some sign is forthcoming very soon from the United States," presidential adviser C. D. Jackson pointed out to Eisenhower in early July, "there could be a terrible letdown in both East and West Germany, which would seriously affect the US position and even more seriously affect Adenauer's position." After the initial surge of riots and demonstrations in East Germany, the US High Commission noted that "whether the SED suffers [a] further, perhaps crippling setback or substantially recovers [its] former power position (which could happen within the next six months) may depend largely on US policy." High Commissioner Conant warned from Bonn that unless some action was taken in the near future, the "Soviet[s] might regain control of the situation and recoup a major part of [their] lost prestige."[29]

By far the most important US program taken in response to the uprising was a large-scale food program for East Germany, which the PSB approved on July 1. US officials thought a program to provide the East

German population with food ideally combined humanitarian motives and political-psychological objectives. The distribution of food at no cost to the East Germans would help to alleviate the immediate crisis "but offer no long-range change in the deteriorating economic condition." The food relief would demonstrate Adenauer's sympathy for his East German brethren. High Commissioner James Conant emphasized that "our primary objective should be to put Adenauer in [a] position to take decisive action with respect to [the] East Zone crisis." By placing the food program officially under West German auspices, as Conant urged from Bonn, the United States could "provide [a] powerful stimulus to the Adenauer election victory" and to Western resolve on the European Defence Community. The food program would also demonstrate continuing US concern for the plight of the East Germans, yet keep the Soviets on the defensive and aggravate antagonisms between the SED regime and the populace.

To maximize the propaganda effect of the program, it was officially announced on July 10 via the publication of an exchange of letters between Chancellor Adenauer and President Eisenhower. Simultaneously published was Eisenhower's note to the Soviets, offering $15 million worth of food aid for the East Germans. Planned as a fait accompli regardless of Soviet reaction, rejection by the Soviets on July 11 came as little surprise. An interdepartmental committee, chaired by Eleanor Dulles, the sister of John Foster and Allen Dulles working as a German hand in the State Department, then decided to support a plan that placed the food packages—labeled "Eisenhower packages"—at the disposal of the federal West German government and Berlin Senate for distribution to the East Germans. The parcels were made available on a "come-and-get-it" basis to East Berliners and East Zoners at various distribution centers in the Western sectors of Berlin easily accessible from the East. The distribution of the packages, each containing flour, lard, condensed or powdered milk, and dried vegetables from the Berlin stockpile and US agricultural surpluses, commenced on July 27.[30]

The aid scheme received an "overwhelming" response from the East Germans. By the end of the first day, the US High Commission could report that the number of applicants for food packages—103,743 packages were issued—had exceeded all expectations, a success attributed mainly to the heavy play that RIAS gave to the operation. By the third day, more than 200,000 parcels were being issued daily. By the end of the program's first phase (August 15), some 865,000 people had come from East Germany and

East Berlin to get food. Since many East Germans carried identity cards belonging to friends and relatives, which allowed them to receive packages for those people as well as themselves, the average applicant collected about three packages. All in all, 2,598,202 parcels were reportedly distributed. By mid-August an estimated 75 percent of East Berlin's population had received at least one parcel. Most important, however, two-thirds of the food went to people living in the Berlin periphery and to "deep zoners." A second program, lasting from August 28 to early October, evoked a similar response. In total, more than 5.5 million food packages were distributed.[31]

Though considered a brilliant success in supporting Adenauer's overwhelming election victory at the September 6 federal elections and making the SED regime's post–June 17 recovery more difficult, the program was a far cry from the ambitious rhetoric of rolling back Communism. Hailed by some as a model for future rollback operations, even a program as limited in scope as the food aid for the GDR ultimately fell prey to anxieties within the administration and among the Western Allies over "pushing too far." For the Eisenhower administration, the lessons of the June 1953 uprising were therefore ambivalent: on the one hand, the Soviet crackdown had demonstrated that the Soviets would not hesitate to secure their sphere of influence by military means, if necessary. Thus, any Western calls for mass protest and unrest would be irresponsible. With a military intervention out of the question, US policy options were severely constrained. Still, to keep alive the spirit of resistance behind the Iron Curtain, the administration also doubled down on its commitment to psychological warfare and covert operations throughout the Soviet bloc, including support for anti-Communist groups operating from the western sectors of Berlin. Not until the 1956 Hungarian Revolution would this conflicted approach face its final reckoning.

NOTES

1. Katja Hoyer, *Beyond the Wall: East Germany, 1949–1990* (New York: Basic Books, 2023). Hoyer cites my "'Keeping the Pot Simmering': The United States and the East German Uprising of 1953," *German Studies Review* 1 (1996): 61–89. For the review by Franziska Kuschel, see *Der Spiegel* no. 20 (May 13, 2023): 38, 39.
2. The best overview is Ilko-Sascha Kowalczuk, *17. Juni 1953: Geschichte eines Aufstandes* (Munich: Verlag C H Beck, 2013), 24–35.
3. On the events of June 17, 1953, see Roger Engelmann and Ilko-Sascha Kowalczuk, eds., *Volkserhebung gegen den SED-Staat: Eine Bestandsaufnahme zum*

17. Juni 1953 (Göttingen: Vandenhoeck & Ruprecht, 2005); Ilko-Sascha Kowalczuk, Armin Mitter, and Stefan Wolle, eds., *Der Tag X: 17. Juni 1953. Die "Innere Staatsgrümdung" der DDR als Ergebnis der Krise 1952/54* (Berlin: Ch. Links, 1995); Mark Kramer, "Der Aufstand in Ostdeutschland im Juni 1953," in *Krisen im Kalten Krieg*, ed. Bernd Greiner, Christian Th. Müller, and Dierk Walter (Hamburg: HIS Verlag, 2008), 80–126.

4. "Text of Eisenhower's letter to Chancellor Adenauer," *New York Times*, July 26, 1953.

5. "Minutes of Discussion at the 150th Meeting of the National Security Council on 18 June 1953," June 19, 1953, reprinted in *Uprising in East Germany, 1953*, ed. Christian F. Ostermann (Budapest: CEU Press, 2001), 227.

6. Murphy to Marshall, June 26, 1948, NARA, RG 59, 740.00119Control (Germany)/6-2648.

7. CIA, "Effect of Soviet Restrictions on the US Position in Berlin," ORE 11–48, June 14, 1948, in *On the Front Lines of the Cold War: Documents on the Intelligence War in Berlin, 1946 to 1961*, ed. Donald P. Steury (Washington, DC: CIA, 1999), 177–80.

8. Enrico Heitzer, *Die Kampfgruppe gegen Unmenschlichkeit (KgU): Widerstand und Spionage im Kalten Krieg*, Zeithistorische Studien 53 (Köln Böhlau, 2015), 41–46; Kai-Uwe Merz, "Kalter Krieg als antikommunistischer Widerstand: Die Kampfgruppe gegen Unmenschlichkeit, 1948–1959," *Studien zur Zeitgeschichte* 34 (München: R. Oldenbourg, 1987), 45–47; Jochen Staadt, "Vergesst sie nicht! Freiheit war ihr Ziel. Die Kampfgruppe gegen Unmenschlichkeit," in *Zeitschrift des Forschungsverbundes SED-Staat* 24 (2008): 60–79; Jochen Staadt, "Ein Historikerreinfall: Die Kampfgruppe gegen Unmenschlichkeit—Desinformation macht Geschichte," in *Zeitschrift des Forschungsverbundes SED-Staat* 33 (2013): 94–111.

9. "Highlights Review of PW Operations (PUB, Policy Staff)," Alfred Boerner to Mrs. Allen, memorandum, March 19, 1952, NARA, RG 59, 511.62A/3-1952.

10. "Notes of Fifth Meeting of Ad Hoc Berlin Committee," by D. W. Montenegro, July 15, 1952, NARA, RG 59, 762A.5/7-1752 (FOIA release to author). On the UFJ, see Frank Hagemann, *Der Untersuchungsausschuss Freiheitlicher Juristen, 1949–1969* (Frankfurt: Peter Lang, 1994); David E. Murphy, Sergei A. Kondrashev, and George Bailey, *Battleground Berlin: CIA vs. KGB in the Cold War* (New Haven, CT: Yale University Press, 1997), 113–26; Stöver, *Die Befreiung vom Kommunismus*, 250–83.

11. A nephew of the theologian Paul Tillich who, as an émigré in the United States, had led the Council for a Democratic Germany. Ernst Tillich had been a member of the anti-Hitler resistance and had spent three years in a concentration camp. Judged by US personnel to be "capable, balanced aggressive," he developed close contacts to US agencies.

12. Bernd Stöver, "Politik der Befreiung?Private Organisationen des Kalten

Krieges: Das Beispiel der Kampfgruppe gegen Unmenschlichkeit (KgU)," in *"Geistige Gefahr" und Immunisierung der Gesellschaft,* ed. Stefan Creuzberger and Dierk Hoffmann (Munich: Oldenburg, 2014), 222.

13. Bernd Stöver, "Zusammenfassung: Das Umbruchsjahr 1953: Ein Resümee," in *1953—Krisenjahr des Kalten Krieges in Europa,* ed. Christoph Klessmann and Bernd Stoever (Cologne: Boehlau, 1999), 213; HICOG Berlin to Department of State, July 1, 1953, NARA, RG 59, 762B.00/7–153; Tel. 564, Ward to FO, June 22, 1953, PRO, FO/371/103840, CS 1016/90.

14. Wolfgang Schivelbusch, *In a Cold Crater: Cultural and Intellectual Life in Berlin, 1945–1948* (Berkeley: University of California Press, 1998), 117, 119–25; Nicholas J. Schlosser, *Cold War on the Airwaves: The Radio Propaganda War against East Germany* (Urbana: University of Illinois Press, 2015), 23–46; Nicholas J. Schlosser, "Creating an 'Atmosphere of Objectivity': Radio in the American Sector, Objectivity, and the United States Propaganda Campaign against the German Democratic Republic, 1945–1961," *German History* 29, no. 4 (December 2011): 610–27; McCloy to Secretary of State, August 24, 1950, NA, RG 59, 511.62B4/8–2450. On the origins of RIAS, see Schanett Riller, *Funken für die Freiheit: Die U.S.-amerikanische Informationspolitik gegenüber der DDR* (Trier: WVT, 2004).

15. Ewing quoted in Schlosser, *Cold War on the Airwaves,* 80.

16. *Der Aufstand der Arbeiterschaft im Ostsektor von Berlin und in der sowjetischen Besatzungszone: Tätigkeitsbericht der Hauptabteilung Politik des Rundfunks im Amerikanischen Sektor in der Zeit vom 16. Juni bis zum 23. Juni 1953,* 3, copy in BA Koblenz, J. Kaiser Papers, NL 18/314; HICOG Berlin to HICOG Bonn, June 17, 1953, National Security Archive, Soviet Flashpoints Collection.

17. The Ewing quote is from Steward Alsop, "Courage in Berlin and Its Reward," *New York Times,* July 20, 1953. The name and details are given in an interview by Ewing, printed in Ilse Spittmann and Karl Wilhelm Fricke, *17. Juni 1953. Arbeiteraufstand in der DDR,* 234–37. See also Hildebrandt, *The Explosion,* 46–69; D. Prowe, *Weltstadt in Krisen. Berlin 1949–1958* (Berlin: Walter De Gruyter, 1973), 113.

18. *Der Aufstand der Arbeiterschaft im Ostsektor von Berlin und in der sowjetischen Besatzungszone.*

19. Quoted in Christian F. Ostermann, ed., *Uprising in East Germany, 1953: The Cold War, the German Question, and the First Major Uprising behind the Iron Curtain* (Budapest: Central European University Press, 2001), 174.

20. Rudolf Herrnstadt, *Das Herrnstadt-Dokument: Das Politbüro der SED und die Geschichte des 17. Juni 1953* (Hamburg: Rowohlt, 1990), 83; Burton B. Lifschultz, CIA-Eastern European Division, to Allen Dulles, July 10, 1953, DDEL, C.D. Jackson Papers, box 74.

21. Ostermann, *Between Containment and Rollback,* 249.

22. Ostermann, 250.

23. Frank G. Wisner to John Bross, June 18, 1953, CIA Records; see also Ostermann, *Between Containment and Rollback,* 250; Workingpaper Prepared in the Eastern Affairs Division, HICOG Berlin Element, June 25, 1953, *FRUS 1952–54,* 7: 1595; "Comment on East Berlin Uprising," June 17, 1953, in *On the Front Lines of the Cold War: Documents on the Intelligence War in Berlin, 1946 to 1961,* ed. Donald P. Steury (Washington, DC: CIA, 1999), 245; "Comment on East Berlin Rioting," *CIA Current Intelligence Digest,* June 18, 1953 (FOIA release to author); Ronny Heidenreich, Daniela Münkel, and Elke Stadelmann-Wenz, *Geheimdienstkrieg in Deutschland: Die Konfrontation von DDR-Staatssicherheit und Organisation Gehlen 1953* (Berlin: Ch. Links, 2016), 43; Ronny Heidenreich, *Die DDR-Spionage des BND: Von den Anfängen bis zum Mauerbau* (Berlin: Ch. Links, 2019), 239–42; George A. Morgan to C. D. Jackson, "Berlin," memorandum, June 18, 1953, DDEL, C. D. Jackson Papers.

24. Ostermann, *Between Containment and Rollback,* 251–52.

25. Minutes of Discussion at the 150th Meeting of the National Security Council on June 18, 1953, June 19, 1953, Dwight D. Eisenhower Library (mandatory review release to author).

26. Tel. 168, Personal from Prime Minister to Coleman, June 22, 1953, UK National Archives, FO/371/103840, CS 1016/85. For an excellent overview of Churchill's position in 1953, see Klaus Larres, "Grossbritannien und er 17. Juni 1953. Die deutsche Frage und das Scheitern von Churchills Entspannungspolitik nach Stalins Tod," in Klessmann and Stoever, *1953,* 155–79.

27. HICOG Bonn to Department of State, July 6, 1953, NA, RG 59, 762B.00/7–653.

28. "Vertrauliche Information," memorandum by FDGB-Bundesvorstand, no. 21, June 13, 1953, German Federal Archives, SED Records, IV 2/5/543.

29. C. D. Jackson to Eisenhower, July 3, 1953, DDEL, C. D. Jackson Papers, box 41; Conant to Secretary of State, June 26, 1953, NARA, RG 59, 762B.00/6–2653.

30. On the food aid program, see Christian Ostermann, "'Die beste Chance für ein Rollback?' Amerikanische Politik und der 17. Juni 1953," in Klessmann and Stöver, *1953,* 115–39.

31. HICOG Berlin to Secretary of State, July 28, 1953, NARA, RG 59, 862B.49/7–2853; HICOG Berlin to Secretary of State, July 27, 1953, NARA, RG 59, 862B.49/7–2753; Edward M. O'Connor to C. D. Jackson, White House Central Files (Confidential File), Subject Series, box 37, DDEL; HICOG Berlin to Secretary of State, August 17, 1953, NARA, RG 59, 862B.49/8–1753; HICOG Berlin to Department of State, September 17, 1953, NARA, RG 59, 862B.49/9–1753.

CHAPTER 4

_____

Abduction City

Abductions by the GDR State Security Service in Cold War Berlin

SUSANNE MUHLE

A DEAD BOAR

On the morning of October 2, 1958, Friedrich Böhm,[1] who worked for the French intelligence service, disappeared in a forested area of West Berlin. Clues at the scene soon substantiated the suspicion that he had been abducted: his dog was found tied to a tree, the dirt on a nearby path showed signs of a struggle, and the leaves on the ground were stained with blood. The West Berlin investigators also found a broken pair of glasses, a watch glass, and a leather case with a comb. These objects, which reinforced the impression of an attack, were identified by the wife of the missing Friedrich Böhm as his property. Investigators also suspected that the carcass of a boar piglet found in the vicinity by a forester was tied to the incident because an examination of its stomach contents revealed that the young boar had not lived in the wild. Even the escape route of the alleged kidnappers was identified: approximately three kilometers from the scene of the crime, tire tracks cut across a grassy area on Potsdamer Chaussee, which skirted the zone border on the West Berlin side, into the territory of the GDR.[2] The GDR Ministry for State Security (Stasi) had meticulously planned the abduction of Böhm but a trail of evidence was left all the same.

Böhm had caught the attention of the Stasi five years earlier. Born in 1910, the trained master blacksmith had left the GDR in 1950 and since lived in West Berlin, where in 1953 he became a full-time employee of the French intelligence service. This employment had been noted in the context of a Stasi operational process in the spring of 1954. An unofficial collabora-tor (IM) of the Stasi with the code name "Schwerin" had made contact with Böhm and had reported on him from then on. In February 1955, Haupt-abteilung II of the Stasi organization, responsible for counterintelligence, took over the operational process with IM "Schwerin," who received the order to establish a friendly relationship with Böhm. Although he had not succeeded in this by the summer of 1955, the Stasi had nevertheless—to some extent with his assistance—managed to get other IMs close to Böhm.[3]

Based on a suspicion of collaboration with British intelligence, in November 1955 Hauptabteilung II/2 created a separate operational process dedicated to Friedrich Böhm with the code name "Tegel." Over the months to follow, eight IMs from the Stasi and the Polish secret service established or strengthened their connections to Böhm.[4] The first abduction plan was hatched five months later, and in April 1956 the IM "Konsul" advanced a proposal to abduct Böhm to East Berlin by force, using three accomplices. In view of an internal assessment rating the chances of winning him over as futile and finding little promise of gaining any future information of any use, the Stasi took up the offer. Under the pretext of meeting an informant, Friedrich Böhm was to be lured into an ambush and rendered unconscious with chloroform or knocked out with a sandbag. A few days later another IM explored the proposed site of the crime.[5] For unknown reasons, how-ever, the planned abduction was not carried out. Instead, with the idea of a future abduction in mind, further investigations were commissioned, and additional IMs were assigned to Böhm: in January 1957 Hauptabteilung II/2 positioned eight IMs close to him, and an additional seven had periodic contact with him. The original abduction plan was expanded in the spring of 1957: after the abduction, two IMs who had good relations with Böhm would go to his apartment, give his wife an anesthetic dissolved in alcohol, and then remove incriminating documents from the apartment.[6]

With the help of the IMs, Hauptabteilung II/2 observed Böhm's activ-ities for the French and other Western intelligence services in the field of economic and military espionage in the GDR and in Poland. Through the same channels, the Stasi also learned about Böhm's various security measures:

his apartment was secured by an alarm system that could be triggered in every room and that was directly connected to the nearest police station. Moreover, a trained guard dog lived in the apartment, and the apartment door was secured with a steel bar. Böhm himself, they noted, did not use public transport but only taxis or his private car, and he carried two pistols with him. The decision to carry out the planned abduction was finally made in the summer of 1957, and Hauptabteilung II/2 was to report the "executed measure" to the minister's deputy, Bruno Beater, by mid-August at the latest.[7] But the report, like the abduction itself, was not forthcoming; Böhm's security measures repeatedly foiled the Stasi's plans. Hauptabteilung II, however, remained committed to its objective of an "active measure."[8]

In June 1958, the now responsible Hauptabteilung II/3 intensified planning and preparations once again: on a pretext, Böhm would be lured into an ambush in the forested area in Berlin-Gatow, where the IM "Tell" who was assigned to him worked as an auxiliary forester. Böhm occasionally went for walks there with his two dogs and got sand for his bird cages. The latter was to serve as a pretext for bringing Böhm, accompanied by IM "Tell," into the forested area in early July 1958. Near the parking lot, two other IMs—disguised as forestry workers—would overpower Böhm, disarm him, and bundle him, wrapped in a tent tarpaulin, into a waiting car. IM "Tell" was tasked with keeping Böhm's dogs under control and "rendering them harmless" with poisoned food and a club. Two further IMs would secure the crime scene. For the subsequent escape to the GDR, they had selected a spot in Groß-Glienicke, in West Berlin, which had been made passable for the occasion; the GDR side was normally blocked by trenches and barbed wire entanglements.[9] The plan received a few modifications and additions in early July 1958: in addition to IM "Tell," a three-person task force under the direction of an IM "Neuhaus" would be deployed. Disguised as forestry workers, these three IMs were to place a dead boar in the access road near the parking lot in order to force Böhm to stop his car and get out. At this point, the attack by the IMs would take place.[10]

It would be three months before a suitable occasion for carrying out the abduction arose: Friedrich Böhm had asked IM "Tell" to cut down a birch tree for him, which the two of them would then pick up. Hauptabteilung II/3 stuck, in the main, to the abduction plan it had devised in July and began preparations: the crime scene, the escape route, and the smuggling point at the border were subjected to another round of reconnaissance, orders were given for the construction of a temporary bridge over a trench at the border crossing, and two automatic pistols with thirty rounds of ammunition each were requisitioned.[11] When Böhm, accompanied by IM "Tell," drove to the parking lot in the Gatow forest on the morning of October 2, the three-person abduction squad around IM "Neuhaus" was already waiting for him. However, they had not been able to place the dead boar on the access road in good time, as had been planned. IM "Tell" led Friedrich Böhm down a trail to the place where the birch he had asked for was supposed to be. Disguised as a forest ranger, IM "Neuhaus" approached the two men, told them about a boar found nearby and led them to the site. An instant later, "Neuhaus" whipped a pistol out of his trouser pocket and threatened Böhm, who nevertheless attempted to defend himself. At this point, the other two kidnapper IMs, who had been hiding in the nearby bushes, joined the fray, using rubber truncheons to beat the desperately flailing Böhm. Amid the fray, a shot was fired from "Neuhaus's" pistol and hit Böhm, but both the shot and his cries for help went unheard in the woods and the morning's heavy rain. The IMs tied up the injured Böhm, bundled him into a VW estate car, removed the bloodstains at the crime scene, and drove him into the GDR via the planned route. They also removed Böhm's car from the scene. In a wooded area just over the sector border, Böhm was transferred from the car of the kidnapper IMs into the vehicle of an official employee of Hauptabteilung II and subsequently taken to the Stasi detention center in Berlin-Hohenschönhausen. At the smuggling point on the border between West Berlin and the GDR, the Stasi promptly restored the changes that had made to the route—the provisional bridge was removed and the barbed wire fence was reinstalled—and the border police was ordered to resume its patrols there.[12]

Just a few hours after his abduction, in the hospital of the Stasi detention center, Friedrich Böhm was interrogated for the first time. Although he had been seriously injured by the gunshot wound and blows, the Stasi interrogators nevertheless interrogated him around the clock, they only discontinued the nightly interrogations when he collapsed from the strain—after fourteen days.[13] Upon completion of the investigations and interrogations, Böhm was accused of initiating "extensive snooping, disruption and espionage activities against the Warsaw Treaty states by creating an extensive network of agents in the territory of the German Democratic Republic and the Polish People's Republic."[14] He had, it was claimed, recruited a total of fifty citizens for the purpose of economic and military espionage in both the GDR and Poland. One witness who leveled severe allegations against him was IM "Tell," who had been involved in his abduction.[15]

On November 10, 1959, the Frankfurt (Oder) district court sentenced Böhm to life imprisonment. He served the first two years of the sentence in East Berlin, followed by three years in a basement cell in Bautzen II; then, finally, he was taken back to East Berlin to serve the rest of his sentence. In September 1972, almost fourteen years after his abduction, Böhm was able to return to the Federal Republic of Germany as part of a *Häftlingsfreikauf* (prisoners' ransom), in which prisoners' freedom was bought by the Federal Republic of Germany.[16] His return was a surprise to many in the Federal Republic, since the rumor had spread ten years prior that he'd killed himself in GDR detention.[17]

ABDUCTIONS IN THE "FRONTLINE CITY OF THE COLD WAR"

Friedrich Böhm was among roughly four hundred people who were abducted from West Berlin and the Federal Republic of Germany and taken to the GDR between 1950 and the mid-1960s. The first half of the 1950s was a high point for abductions, most of which, beyond those perpetrated by the Soviet secret service, were carried out by the Stasi established in February 1950. Under the regime of the SED dictatorship, the Stasi unified three functions by serving as a political secret police, a criminal investigation body (with its own detention centers), and an intelligence service. As the "shield and sword of the party," the Stasi was dedicated to the enforcement of SED rule—both within the GDR and outside its borders. This was reflected in its abduction practices in the 1950s.

The main scene of these abduction campaigns was the divided city of Berlin, where the sector border, still largely open until the wall was built in 1961, could be crossed by car or even S-Bahn commuter trains and the underground system.[18] Located in the middle of the GDR and with its special status as a city under the control of the Four Powers, Berlin was a constant thorn in the side of the SED leadership—and not only because it offered a loophole for escape from the SED dictatorship, which was used by hundreds of thousands of people after the closure of the inner-German border in 1952. From the perspective of the SED government, the divided city was rife with potential to have its rule destabilized—a notion that was also well understood in the West. In 1953, the head of the West Berlin office of the Federal Ministry of All-German Affairs, Karl Magen, delivered the following speech, with considerable pathos, before the All-German Committee of the Bundestag: "For the people of the Soviet-occupied territory, West Berlin is the spiritual foothold to which they hold fast and from which they receive fresh impetus for their resistance to the Eastern ideologues. West Berlin is at one and the same time not only the showcase of the West toward the East, but also the forward observation post toward the Soviet zone."[19]

The observation post worked in both directions. The border in Berlin, which prior to 1961 was still porous, facilitated the deployment of agents and informants, and the flow of refugees from East to West was ripe for exploitation for the purposes of espionage. For the Western intelligence services, this meant a broad spectrum of information; for their Communist counterparts, it offered a good opportunity to smuggle agents into the West.

The divided city was not only a gathering place for intelligence services; in the west of the city there were also active anti-Communist organizations such as the Investigative Committee of Free Jurists (Untersuchungsausschuss Freiheitlicher Juristen, or UFJ), the Eastern offices of West German political parties and the militant Fighting Group against Inhumanity (Kampfgruppe gegen Unmenschlichkeit, or KgU). They not only used refugees and people seeking help to gain information from the GDR, but they also maintained informants in the GDR and had leaflets distributed there, for example, or even conducted explosive attacks and sabotage. They passed on the information they obtained, not only to government agencies such as the Federal Ministry for All-German Affairs, but also to Western intelligence agencies, foremost among which was the CIA. The example of the KgU illustrates the close interlinking between the actors, which had an infrastructure for intelligence activities and stored the intelligence gained in a central file system that was in line with intelligence service standards and was taken over by the Federal Intelligence Service (BND) after the dissolution of the KgU in 1959. Anti-Communist groups, state agencies, and intelligence services in the West formed an "informal network of liberation politics."[20] Their collaboration illustrates the sense of threat engendered by the clash of competing systems, not only in the GDR, but also in the young Federal Republic of Germany, and how it shaped the atmosphere in the divided city of Berlin. The fear in the West of political infiltration and destabilization fueled an anti-Communism that was promoted by the state and at times took on troubling proportions in terms of its implications for the liberal-democratic order.[21]

"FORCED ON US BY THE OPPONENT"

It was not entirely without basis that the anti-Communist organizations were regarded by the GDR secret police as every bit as much "hostile agent centers" as the Western intelligence services themselves. Above all, however, the comparison reflected the Stalinist conception of the enemy held by SED dictatorship: the lack of loyalty among the population, which led to serious crises particularly in the 1950s, did not fit with the socialist worldview. Political opposition could only be initiated from "outside" and was thus elevated to the global level of the international class struggle. All critics and opponents of the regime—regardless of whether they were actually connected to Western intelligence or the form they took—were depicted as "agents" in the services of the "class enemy." This radical friend-or-foe thinking and the conviction of having the "revolutionary right" to establish a "dictatorship of the proletariat" by any means were the basis for the severe repressive measures in the GDR and the abductions carried out by the Stasi in the West during the consolidation phase of the SED dictatorship.

More than half of the abductions took place in the first three years after the founding of the Stasi, when it was under the leadership of Wilhelm Zaisser and was still under an extraordinary degree of Soviet influence. After the uprising in 1953, Zaisser fell into disrepute with the party leadership and was replaced by Ernst Wollweber, marking the beginning of a special phase of repression in the GDR. Roughly 25 percent of the abductions came during his time in office from 1953 to 1957. As a committed Stalinist, Wollweber regarded the liquidation of "enemies" and "traitors" as completely legitimate.[22] "Concentrated blows," he asserted, "should be used to target and crack down on enemy and agent centers" in the West.[23] Centrally organized mass arrests and propaganda campaigns were planned in the GDR, while attempts at infiltration and abduction were planned in the West—particularly in West Berlin. The target of this offensive was Western intelligence services and anti-Communist organizations, and between 1953 and 1955 three waves of arrests—code-named "firework," "arrow," and "lightning"—led to the arrest of hundreds of actual and alleged agents and opponents of the regime. The arrest sweeps were accompanied by propaganda campaigns in the press and radio as well as show trials.[24]

The "concentrated blows" led to a further increase in the total number of abductions, including violent abductions, in 1954–55, after which numbers showed a downward trend. After the timid effort toward de-Stalinization, the crisis at the head of the state security apparatus in 1956–57, and the change from Ernst Wollweber to Erich Mielke[25] in November 1957, there was another small increase in abductions, but at a low level. Under Mielke, the Stasi changed the strategy and orientation of its work according to the ideas of the party and state leader Walter Ulbricht. Mielke moved away from Wollweber's focus on the West and instead instituted stronger surveillance and persecution within the GDR. And in view of its constant efforts to achieve international recognition for the GDR, the Stasi refrained somewhat from using methods that were all too obviously violent in nature. Gradually—and especially after the consolidation of the SED dictatorship by the building of the Berlin Wall—the task and scope of the Stasi "went from offensive repression aimed at asserting party rule to defensive repression with the objective of preserving and securing the structures of its power."[26]

This was reflected in the statement Stasi department head Josef Kiefel made in the mid-1960s to an IM who was requesting further deployments as a kidnapper: "Today we can no longer use such working methods as we were obliged to use ten, eight and even six years ago because they were forced on us by the opponent."[27] Former Stasi officers, firmly rooted in their old antipathies, presented similar arguments as late as 2010: through the early 1960s, they asserted, there had been a few cases of abduction, performed "in a period of rampant terror and massive incitement and spying against the GDR, which was developing under difficult and unique conditions." The abductions, they said, had been of people "who had committed serious crimes against the GDR and had to answer for them before GDR courts."[28]

How serious were the "crimes" of those who were abducted? The scope and the effectiveness of the activities by the abduction victims for Western intelligence services and anti-Communist organizations can scarcely be determined from the existing documentary basis, not least because the files of the Western intelligence services are largely inaccessible. In a sizable number of cases, however, Stasi documents show that the Stasi had notable difficulties in proving the abducted person's espionage activities and actually had to manufacture evidence to obtain a conviction. Overall, it is questionable whether the Western secret services and anti-Communist organizations in West Berlin were really as threatening to the existence of the SED dictatorship as the party leadership and state security apparatus feared. The GDR espionage of the BND in the 1950s, for example, is judged by Ronny Heidenreich to be "largely dysfunctional and deficient." Due to a lack of professionalism and inadequate security precautions, the employees and informants had been literally burned up.[29]

A closer look at the group of roughly four hundred abductees reveals that many had previously left or fled the GDR to go to the West and had previous or newly established connections with Western intelligence services or anti-Communist organizations. As a fixed component of the emergency admittance procedure in the Federal Republic, such contact was inevitable for GDR refugees. But some were also actively involved in the circles of Western intelligence services or in anti-Communist organizations. Their motives were diverse, ranging from financial interests and personal benefits to political motives, such as the intention to oppose the Communist regime in the GDR in this manner. The position they occupied in the intelligence services or organizations in question and the scope of their activities were of little concern to the kidnappers: employees in subordinate positions or contact persons, who were not part of the full-time staff at all, were as likely to be targeted as leaders. Each abduction was regarded as having the potential to weaken the respective organization—not only through the loss of the workforce, but through the knowledge and informants of the abducted person.

The aim, however, was also to deprive the Western intelligence services and anti-Communist organizations of their base in another respect: employees and informants were to be discouraged from continuing their work due to the evident danger of their activities. And the public was to be made aware of the carelessness and irresponsibility demonstrated by these institutions and organizations. This effect of deterrence and discreditation was just as important, if not more important, than punishing the abductees and exposure of their connections. The abductions—above all the violent ones—were a demonstration of power that began with the disregarding of the state border and the special status of West Berlin.

This deterrence function was even more pronounced in the case of another group of Stasi abduction victims, namely those who were members of the SED, the East German police (Volkspolizei), the East German army (NVA), or the Stasi before fleeing from the GDR.

"Every traitor to our just cause hastens their own fate," announced Stasi chief Ernst Wollweber in an internal order in 1955 after two escaped Stasi employees had been abducted from the Federal Republic and executed. "He will be apprehended, no matter how safe a hiding place he believes himself to be in, and will under no circumstances escape his just punishment, for the power of the working class extends over all frontiers."[30] It was a clear threat to any defectors in their own ranks; after all, the enormous movement of people fleeing from the GDR in the 1950s did not spare the party and state security apparatus. The "retrieval"—as the Stasi euphemistically called the abductions—of such special GDR refugees was intended to prevent Western authorities from being able to make use of these former officials and their knowledge. Injured egos and personal desires for revenge in the state security apparatus also played a role here. Above all, as illustrated by internal statements such as the order cited above, the abductions served primarily as a demonstration of power and deterrence.

The Stasi certainly wanted to be perceived as the author of the activities, but nevertheless they organized the abduction campaigns with the utmost secrecy, and in order to minimize the foreign policy damage to the SED government, vehemently denied them when they came to light. The responsible actors in the SED regime were cognisant of the territorial limits of their sphere of activity, even if they did not recognize them regarding West Berlin: they could not make any official arrests in West Berlin or in the Federal Republic, not least because the people they would be arresting were citizens of West Berlin or West Germany. They therefore had to resort to the conspiratorial means of abduction, hiring henchmen in West Berlin for that purpose. This approach also gave them the ability to deny abductions, to declare them as arrests on GDR territory, or to present abductees as defectors.

The Stasi employed a variety of abduction methods: they used fake telegrams and letters, or the help of relatives or acquaintances, to lure people into the territory of East Berlin under various pretexts in order to arrest them on the spot. They assigned IMs to people to be abducted to induce them, under the influence of alcohol, to enter the Eastern sector or to bring them there by force using sedatives or violence. To achieve this, it was necessary for the IM to have an existing trusting relationship with the person, or to establish one at the behest of the Stasi. So the Stasi needed to have people either in place around the intended abductee or who could penetrate their private circles inconspicuously. Not infrequently, it also specifically recruited people from the criminal milieu in West Berlin for use in abduction operations, especially the ones to be carried out by force. From the Stasi's perspective, not only did such people have the requisite willingness to use violence and unscrupulousness, but employment of them offered the advantage of making it easier to conceal failed abduction attempts. In view of the criminal background of the perpetrators, the West Berlin police could easily incorrectly infer that the incident was an attempted mugging. The operatives themselves were usually motivated by a desire for validation or financial interests.[31]

The abduction victims often suffered draconian punishments, and many were only able to return to the West after years of imprisonment in the GDR. For many of them there was no return. Of those abducted, twenty-four received the death penalty and were executed, among whom sixteen were sentenced before 1953 by Soviet military tribunals and then executed by shooting in Moscow. Of the remaining eight executed abductees, one was a Western secret service agent, one was a border police officer, and six were Stasi employees who had fled the GDR. At least ten further abduction victims died in GDR imprisonment due to illness, physical abuse, or suicide. The victims of the abductions and their relations were often scarred for life.

REACTIONS IN THE WEST

In the respective organizations, but also in the West German—and particularly West Berlin—public, the abductions caused not only outrage but also uncertainty and fear. The governments, investigating authorities, secret services, and anti-Communist organizations there were faced with two main tasks. On the one hand, they had to search for the abducted person and offer them and their families support. On the other they had to take measures to protect their own citizens, as well as their own employees and contacts.

The driving force behind campaigns to find abductees was mainly their families, who often waited for weeks, or even months, without information about exactly what had happened. There is no doubt that Western intelligence services were also activated. However, without access to Western secret service documents, it is very difficult to say anything about the scope of their work or the methods they applied.[32] The police investigated in the same they did any missing persons case, but they soon reached the boundaries of what was possible—in this case, of course, coming up against the very real boundary presented by the inner-German border. All traces of the victims and those involved in the abduction ended at the sectoral or zonal border, making it impossible to follow them any further. No help could be expected from the GDR; in fact, quite the opposite was true. Unless there were eye-witnesses, the West Berlin or West German investigators could not even be fully certain that an abduction had taken place. In addition, suspicion that a person had been abducted was often accompanied by the suspicion that they might have committed treason. Had the person really been abducted? Or had they gone of their own free will? Were they perhaps even an agent working for an Eastern secret service who had simply gone back to the people who had sent them in the first place? The GDR fueled this uncertainty by publishing corresponding newspaper stories, which often presented those who had been abducted as spies who had been caught red-handed and arrested in the GDR, or as repentant returnees or even defectors.

The complexity of such investigations can be seen in the example of Hans Keller,[33] an employee of the US intelligence who was abducted and who in April 1957 was sentenced to life imprisonment by the Local Court Potsdam. Following his sentencing, the Stasi published a brochure about him titled "Manhunters serving the USA." Written in the style of a spy novel, it reported the "facts" about his crime and his punishment.[34] One evening in October 1956, Hans Keller and his wife had allowed themselves to be persuaded by his sister to take home an underground train that went through the Eastern sector. But at the first station they reached in East Berlin, they were arrested.[35] Before his disappearance, the West Berlin police had been investigating him on suspicion of treasonous activities. This suspicion arose because he was constantly hanging around the area near a railway station in West Berlin, close to the border, where he could be seen observing people and buildings. What is more, in the summer of 1956 two of his informants had been arrested and sentenced in East Berlin. However, he had been able to provide evidence to the West Berlin police that he was working on the orders of the US intelligence, and that his job was to get hold of information about people from East Berlin.[36] Now, following his disappearance, police investigations concluded that Keller and his wife had gone to East Berlin of their own free will, which seemed to confirm their suspicions that he was a double agent. It was assumed that he had recruited a number of agents for the US intelligence and had then betrayed them to the Stasi when he was "deactivated" by the Americans.[37]

It was not until four years later that the West German law enforcement authorities realized—with the help of a witness who came from the GDR in the spring of 1961—that it was not Hans Keller, but his sister, who worked as his secretary, who had betrayed him. For a monthly sum of 400 DM/West, she had allegedly revealed to the Stasi the names of an estimated four hundred people her brother had been in contact with. Around a hundred fifty to two hundred of these contacts are said to have been arrested as part of a large-scale campaign of arrests in July 1956 later being sentenced to terms of imprisonment that were sometimes lengthy. In October of the same year, this woman delivered her brother to the Stasi, for which she received a bonus of 5,000 DM/West. Berlin's High Court sentenced her in November 1963 for "treasonous relations in coincidence with profit-motivated cunning abduction, severe unlawful imprisonment and casting political suspicion" to nine years in prison, five years' loss of honor, and a fine of 14,200 DM/West.[38] Hans Keller himself had, in April 1957, been sentenced to life in prison by the Potsdam District Court, but the Federal Republic bought his release in September 1964.[39]

The investigations into abductions at a political level in West Berlin and in West Germany were influenced by considerations over whether a disappearance had been an abduction. The authorities wanted to avoid the embarrassment of seeking to assist somebody who seemed to have been abducted but then turned out to be a defector or even a returning agent. A remark in a CIA document also reveals that West Berlin politicians were sometimes urged to exercise restraint: "USCOB desirous unofficially inform Mayor Reuter that Hoeher was German intelligence agent who took own risks of kidnapping and that this not another Linse case to be made political cause celebre by West German authorities."[40] Wolfgang Paul Höher is a special case that highlights all the imponderables associated with the disappearance of Western agents. Höher, a journalist and employee of the Gehlen organization, disappeared from West Berlin in February 1953. The records of the Stasi, the BND, and the CIA do not clearly indicate whether he was abducted or went to the GDR voluntarily as a double agent. Either way, he appeared as a prosecution witness in East Berlin in several show trials against agents of the Gehlen organization. After a brief imprisonment, he was initially active in the GDR for the KGB and the Stasi. In 1957, the CIA attempted without success to recruit Höher under pressure after his wife fled East Germany for the West. Höher died in Leipzig in October 1959 at the age of forty-five.[41]

In general, most of the initiatives to free abductees were not successful. Inquiries and protests—also by the Western powers—usually came to nothing. The authorities responsible in the GDR denied having any knowledge whatsoever about the whereabouts of people who had disappeared, or they maintained that a perfectly legal arrest had been made on GDR territory. In this respect, it is important to remember that, at that time, intergovernmental relations had not yet been established between the Federal Republic and the GDR. The West German government often had no choice but to support the imprisoned abductees from a so-called "legal protection office." While they could not provide legal representation of any kind in court proceedings, as the GDR courts forbade this, they could observe—to the extent possible—the prisoners' situation and make efforts to achieve an early release. Buying the release of political prisoners, an activity that the West German government was involved in from 1963–64 onward, did provide more scope for maneuvering and lead to the release of several abduction victims from prison in the GDR.

Faced with its lack of power, political leaders and public offices, as well as the pertinent organizations in West Berlin and in the Federal Republic, undertook various measures to protect their own citizens and/or employees and contacts. The department responsible in West Berlin's police headquarters provided advice to people at risk and either warned them not to go to East Berlin under any circumstances or told them not to agree to meet people near the border. Political actors who were at risk could apply for special police protection at any time. Those at high risk were placed under surveillance by the closest police station, and if it was suspected that an abduction might be imminent, special officers were sent to protect the person in question night and day. The heads of West Berlin's refugee camps could also request increased police protection.[42]

A vital part of the protection measures carried out by the state, and especially by the police, to combat the abductions was to secure the borders between the zones and the sectors, which fell under the remit of the West Berlin constabulary.[43] In view of the many abductions, they increased their patrols there at the beginning of the 1950s, sometimes using motorized police squads, and they set up emergency telephones on streets close to the border. Following the spectacular, violent abduction of the UFJ lawyer Dr. Walter Linse in 1952, West Berlin's Senate arranged for various security measures along the border. Barriers both movable and permanent, such as stone blocks, ditches, and steel structures, blocked the road crossings between East and West Berlin. And more West Berlin police were deployed on the sectoral and zonal borders.[44]

Due to Berlin's Four Power status, the West German government faced certain restrictions in their protective measures. All demands, for example, that the police and customs officers be better armed along the sectoral and zonal borders required the consent of the Western Allied powers. The government of West Berlin requested, for instance, that Western Allied military posts be deployed, that the police be better armed, and that there be more extensive controls of vehicles traveling in the direction of East Berlin.[45] But the Allied Kommandatura was not willing to budge from the rule that police could only be armed with wooden batons, only some being provided with pistols. Police were only permitted to use carbines at the zonal borders, not at the sectoral ones. Nevertheless, to support the police of West Berlin and to prevent abduction attempts, the western city commanders decided to set up reinforced patrols by Allied military police on the sectoral and zonal borders.[46] The issue of arming West Berlin's police at the border remained a point of contention in the following years, and the Western powers maintained a restrictive policy in the matter.

Besides security measures along the sectoral and zonal borders, there were also legal regulations aimed to protect West Berliners and the West German population. In June 1951 the Berlin Parliament passed a "law for the protection of personal freedom," which extended and tightened the law passed in September 1949 pertaining to the abduction of people from West Berlin. At that time, the German federal government also realized that there was a need for action. The federal parliament, the Bundesrat, passed the "law for the protection of personal freedom" as part of federal legislation, and it entered into force throughout Germany in July 1951 as Section 234a of the German Criminal Code. This laid the legal foundations for the criminal prosecution of perpetrators and their accomplices, although the law proved very difficult to enforce. Even identifying perpetrators and accomplices could be very difficult, depending on how the abduction had been carried out. And even if there were suspicions of abduction, the ultimate evidence was often missing—especially as the victims and therefore the main witnesses for the prosecution had disappeared—or the perpetrators could not be reached, as they had escaped to the GDR. This is also illustrated in the abduction of Friedrich Böhm in West Berlin (see above). It was correctly re-constructed following successful investigations, and this resulted in an arrest warrant being issued for IM "Tell" in mid-November 1958 for violating the law on the protection of freedom. However, the trial at the Regional Court Berlin had to be temporarily suspended a few days after it got underway, as the relevant parties were absent. IM "Tell" and his family had disappeared from West Berlin.[47] In a few abduction cases, however, it was possible to prosecute the perpetrators before 1989.

Outside of official state measures, the Western secret services and anti-Communist organizations also took their own measures to protect persons (and the information they had) who worked for them and who were at risk. One of these, for example, was to secure their offices with alarm systems. In addition, employees were only allowed to use means of public transport that West Berlin was in charge of, and they were not able to travel further than the last stop before the sectoral border.[48] Several organizations would have liked to arm some of their particularly vulnerable employees. After the abduction of his employee Dr. Walter Linse, the head of the UFJ demanded that all citizens in public service of the divided city of Berlin be permitted to carry weapons.[49] Other organizations, such as the Association of Political Refugees from the East (Vereinigung Politischer Ostflüchtlinge, or VPO), made similar pleas, demanding special police protection and gun permits for vulnerable people.[50] In 1952 a request for the issuance of gun permits was also submitted to the Berlin Parliament as an emergency motion, establishing the same regulations for carrying weapons in Berlin as in the territory of West Germany, and was passed unanimously. Following that, the Berlin Senate tried to negotiate this with the Allied Kommandatura, but the Kommandatura remained very reticent on the matter.[51] There were repeated negotiations in the following years, but because the Allies again refused to issue regular pistols, gas pistols remained the only legal weapon that was permitted for purposes of self-defense. The Stasi noted in several abduction cases that the victims were in possession of blank guns.[52] The UFJ, for example, handed out pistols of that kind to their employees, leading one of them to comment: "I do not consider gas pistols to provide anywhere near sufficient protection, and I request as always to be issued a pistol with a calibre of 7.65."[53] This was an opinion obviously shared by other UFJ employees. After one of their colleagues, Erwin Neumann, was violently abducted in 1958, the West Berlin police found a revolver and a pistol in his apartment.[54]

* * *

To the present day, people who formerly held positions of responsibility in the party or Stasi apparatus in the GDR, have never tired of justifying abductions as usual secret service practices and as a means of defense in the Cold War rivalry between political systems. There is no doubt that other states and their secret services all over the world use such methods and carry them out using very similar means. However, not many have achieved the dimensions of around four hundred abductions in a good ten years. And the Stasi files provide an insight into abduction practices.

The Stasi's abduction practices were fed by the East-West conflict and the rivalry between its political systems on German territory (and the fight between their respective secret services). However, it was based at the same time on the Stalinist concept of the enemy and was part of the repressive system with which the SED tried to gain stability for its crisis-torn leadership in the 1950s. It was therefore directed, not only against Western secret services and political opponents, but also against those among their own ranks who were seen as defectors.

Once the SED dictatorship had consolidated itself—particularly by building the Berlin Wall in 1961—the Stasi moved away from the praxis of abduction. The abductions were no longer seen as being urgent enough to make the collateral damage in the GDR's struggle for international acceptance worthwhile. The act of "voting with their feet"—that is, citizens leaving the GDR en masse—had come to an end. Closing in its own population gave the SED regime more stability and led to a relaxation in the rivalry between the two systems. The hermetic sealing and cementation of their division also cut off the inflow of potential employees to the secret services and the (already weakened) anti-Communist organizations in the West, making their work more difficult. From then on, the Stasi only saw the need to carry out such violent cross-border methods like abductions in very few cases—for example, in the case of defected Stasi employees. When weighing the benefits and harms of such activities, the fear of negative (foreign) political consequences for the GDR predominated. The violent practice of having people disappear, however, remained a working method used by the Stasi and, in a few individual cases, even turned into a murder plan. This is also related to the fact that Stalinists remained in leading positions (especially Erich Mielke as minister for state security).

In the Federal Republic, and in West Berlin in particular, the Stasi abductions caused outrage and—especially in the divided city—a feeling of insecurity. They highlighted on the one hand the unscrupulousness, the apparent ubiquity, and the cross-border danger of the Communist power bloc and its secret services. On the other hand, they also highlighted the powerlessness of the Federal German and the Western Allied governments and their public authorities. Accordingly, while the SED dictatorship was publicly criticized as the culpable party, the actors in the West—the police and political leaders in Bonn and West Berlin, as well as the Western Allies—were also criticized for their inability to effect protective measures, while the Western secret services and anti-Communist organizations also faced criticism for their activities.

It was only when the Berlin Wall was built that the various secret services and anti-Communist organizations severely reduced their activities in Berlin, while by that time the latter had already lost a great deal of importance. At the beginning of the East-West conflict, all groups involved were united in the face of a perceived common threat, a perception shared by the public at large. During the 1950s, however, their work and the methods they used were critically questioned by the public—especially with an eye to the persecuted and arrested people who were the victims of such activities. The Stasi abductions certainly played a considerable role in this.

NOTES

1. The name is a pseudonym.
2. The following sources (except for the final two newspapers) are found in the collection BArch (Bundesarchiv / Federal Archives), MfS, AP 21826/80. Report, Dept. I 4 KJ 1, 3.10.1958, 13–18; Note, Dept. I 4 KJ 1, 4 October 1958, 37; Report, Dept. I 4 KJ 1, 4 October 1958, 38–39; Report, Dept. I 4 KJ 1, 6 October 1958, 46–47; Report, Dept. I 4 KJ 1, 6 October 1958, 48–50; Report, Dept. I 4 KJ 1, 9 October 1958, 66–67; Expert opinion, Regional Office for Foodstuffs, Medicines, and Forensic Chemistry, 15 October 1958, 82; "Wieder Menschenraub in Berlin?" [Another abduction in Berlin?], *Frankfurter Rundschau,* 6 October 1958; "Perfektion im Gatower Menschenraub" [Perfection in Gatow abduction], *Spandauer Volksblatt,* 9 October 1958.
3. Final Report, Stasi, May 20, 1959, BArch, MfS, AOP 20495/62, vol. 7, 316–42, here 316–19; Interrogation record, West German Police, 19 December 1972, BArch, B 209/1070, no page nos; Report, HA II/2, February 3, 1955, BArch, MfS, AOP 1011/57, vol. 2, 97; Operative plan, HA II/2, July 5, 1955, BArch,

MfS, AOP 1011/57, vol. 2, 188–89; Final Report, HA II/2, June 28, 1957, BArch, MfS, AOP 1011/57, vol. 2, 250; Status Report, HA II/2, October 19, 1955, BArch, MfS, AOP 20495/62, vol. 1, 21–27; Report, HA II/2, November 24, 1955, BArch, MfS, AOP 20495/62, vol. 1, 81–82.

4. Decision, HA II/2, November 5, 1955, BArch, MfS, AOP 20495/62, vol. 1, 11–12; Status Report, HA II/2, July 27, 1956, BArch, MfS, AOP 20495/62, vol. 1, 289–309.

5. The following sources are found in the collection BArch, MfS, AOP 20495/62: Report, IM "Konsul," April 20, 1956, vol. 1, 213–14; Report, IM "Kettenbach," May 2, 1956, 215–16; "Proposal for Extracting English and NATO Residents," HA II/2, June 6, 1956, vol. 2, 128–34; Amendment to the abduction plan, HA II/2, September 20, 1956, 234; Information Report, HA II/2, September 25, 1956, 242–50.

6. The following sources are found in the collection BArch, MfS, AOP 20495/62: Report, HA II/2, October 24, 1956, vol. 2, 268–71; Operative plan, HA II/2, January 15, 1957, vol. 3, 172–87; Follow-up plan for "extracting residents," HA II/2, February 5, 1957, 198; Operative plan, HA II/2, March 13, 1957, vol. 4, 35–41.

7. Memorandum, HA II Head Office to HA II/2, July 2, 1957, BArch, MfS, AOP 20495/62, vol. 6, 107. Cf. Status Report, HA II/2, May 1, 1957, BArch, MfS, AOP 20495/62, vol. 4, 158–71, here 163–64; Proposal, HA II/2, June 25, 1957, BArch, MfS, AOP 20495/62, vol. 5, 227–28; Report, HA II/3, February 13, 1957, BArch, MfS, AOP 228/60, vol. 1, 32–34; Information Report, HA II/3, August 25, 1958, BArch, MfS, AOP 228/60, vol. 2, 8–26.

8. The following sources are found in the collection BArch, MfS, AOP 20495/62: Proposal, HA II/2, October 1, 1957, vol. 6, 109–10; Proposal for the "Execution of Active Measures," HA II/2, December 16, 1957, 215–17; Information Report, HA II/3, July 25, 1958, vol. 7, 17–47.

9. The following sources are found in the collection BArch, MfS, AOP 20495/62, vol. 14: Report, HA II/3, June 26, 1958, 200–202; Report, IM "Fischer," June 27, 1958, 203–6; Action plan, HA II/3, June 27, 1958, 185–94.

10. Follow-up plan, HA II/3, July 3, 1958, BArch, MfS, AOP 20495/62, vol. 14, 195–99; Meetings Report, HA II/3, July 1, 1958, BArch, MfS, AOP 20495/62, vol. 14, 211–14; Report, IM "Neuhaus," July 1, 1958, BArch, MfS, AIM 13009/86, A-file vol. 2, 98–100; Meetings Report, HA II/SR 3, July 3, 1958, BArch, MfS, AIM 13009/86, A-file vol. 2, 96 f.

11. The following sources are found in the collection BArch, MfS, AOP 20495/62, vol. 14: Report, HA II/3, September 23, 1958, 225 f.; Additional plan, HA II/3, September 30, 1958, 227–32; Memorandum, HA II/3, October 1, 1958, 210.

12. Report, IM "Neuhaus," October 2, 1958, BArch, MfS, AIM 13009/86, A-file vol. 2, 118–20; Report, IM "Neuhaus," October 3, 1958, BArch, MfS, AIM 13009/86, A-file vol. 2, 121–23; Meetings Report, HA II/SR 3, October 17, 1958, BArch, MfS, AIM 13009/86, A-file vol. 2, 126–27; Report, HA II/3, October 2,

1958, BArch, MfS, AOP 20495/62, vol. 14, 233–36; Report, HA II/3, October 4, 1958, BArch, MfS, AOP 20495/62, vol. 14, 237–38; Interrogation record, West German Police, December 19, 1972, BArch, B 209/1070, no page nos.

13. Report, West German Police, December 19, 1972, BArch, B 209/1070, no page nos.

14. Final Report, Stasi, May 20, 1959, BArch, MfS, AOP 20495/62, vol. 7, 316–42, here 316–17.

15. Final Report, Stasi, 316–42.

16. Interrogation record, West German Police, December 19, 1972, BArch, B 209/1070, no page nos.

17. Bundesministerium für gesamtdeutsche Fragen, *Der Staatssicherheitsdienst: Ein Instrument der politischen Verfolgung in der sowjetischen Besatzungszone Deutschlands* (Bonn: Bundesministerium für gesamtdeutsche Fragen, 1962), 45.

18. On the surveillance of the sector and zone border in the 1950s, cf. Gerhard Sälter et al., *Die vergessenen Toten: Todesopfer des DDR-Grenzregimes in Berlin von der Teilung bis zum Mauerbau (1948–1961)* (Berlin: Ch. Links Verlag, 2016), 53–89.

19. Quoted in Stefan Creuzberger, *Kampf um die Einheit: Das gesamtdeutsche Ministerium und die politische Kultur des Kalten Kriegs 1949–1969* (Düsseldorf: Droste, 2008), 126.

20. Bernd Stöver, *Die Befreiung vom Kommunismus. Amerikanische Liberation Policy im Kalten Krieg 1947–1991* (Köln: Böhlau, 2002), 269, also 258–69; Siegfried Mampel, *Der Untergrundkampf des Ministeriums für Staatssicherheit gegen den Untersuchungsausschuss Freiheitlicher Juristen in Berlin (West)* (Berlin, 1999); Enrico Heitzer, *Die Kampfgruppe gegen Unmenschlichkeit (KgU): Widerstand und Spionage im Kalten Krieg 1948–1959* (Köln: Böhlau, 2015); Ronny Heidenreich, *Die DDR-Spionage des BND: Von den Anfängen bis zum Mauerbau* (Berlin: Ch. Links Verlag, 2019), 219–36; Wolfgang Buschfort, *Parteien im Kalten Krieg: Die Ostbüros von SPD, CDU und FDP* (Berlin: Ch. Links Verlag, 2000), 29–68, 79–142, 213–37.

21. Michael Lemke, *Vor der Mauer: Berlin in der Ost-West-Konkurrenz 1948 bis 1961* (Köln: Böhlau, 2011), 177–81; Creuzberger, *Kampf,* 16; Bernd Stöver, *Der Kalte Krieg 1947–1991: Geschichte eines radikalen Zeitalters* (München: C. H. Beck, 2007), 232–33; Till Kössler, *Abschied von der Revolution: Kommunisten und Gesellschaft in Westdeutschland 1945–1968* (Bonn: Droste, 2005), 223–97, 315–69, 435–46.

22. Roger Engelmann, "Wollweber, Ernst," in *Das MfS-Lexikon,* ed. Helge Heidemeyer et al. (Berlin: Ch. Links Verlag, 2011), 343–45.

23. Lecture by Ernst Wollweber at a central official conference of the SfS, November 11–12, 1953, quoted in Karl Wilhelm Fricke and Gerhard Ehlert,

"Entführungsaktionen der DDR-Staatssicherheit und die Folgen für die Betroffenen," in *Deutschland im geteilten Europa: Materialien der Enquete-Kommission, Bd. VIII.2,* ed. Deutscher Bundestag (Berlin, 1999), 1174.

24. Karl Wilhelm Fricke and Roger Engelmann, *"Konzentrierte Schläge": Staatssicherheitsaktionen und politische Prozesse in der DDR 1953–1956* (Berlin: Ch. Links Verlag, 1998), 7–8, 29, 38, 42–60; Heidenreich, *DDR-Spionage,* 253–63.

25. For Erich Mielke's biography, cf. Jens Gieseke, "Erich Mielke (1907–2000): Revolverheld und oberster DDR-Tschekist," in *Konspiration als Beruf: Deutsche Geheimdienstchefs im Kalten Krieg,* ed. Dieter Krüger and Armin Wagner (Berlin: Ch. Links Verlag, 2003), 237–63.

26. Jens Gieseke, *Mielke-Konzern: Die Geschichte der Stasi 1945–1990* (Stuttgart: DVA, 2001), 175.

27. Report on the discussion between Josef Kiefel and IM "Neuhaus," February 1965, BArch, MfS, AIM 13009/86, P-file vol. 1, 353–61, here 354.

28. Werner Großmann and Wolfgang Schwanitz, *Fragen an das MfS: Auskünfte über eine Behörde* (Berlin: Edition Ost, 2010), 295–96.

29. Heidenreich, *DDR-Spionage,* 627. Cf. pp. 629–30.

30. Order no. 224/55, Ernst Wollweber, August 5, 1955; BArch, MfS, GH 108/55, vol. 6, 3–4, here 4.

31. For detailed research on the kidnapper-IM, cf. Susanne Muhle, *Auftrag Menschenraub: Entführungen von Westberlinern und Bundesbürgern durch das Ministerium für Staatssicherheit der DDR* (Göttingen: Vandenhoeck & Ruprecht, 2015), 369–593.

32. Unfortunately, even the latest research on the BND and the Verfassungsschutz does not provide any information here. In one case, Wolfgang Paul Höher, some corresponding CIA documents have been preserved. Cf. NARA, 640446, box 52, folder 6 and box 53, folder 1.

33. The name is a pseudonym.

34. *Menschenjäger im Dienste der USA* [Manhunters in the service of the USA], ed. Stasi Dept. Agitation, East Berlin 1957, BArch, MfS, ZAIG 18533. "Menschenfalle flog auf" [Mantrap revealed], *Neues Deutschland,* April 16, 1957; "Lebenslänglich Zuchthaus für Menschenhändler" [Life imprisonment for human traffickers], *Neues Deutschland,* April 21, 1957; "Wieder lebenslänglich" [Another life sentence], *Welt am Sonntag,* April 21, 1957.

35. "Neun Jahre Zuchthaus für führende Agentin des SSD" [Nine years in prison for SSD agent], *Tagesspiegel,* November 19, 1963; Fricke and Ehlert, "Entführungsaktionen," 1202.

36. The following sources are found in the collection BArch, B 137/32151: Query, Police Commissioner in Berlin Dept. 1 at the Legal Protection Office, June 21, 1957, 8; Note, Dept. I 4 KJ 1, August 4, 1956, 27; Final Report, Dept. I 4 KJ 1, August 17, 1956, 28; Report, Dept. I 4 KJ 1, November 9, 1956, 51–53.

37. Memorandum, Attorney General at the Regional Court Berlin to the Chief Federal Public Prosecutor at the Federal Supreme Court, March 8, 1957, BArch, B 137/32151, 29–30.

38. "Neun Jahre Zuchthaus für führende Agentin des SSD" [Nine years imprisonment for leading SSD agent], *Tagesspiegel,* November 19, 1963; "400 Menschen und den Bruder an den SSD verkauft" [400 people and her brother sold to the SSD], *Berliner Morgenpost,* October 31, 1963; "Anklage gegen West-Berlinerin: Den Bruder an den SSD ausgeliefert" [West Berlin woman charged with handing over her brother to the SSD], *Tagesspiegel,* November 1, 1963; "Den Bruder für 5000 DM verraten" [She betrayed her brother for 5,000 DM], *Telegraf,* November 1, 1963; "Unter Ausschluss der Öffentlichkeit: Prozess gegen SSD-Agentin begann—Bruder für 5000 DM verraten" [Trial held in camera: Proceedings begin against SSD agent—betrayed her brother for 5,000 DM], *Tagesspiegel,* November 16, 1963; "Sühne für Bruderverrat" [Atonement for betraying her brother], *Telegraf,* November 19, 1963; "Sühne für gewissenlosen Verrat" [Atonement for unscrupulous betrayal], *Die Welt,* November 19, 1963.

39. "Wieder lebenslänglich" [Life imprisonment again], *Welt am Sonntag,* April 21, 1957; "Lebenslänglich Zuchthaus für Menschenhändler" [Life imprisonment for human traffickers], *Neues Deutschland,* April 21, 1957; Letter, Legal Protection Office to Federal Minister of All-German Matters, February 28, 1966, BArch, B 137/32151, 77.

40. Classified Message, SB REP Berlin to Director CIA, February 20, 1953, NARA, 640446, box 52, folder 6, 39. The Linse case mentioned above involves the forcible abduction of a lawyer from West Berlin in July 1952.

41. Report, Stasi, February 10, 1959, BArch, MfS, BV Leipzig, AIM 355/61, P-Akte, 68–69; Criminal complaint against Horst K., ZERV 215, February 6, 1998, Berlin public prosecutor, AZ 29 Js 68/95 Bd. IIIa, 110; Report "Abduction of Wolfgang Hoeher," February 1953, NARA, 640446, box 52, folder 6, 23–24; Report "Abduction of Hoeher," February 17, 1953, NARA, 640446, box 52, folder 6, 25–26; Report, Chief of Base Pullach to Chief EE, January 21, 1954, NARA, 640446, box 52, folder 6, 176–77; the following sources are all from the collection NARA, 640446, box 53, folder 1: Agent Report, CIC, October 27, 1955, 44; Report, Headquarters 66th CIC Group, January 4, 1956, 57–59; Operational Cadory Cart, CIA, January 31, 1956, 62; Report, CIA, April 5, 1956, 81–82; Summary of Information, CIA, May 11, 1956, 85; Report with details of the abduction, August 29, 1957, 144–47; Letter to Wolfgang Höher, 1957, 194–96; Classified Message, BND to CIA, November 25, 1957, 200; Report, Chief of Base Munich to Chief EE, January 17, 1958, 211–15; Dispatch, Chief of Base Munich, October 22, 1959, 223; Fricke and Engelmann, *Staatssicherheitsaktionen,* 124; Heidenreich, *DDR-Spionage,* 251–54.

42. "Berlin wird immer gefährlicher: 223 Menschen verschwanden in 10 Monaten / Polizei 'beschattet' Gefährdete" [Berlin becoming increasingly dangerous:

223 people disappear in 10 months / Police "shadow" potential victims], *Frankenpost,* November 24, 1951; Record of the confrontation between Friedrich Böhm and IM "Tell," Stasi, spring 1959, BArch, MfS, AOP 20495/62, vol. 11, 125–33, here 129; Letter, Federal Minister of All-German Matters to the Federal Chancellor's Office, October 6, 1952, BArch, B 136/6539, no page nos.

43. Annual Report of the Berlin Police Force, 1953, LAB (Landesarchiv Berlin), Zs 505, 159; Annual Report of the Berlin Police Force, 1955, LAB, Zs 505, 13.

44. Letter, BMG (Federal Minister of All-German Matters) to the Federal Chancellor's Office, October 6, 1952, BArch, B 136/6539, no page nos.; "Entführungen müssen ein Ende haben: Berliner Senat sichert Grenzübergänge zur Sowjetzone und zum Sowjetsektor" [Abductions must end: Berlin Senate secures border crossings to the Soviet Zone and the Soviet Sector], *Tagesspiegel,* July 9, 1952; "Berlin schützt sich gegen Terrorakte" [Berlin protects itself against acts of terror], *Neue Zeitung,* July 9, 1952; "Da könnt ihr lange kratzen: Eisenträger wachsen aus der Erde—Schutzmaßnahmen gegen Menschenraub" [Protection measures: Iron girders grow out of the soil—measures taken to stop abductions], *Die Welt,* July 19, 1952; "Neuntausend sind echt" [Nine thousand are real], *Der Spiegel,* no. 32/1952, 6; Note, Federal Ministry of Justice, July 14, 1952, BArch, B 141/12195, 7–11; Report, Federal Chancellor's Office, January 19, 1955, BArch, B 136/6539.

45. Emergency motion by the factions of the SPD, CDU and FDP, Berlin Parliament, July 16, 1952, LAB, B Rep. 228, no. 1004, no page nos.; Stenographic Report of the 51st Session of the Berlin Parliament, July 17, 1952, LAB, B Rep. 228, no. 998, 548–90, here 549–51; "Schwerste Strafe für Menschenräuber: Abgeordnetenhaus für Militärposten und bessere Bewaffnung der Polizei" [Severe punishments for kidnappers: Berlin Parliament in favour of military posts and for better arming police], *Tagesspiegel,* July 18, 1952.

46. Letter, Federal Minister of All-German Matters to the Federal Chancellor's Office, October 6, 1952, BArch, B 136/6539, no page nos.; Annual Report of Berlin Police Force, 1953, LAB, Zs 505, 159.

47. The following sources (except for the final two) are found in the collection BArch, MfS, AP 21826/80: Report, Dept. I 4 KJ 1, October 3, 1958, 13–18; Note, Dept. I 4 KJ 1, October 4, 1958, 37; Report, Dept. I 4 KJ 1, October 4, 1958, 38–39; Report, Dept. I 4 KJ 1, October 6, 1958, 46–47; Report, Dept. I 4 KJ 1, October 6, 1958, 48–50; Report, Dept. I 4 KJ 1, October 9, 1958, 66–67; Report, Dept. I 4 KJ 1, October 23, 1958, 85–91; Arrest warrant, Local Court Tiergarten, November 11, 1958, 95–96; Internal Memorandum, BMG Dept. II.1 to BMG Bonn, November 13, 1958, BArch, B 137/1063, no page nos.; Internal Memorandum, BMG Dept. II.1 to BMG Bonn, July 16, 1959, BArch, B 137/1063, no page nos.

48. Buschfort, *Parteien,* 184–85.

49. "Berlin schützt sich gegen Terrorakte" [Berlin protects itself against acts of terror], *Neue Zeitung*, July 9, 1952.

50. Letter, VPO to Federal Chancellor Konrad Adenauer, July 9, 1952, BArch, B 136/6539, no page nos. The Federal Ministry of Justice makes sure that it demands that the Senate and the Allied Commanders of Berlin undertake all conceivable security measures (also for the personal protection of those at risk). Cf. reply letter, Federal Ministry of Justice, July 19, 1952, BArch, B 141/12195 8/1: 20–21; Renewed demands by the VPO for arms Cf. Letter, VPO to the Police Commissioner of Berlin, December 29, 1952, BArch, B 141/12195 8/1, 55.

51. Stenographic Report of the 51st Session of the Berlin Parliament, July 17, 1952, LAB, B Rep. 228, no. 998: 548–90, here 550; Letter, BMG to the Federal Chancellor's Office, October 6, 1952, BArch, B 136/6539, no page nos.

52. Report, Dept. III, March 18, 1955, BArch, MfS, BV Potsdam, AOP 329/552, 40–44, here 40; Abduction plan, Dept. III, March 4, 1955, BArch, MfS, BV Potsdam, AOP 329/552: 24–30; Report, Stasi, October 20, 1953, BArch, MfS, AOP 1539/65 5: 36–51, here 48; Interrogation record, Stasi, April 28, 1954, BArch, MfS, AU 402/54 2: 150–51, here 150.

53. Certificate, UFJ, July 23, 1952, BArch, B 209/29, no page nos. Around twenty-five attestations with identical wording are in the file pertaining to the temporary issue of gas pistols from the period July to November 1952.

54. Memorandum, Attorney General at the Regional Court Berlin to Dept. I 4 KJ 2, November 17, 1958, BArch, MfS, AP 21882/80, 305.

PART II

CRISIS, 1958–1971

CHAPTER 5

The Never-Ending Berlin Crisis and the Limits of Alliance Politics

ERIN MAHAN

The early 1960s have long been regarded as a period of Cold War crises. Berlin was one prominent hotspot—"the one place in the world where the two superpowers faced each other continuously eye to eye."[1] Yet to call Berlin a "crisis" is somewhat of a misnomer. In reality, the question of Berlin was a perennial problem that had plagued the victorious powers of World War II since their agreement in 1945 for the joint administration of the former German capital. Access and other occupation issues had existed since the end of World War II. Soviet harassments and threats to end Western access to Berlin were not a new phenomenon, but the previous flash point of the blockade of 1948 was before the perils of the nuclear age loomed. The problem of Berlin festered for another decade until beginning in November 1958, the North Atlantic Treaty Organization faced a renewed predicament from the East, when the Soviets used the threat of signing a separate peace treaty with the German Democratic Republic (GDR) to force the NATO

The views expressed in this chapter reflect those of the author and not that of the US government. The public release clearance of this chapter by the Department of Defense does not imply official endorsement of the material.

powers out of West Berlin. Initially, Soviet premier Nikita Khrushchev set a six-month ultimatum to reach an agreement with the West, and then let it pass in 1959 when the administration of President Dwight Eisenhower refused to give up the US position in the former German capital. Khrushchev renewed his threat with Eisenhower's young successor, John F. Kennedy, at a superpower summit in Vienna early June 1961. The Soviet signing of a separate peace treaty with the GDR would not by itself mean war. The United States, however, feared that once the Soviets renounced their wartime occupation rights the East Germans would demand the withdrawal of the Western powers from Berlin. The Kremlin would denounce the hard-won understandings that permitted the West to reach Berlin, an enclave 110 miles inside of East Germany, by car, rail, or road. It would be East German interference with Allied access to Berlin, backed by Soviet power, which could possibly spark a war.[2]

The narrative and analysis of Kennedy's approach to Berlin have generated hundreds of accounts from almost every angle. One commonality running through the vast literature on the building of the Berlin Wall and its aftermath is the interplay and complexities of alliance politics for both superpowers. Neither Washington nor Moscow operated in isolation. For the Kennedy administration, the West European powers played a complicating role in shaping the contours of a Berlin solution before and after the erection of the wall. While it is tempting to try to challenge the dichotomy that posits diametrically opposed versions for Western Europe—Anglo-American "Atlanticism" or French-driven Gaullism—there is insufficient documentary evidence to support other narratives. In other words, European policy was essentially divided between two camps on strategic visions for the Continent and alliance issues: an economically and integrated Western Europe that included Great Britain as part of the Common Market and de facto dominance with the US in NATO or a continental approach in which de Gaulle's France would direct West European affairs with the Federal Republic of Germany in a "junior" partnership. By the late 1950s, the Atlantic alliance began polarizing over, first, preserving Western access and rights to Berlin and, second, responding to French and West German demands for *Mitbestimmung,* or a share in nuclear decision-making. And by the early 1960s, a quadrilateral saga among the four major NATO powers played out against the backdrop of the ongoing Berlin crisis. In this regard, the analysis offered here attempts to move beyond the conventional interpretations of the Berlin crisis and the NATO alliance, which hold that despite US and French differences over the best deterrence strategy to pursue against the Soviet Union, de Gaulle always firmly supported Kennedy during both Berlin crisis and Cuban Missile Crisis. Although on the surface the French general did stand with NATO, his actions had lasting effects that strained the alliance for years to come.[3]

Neither British prime minister Harold Macmillan nor West German chancellor Konrad Adenauer were passive actors during either the Berlin crisis or larger NATO debates. Yet the reality was that Britain was largely preoccupied with its bid to join the European Economic Community (EEC), commonly known as the Common Market. At a time when de Gaulle was exerting pressure on Adenauer to oppose negotiations with the Soviets over Berlin, Macmillan and Kennedy believed Britain's entrance into the EEC could offset French influence on West Germany. Adenauer had long supported a unified, "integrated" Western Europe, but he was greatly disturbed by what he feared was Macmillan's apparent willingness to "sell out" West Germany for peace with the Soviet Union in central Europe. The chancellor was also increasingly disturbed by Kennedy's calls to revise NATO nuclear strategy by an increased reliance on conventional military capabilities, or what is widely known as flexible response. Adenauer was willing to entertain de Gaulle's conception of a "little Europe," which excluded Britain from the EEC, if de Gaulle were to maintain a hard-line stance against negotiating with the Soviets over Berlin. De Gaulle hoped to wean the German chancellor from US tutelage in NATO. The French president delighted in opportunities to capitalize on Adenauer's annoyance with the new young American president, who had omitted the issue of Berlin's security in his first address to Congress on February 6, 1961.[4]

During President Kennedy's early months in office, before the Vienna summit, he was preoccupied with more pressing concerns and crises, namely in Laos or Cuba, and his knowledge of West German affairs and the Berlin question in particular was minimal. Journalist Theodore White, who chronicled the American 1960 presidential campaign, noted how the candidate "talked about Berlin, very slowly, as if picking his own way through his thoughts."[5] In the most general terms, the new president viewed Berlin as a test of Western credibility because it was the one place, the one hotspot, where all the major powers had vested interests. How that intangible test would play out in concrete terms was initially unclear. Kennedy's team worried that the Kremlin's demand for unilaterally abrogating the Western powers' post–World War II occupation rights to their sectors in Berlin would generate dissension among Britain, France, and the US governments, who held highly divergent positions on how to counter the Soviet threat. Khrushchev would then capitalize on that disunity to oust the Western powers from Berlin.[6]

The Kennedy administration inherited a NATO contingency-planning structure established during the 1958 Berlin crisis. The three Western powers code-named their planning staff "LIVE OAK" and also convened the Washington Ambassadorial Group (WAG) to formulate operational plans. Even a month before Kennedy's fateful summit with Khrushchev, Secretary of Defense Robert McNamara had warned his commander in chief that NATO contingency plans for ensuring continued access to Berlin were "deficient" against even East German forces acting without Soviet backup.[7] The US realized that revamping NATO planning efforts would be an arduous task. Dean Rusk, JFK's secretary of state, cautioned about "the crucial role that France plays in the dialogue with the Soviet Union on Berlin." He feared that de Gaulle might pursue an independent line that could encourage the Kremlin to take a divide-and-conquer approach toward abrogating Western rights in Berlin. As one longtime NSC staffer quipped, "Uncle Charlie [Charles de Gaulle] was the real nut to crack in revitalizing NATO." And he and others within the Kennedy administration decried the "obduracy of an obsessed old man."[8] Compounding friction between the French president and NATO was the election by that body's council of Dirk Stikker from the Netherlands as the new NATO secretary general on April 18, 1961. De Gaulle held nothing but disdain for someone he perceived as well below his position and from a "lesser" European country, the Netherlands. In fact, France tried for months to block his candidacy. When it did go through, de Gaulle refused to meet with the new secretary general until July 12, 1961, and then only once for a mere thirty minutes.[9]

While Western contingency planning within NATO continued laboriously and tortuously through LIVE OAK and the WAG shell, the Kennedy administration's internal deliberations occurred primarily along two tracks: a Berlin task force grafted onto the National Security Council and an interdepartmental coordinating group headed by the former secretary of state to President Harry S. Truman, Dean Acheson, who had managed the Berlin blockade of the late 1940s. Before the wall was erected in August

1961, Acheson's hard-line group seemed to dominate administration planning during the early summer months in part because the former secretary of state had been leading strategic planning for NATO in the spring. On June 28, 1961, in a report to the president, Acheson advocated preemptive military measures such as calling up the reserves, increasing conventional forces in Europe, conducting troop exercises, resuming nuclear testing and U-2 flights, increasing the defense budget; and declaring a state of national emergency. Most importantly, Acheson's report concluded that the United States must make it unequivocally clear that it would defend the status quo in Berlin with nuclear weapons.[10]

Acheson's report sparked heated debate within the administration. Kennedy hoped for coherent advice that would allow him to modulate the US response. He heard instead a cacophony of voices from his best and brightest. The deputy special assistant to the president for national security affairs, Walt W. Rostow, hardly a dove, criticized taking such a hard-line position without stating a political objective that justified "incinerating the world" over access to Berlin. Influential NSC adviser McGeorge Bundy agreed that "nuclear weapons should not be pursued."[11]

Acheson's stance of placing primary emphasis on a nuclear deterrent, which increasingly lost ground within the Kennedy circle, resonated strongly with de Gaulle and Adenauer. The former secretary of state had known the West German chancellor for decades and described him to the young US president as "worried to death—just completely worried" over Berlin. The chancellor's concern that the Kennedy administration was moving toward a NATO strategy that placed a higher premium on conventional weapons in central Europe than on nuclear deterrence left him afraid that Germany would become the chief theater of war. He privately declared, "What the Americans do not see is that for Germany there is no difference between an atomic arsenal and a conventional war on our own soil. To be roasted at a thousand degrees or burned at ninety, the result is exactly the same." To Acheson, he argued that specifying in advance when the West would use nuclear weapons, or "raise the threshold" for nuclear war, as it was called, would only allow the Soviets time to nibble at NATO territory during the pause between conventional and atomic weapons. The Soviets could thereby present the West with a fait accompli.[12]

Through the early summer months of 1961, the Western leaders were unable to agree on a common approach to the Berlin conundrum. Kennedy feared that a failure to provide a coordinated formal response to the Soviet ultimatum issued through an aide-mémoire at the Vienna summit would only strengthen Khrushchev's hand. Kennedy was aware that he had to factor in the positions of the other NATO allies in determining pace and scale of a US mobilization. And yet those Allied positions reflected confusion and disarray. When Kennedy privately queried his Joint Chiefs of Staff on July 18 about whether NATO forces were sufficiently strong to follow a ground probe with nonnuclear air action, the generals replied that only if the alliance members acted in concert. And when the president then asked whether additional American divisions could be employed effectively if NATO allies failed to augment their own forces, he was told no.[13]

Rather than wait for the meeting of NATO foreign ministers scheduled for early August, on July 25 Kennedy went ahead and responded to the Soviet threat during a televised address to the American public. Speaking solemnly, he stressed the importance of Berlin as the acid test of US credibility—"the greatest testing place of Western courage and will."[14] Kennedy's speech was also a call for military preparedness to bolster that credibility of Western resolve. Soon thereafter, he requested an additional $3.25 billion for the US defense budget, activated several National Guard units, and improved conventional weapons capabilities. In the ensuing months, the United States would increase its forces in Western Europe from 228,000 to 273,000 and deploy eleven air force fighter squadrons. Yet American military mobilization could not occur overnight, and two weeks before the wall began to go up, Secretary of Defense McNamara stressed in congressional hearings that the best long-term deterrence to any Soviet move against West Berlin access rights was a steady increase in NATO conventional forces.[15]

Kennedy's uncompromising tone during his television address and his follow-on actions did little to mollify de Gaulle and gave Macmillan cause for concern that the two superpowers were moving inexorably to the brink of nuclear confrontation. The cautious British position only widened the gulf between Macmillan on the one side and de Gaulle and Adenauer on the other. The prime minister viewed the crisis within his overarching aim of a détente between East and West. No less than de Gaulle, Macmillan envisioned himself as a leader of a mediating third force of Europe between the superpowers. On July 28, 1961, three days after Kennedy's address to the nation, Macmillan's cabinet decided that "there might be advantages in according de facto recognition to the GDR, especially if it led to an increase in its contacts with the West that might serve to undermine the communist hold on the country."[16]

Macmillan's views leaked to Adenauer's circle of advisers. The British prime minister's apparent eagerness to negotiate heightened the chancellor's fears that the UK would sell out West Germany in order to achieve an empty détente with the Soviet Union. Suspicious of perceived British fickleness toward West Germany, and worried by British consideration of withdrawing Royal Air Force fighter squadrons from the FRG, Adenauer became increasingly convinced that Britain would disengage militarily from Europe and neutralize Germany or, even worse, divide it permanently as a price for an illusory détente.[17] De Gaulle capitalized on Adenauer's disenchantment with Macmillan to strengthen his own hand in European affairs. The French president reinforced Adenauer's suspicion that the prime minister would sell out Western rights in Berlin and argued that Macmillan's temporizing demonstrated that the British were not European-minded and did not belong in the European Economic Community. De Gaulle's unyielding stance on Khrushchev's ultimatum was not all bluff and bluster. His European strategy of cementing a Franco-German rapprochement required no compromise with the Soviets. Ensuring that Adenauer stayed in power, the key in de Gaulle's mind to collaboration between Paris and Bonn was also the best way to prevent Germany from turning eastward. De Gaulle worried that any appearance of Western weakness, as demonstrated by a willingness to negotiate over Berlin, could only harm Adenauer's domestic political situation. The Bundestag elections were to be in September 1961, and a prospective separate peace treaty with the GDR, which might consolidate the division of Germany, promised to be a key issue. If Western discussions with the Soviets legitimized the GDR, Adenauer might face political defeat.[18]

De Gaulle believed that his tough "verbal" stance would preclude the West ever having to fight over Berlin. Since the 1958 crisis, he had perceived himself as the West's Jeremiah by constantly warning that negotiation would lead to concessions, perhaps allowing Berlin to become a neutral "free city," as the Soviets proposed. De Gaulle—and Adenauer, for that matter—were also captives to history. Remembering the events leading up to World War II, de Gaulle insisted that such a neutralist solution for Berlin would symbolize another "Munich" and open up a slippery and dangerous slope leading to a neutral Germany, which would in his mind eventually succumb to pressures from the East. Negotiations—an indication in de Gaulle's (and Adenauer's) mind of Western weakness—would encourage the Kremlin to deny Western access into the city without expecting more than an idle protest from NATO.[19]

In reality, de Gaulle's bombastic stance on Khrushchev's Berlin ultimatum belied France's limited defense capabilities. De Gaulle had long mastered the use of rhetoric to compensate for French military weakness. Bogged down in the last phases of the war in Algeria, French forces could not easily be deployed to central Europe. By insisting that Khrushchev was bluffing over terminating Western access to its Berlin sectors, de Gaulle did not need to admit that France's military inferiority left him no alternative. Moreover, the strategic value of France's nascent nuclear deterrent (discussed below) lay in de Gaulle's professed willingness to use it. The Berlin crisis reinforced de Gaulle's insistence on integrating the doctrine of *dissuasion du faible au fort* (deterrence of the strong by the weak) into his larger military and diplomatic strategy, which was based more on resolve than on capabilities.[20] If Khrushchev were to back down over Berlin, as he had done in 1958, the French president could appear to be the wise statesman. And if he were wrong and Soviets were not bluffing, de Gaulle knew the West could not match Soviet conventional military power, especially in a ground force engagement in central Europe.[21]

France's refusal to entertain the possibility of negotiations created difficulties within the NATO alliance. After tabling drafts of a possible tripartite response to the Soviet aide-mémoire on its threat to sign a separate peace treaty with the GDR, the French government made it clear that it intended to send an independent reply to Moscow. On July 5, 1961, the French foreign minister Couve de Murville met the Soviet foreign minister, Andrei Gromyko, in Moscow, where he chastised the Soviets for manufacturing a crisis, arguing that no Western action had occurred in Berlin to warrant a change in the status quo.[22]

Although a crisis over Berlin was on the horizon throughout the summer of 1961, precisely how and when the Soviets would act was unclear. The bleeding from East Germany to the West became a hemorrhage during July and the first twelve days of August, as 30,000 refugees fled to the sectors controlled by Britain, France, and the United States. East German forces began erecting barriers in the stealth of the early morning hours of August 13, 1961. While it may seem inconceivable that the early erections of barriers that became the Berlin Wall caught the Western powers off guard, the timing did come as a complete tactical surprise. The month of August is typically the time for government officials to take vacations: Kennedy was in Hyannis Port, Macmillan was in Scotland; de Gaulle was outside Paris.[23]

Kennedy is alleged to have felt a mixture of shock and relief, supposedly exclaiming privately to his aides, "Why would Khrushchev put up a wall if he really intended to seize West Berlin? This is his way out of his predicament. It's not a very nice solution, but a wall is a hell of a lot better than war." Although such sentiments were not expressed by JFK in his privately taped presidential recordings, it is conceivable that he expressed this relief only one-on-one with confidants rather than in meetings. His secretary of state, Dean Rusk, issued a public statement on August 13, when East Germans began erecting barriers: "Available information indicates that measures taken thus far are aimed at residents of East Berlin and East Germany and not at the allied position in West Berlin or access thereto." The administration did not leap into immediate action.[24]

Adenauer's initial response to the beginning of the sealing of the border between East and West Berlin was also muted. He opted not to travel to West Berlin, a decision many in his own country saw as showing a lack of solidarity. Instead, he continued his campaigning for reelection, the election being less than a month away—thereby making what would be the most serious political blunder of his career by not only appearing callous to the fate of the East Germans by not traveling to West Berlin but also by impugning the character of the mayor of West Berlin, Willy Brandt, who was of the rival Social Democratic Party, during the campaign. Adenauer would pay the ultimate political cost; his CDU would lose its majority in the September 1961 Bundestag elections, and even though he remained chancellor, his influence waned, and he would step down from the chancellorship in 1963.[25]

Once West Berlin mayor Brandt requested that the US dispatch troops to the city, located deep in East German territory, as a way to show American solidarity with the FRG, the Kennedy administration complied. At Kennedy's instruction, on August 20 the US government sent a Seventh Army battle group of 1,200 troops down the autobahn under the command of Gen. Lucius Clay, hero of the Berlin blockade of 1948, to convey American resolve to defend the Western sectors. Fortunately, the convoy proceeded to Berlin unchallenged as it passed through GDR territory. Then, on August 25, the secretary of defense issued mobilization orders of 46,500 troops to round out six divisions and provide support for the US Army, Europe; 6,400 for the US Navy's forty destroyers and eighteen patrol squadrons; and 23,700 for the US Air Force to activate thirty-three tactical, transport, and reconnaissance squadrons.[26]

De Gaulle, like all his Western counterparts, did not advocate destroying the wall. In fact, none of the Western powers advocated challenging the Berlin Wall builders. Gen. Lyman Lemnitzer, chairman of the Joint Chiefs of Staff, privately characterized the collective NATO reaction: "Everyone appeared to be hopeless, helpless, and harmless."[27] Although he publicly supported Washington, the French president privately scorned Kennedy's dispatch of 1,200 troops down the autobahn. While the US wanted to use the troop dispatch to test whether Khrushchev would cut off Western access, de Gaulle thought it was an unnecessary provocation.[28]

The larger effects of the protracted crisis in Berlin on the NATO alliance were considerable, and they exacerbated intra-alliance debates over its strategic posture. For the Kennedy administration, the ongoing crisis catapulted NATO strategy ahead of other European concerns, including plans for expanding the Common Market through Great Britain's admission. Kennedy believed that the immediate threat to Berlin required defining NATO's nuclear posture and preparing for armed combat short of a full-scale nuclear attack. In the event that the Soviets tried to block Western access to Berlin, NATO needed sufficient conventional ground forces and arms with air and sea lift to counter a Soviet conventional arms threat.[29] In theory, the American rationale for increasing conventional capabilities—tanks, artillery, troops—was twofold. First, it would demonstrate US willingness to bear the costs of escalating the arms race if the Soviets tried to force the Western powers from Berlin. Second, a buildup would convince the European allies that the United States was committed to sacrificing its own men to fight in Europe.[30]

Kennedy's military advisers expressed concern about the credibility of graduated responses—so-called flexible response. Gen. Lyman Lemnitzer, chairman of the Joint Chief of Staff (JCS), advised the president to clarify *when*—at what stage—the United States would use nuclear weapons if the Soviets moved on Berlin. Kennedy acknowledged the ambiguity surrounding the issue of when but maintained that "the critical point was to be able to use nuclear weapons at a crucial moment before the Soviets used them." Gen. Curtis LeMay, also on the JCS, told the president that only the NATO air bases in Spain allowed the United States to take off without previous consultation. Kennedy worried about the feasibility of consulting France and Britain about the decision to deploy nuclear weapons before the Soviets unleased theirs. The ambiguity in this debate over graduated responses reflected what one historian has pointed to as a gap between the political and strategic value of what became known as the Kennedy administration's "flexible response."[31]

Despite the ambiguity surrounding the Kennedy administration's theorizing about graduated NATO responses, throughout the ongoing crisis the US asked the major West European allies to complement its efforts in augmenting conventional military capabilities on the Continent. Kennedy, who had campaigned on a platform of personal sacrifice, extended his clarion call for burden sharing beyond the nation's borders to ask not what the United States could do for Western Europe but what Western Europe could do for the United States in its common fight against international Communism. In mid-July 1961, Kennedy informed de Gaulle, Macmillan, and Adenauer that he intended to request a supplementary military budget from the American Congress to increase US forces in central Europe. Kennedy reminded them that the number of NATO divisions in central Europe was well below the levels agreed to by the Western powers in 1958 under NATO directive MC 70 and its revised directive, MC 26/4. Soviet divisions outnumbered NATO counterparts by twenty-two to sixteen. Moreover, the Soviet Union's ability to mobilize additional manpower so far exceeded Western capabilities that NATO would be unable to engage in combat for more than three or four weeks. In short, such unequal conventional capabilities would likely not deter Soviet action in Berlin.[32] What Kennedy did not share were assurances that his own secretary of defense had told him privately: if NATO members followed the guidelines prescribed in 1958, then the alliance "would be prepared to launch non-nuclear warfare on a scale which would indicate their determination and which would provide some additional time for negotiation before resorting to nuclear warfare."[33]

Although Paris assured Washington that it would meet its NATO MC 26/4 goals and that it might also allow nuclear stockpiles on French soil, the Kennedy administration believed that France and the major West European powers were delaying agreement on a coordinated military strategy. The US president's brother and attorney general, Robert Kennedy, later recalled that "the French were the ones who gave us the most difficulties. The British were not much better. But the French!" In the area of conventional military measures, the French government took relatively minimal preparations for continued East-West conflict over Berlin. The French military determined that it was impossible to deploy six French divisions, as specified in NATO's MC 70 and 26/4. All the French managed was the shift of two divisions from Algeria to the metropole for quick transfer to West Germany in the event of military incidents in Berlin.[34]

De Gaulle resented US calls for conventional weapons buildup. In a private memorandum circulated among his advisers, he fumed that a war over Berlin would rapidly turn French territory into a bloody battlefield: "America can lose the battle of Europe," he noted with bitterness, "without disappearing." French generals and civilian officials at the Ministry of Defense shared their president's resentment. They believed that conventional weapons lacked both political and strategic credibility as a deterrent, reasoning that the Kremlin knew the United States would never escalate a conventional war to a nuclear one unless the Soviets struck first with nuclear weapons. Yet they also refused to recognize that, for the US, the use of force over the Berlin crisis could escalate to the choice between unleashing nuclear weapons or capitulating.[35]

The ongoing problem of Berlin had decisive effects on French military policy, which conceived of foreign policy in terms of *realités* and *trucs*—the latter term a pejorative for amorphous "things." For de Gaulle, NATO was a partial realité and a partial truc; it was a temporary annoyance, necessary only while he maneuvered to implement his grand design of placing France at the helm of an independent Europe. He scorned the other continental nations that accepted what he deemed a permanent US military protectorate. For de Gaulle it was simply a means for the United States to maintain dominance. Attempts by the United States to accommodate and circumvent French nationalist aspirations were difficult because the French president frequently conflated his aims and his tactics. At times de Gaulle posited demands for tripartism as a means of reorganizing NATO in order to achieve French participation in nuclear targeting and strategy. Yet on other occasions tripartism was an end in itself because it conferred great power status.[36]

Likewise, French possession of a nuclear arsenal, a *force de frappe,* constituted both a role and a capability. De Gaulle strove to ensure France's security and influence in world affairs primarily through the development of an independent nuclear capability. Yet in the same way that he insisted upon tripartism, he often framed his pursuit of a force de frappe in symbolic terms as the keystone to his foreign policy. His detractors felt that he simply believed the syllogism that great nations have nuclear weapons; France is a great nation, so therefore France must have nuclear weapons.[37] In other respects, de Gaulle was convinced that a nuclear arsenal would provide political and diplomatic leverage as a *force de persuasion* that could end the humiliation of stationing US troops on French soil and permit strategic independence between the superpowers. The French also believed a force de frappe would ensure its supremacy on the Continent. By solidifying Franco-German rapprochement, France with a force de frappe would be the dominant continental partner while supposedly satisfying West German nuclear ambitions by offering it nuclear protection.[38]

Hoping to prevent a further schism between Gaullist France and the United States, the Kennedy administration attempted to give the concept of tripartism some de facto acknowledgment. For example, before the building of the Berlin Wall, in June 1961, Kennedy had suggested that the three Western leaders meet the following autumn if the crisis became more serious. He also promised de Gaulle that "in the event of any emergency such as increased tension or the threat of war, the United States will take every possible step to consult with France and other allies unless an attack were so imminent that our survival is threatened."[39]

Such verbal assurances were not what de Gaulle wanted to hear, especially after the beginnings of the building of the wall. His real concern was not consultation per se but lack of French control over NATO's nuclear forces. Although pledging allegiance to NATO, French generals chafed under the NATO chain of command established for an outbreak of hostilities in Berlin. They resented taking orders—in English nonetheless—from the United States (in April 1959, the West had agreed that the occupying commanders in Berlin would be under the orders of the Supreme Allied Commander, Europe [SACEUR]). And because the NATO secretary general received orders from Washington, the French complained that any action taken in Berlin would be "more American than tripartite." They fumed particularly over exclusion from nuclear targeting and control of weapons.[40]

Unbeknownst to Washington, de Gaulle began formulating plans that would culminate in the withdrawal of French forces from NATO in 1966. As long as a direct threat loomed over Berlin, however, he would allow US forces to remain and use French territory for logistical purposes. Beyond that point, he insisted that French territory would not be at US disposal unless the Atlantic alliance was revised along several lines. First, he wanted all US forces and logistical support units within France to be under the authority and control of his government, not NATO's supreme commanders. In effect, he planned to reject the NATO framework and revert to bilateral arrangements. He also left open for further consideration whether he would allow the storage of strategic weapons in France for use by US squadrons in the event of a flare-up in central Europe.

Perceived American unilateralism concerning Berlin was also decisive in fueling de Gaulle's determination to develop an independent nuclear capability. He declared unequivocally that under no circumstances would France put nuclear weapons at the disposal of NATO. Although the French president recognized that Washington, London, and Paris needed to coordinate nuclear strategy, he insisted on a tripartite body independent of NATO to coordinate Western strategy. During this period of the Berlin crisis, however, de Gaulle realized that his infant nuclear program had no military or deterrent value for the present threat looming over the divided city within central Europe.[41]

In essence, de Gaulle's strategic formulations were driven and accelerated by the ongoing Berlin problem. The Berlin Wall was not built overnight nor even over several months. As construction went on and East Germans attempted to escape, Berlin continued to be a dangerous place throughout the early 1960s and beyond. The tactical differences that arose between France and the United States over how best to shape a credible deterrent to the Soviets had a divisive impact on relations between the two allies and far-reaching implications for the Western alliance as a whole. The US and UK approach toward the Berlin crisis heightened Adenauer's fears of abandonment, which facilitated de Gaulle's strategy of tying West Germany firmly to France—the first steps being the 1963 Franco-German Treaty of Friendship and a French veto of the UK's Common Market bid. Moreover, the growing Franco-German entente thwarted the formulation of a NATO strategic doctrine based on graduated responses ranging from conventional to tactical nuclear and strategic levels. On one occasion, Kennedy exclaimed in exasperation to the French ambassador: "That great Franco-German entente. We are always subject to very sharp criticism by the Germans for not doing one thing or another. . . . But we are doing everything we committed to under NATO . . . and France isn't even close to filling its NATO commitment."[42]

Under NATO policy directives MC 70 and 26/4, France was committed to contributing four divisions but produced only two and a third. Just as deplorable from the US perspective, the West Germany requirement of 750,000 armed forces, needed to fulfill a commitment of twelve divisions under MC 26/4, failed to materialize. In short, the problem of Berlin created an insurmountable obstacle to making Kennedy's declarations of a shift in NATO strategy to flexible response a reality of actual doctrinal implementation. Kennedy articulated his rationale for flexible response to his predecessor, Eisenhower:

> When we have this problem of maintaining our position in Berlin, where you may be using sort of gradually escalating force to maintain yourself in Berlin, you can't suddenly begin to drop nuclear weapons the first time you have a difficulty. . . . And it's very valid reason for our emphasizing the necessity of their [West Europeans] building up conventional forces. You can't go up the autobahn waving an atom bomb. And say, the first time a bridge is blown out in front of you, you can't begin a nuclear exchange with the Soviet Union over getting to Berlin.[43]

Yet due in part to French and West German opposition, the so-called flexible response doctrine remained in the theoretical realm rather than becoming actual NATO strategy.

From the summer of 1961 until Kennedy's assassination in November 1963, his administration dealt frequently, if not at times daily, with the ongoing crisis over Berlin. For the Kennedy administration, the Berlin crisis catapulted the German question and NATO strategy ahead of other European concerns, even temporarily ahead of the president's preoccupation with the balance of payments deficit and aspirations of achieving Britain's inclusion in the European Economic Community. Burden-sharing requests shifted to increased US demands for conventional military capabilities in Europe with an insistence that NATO pay its fair share. The Berlin problem delayed a coordinated, comprehensive policy on Western Europe, whose unfulfilled vision became known as the "grand design."

For de Gaulle, the Berlin crisis had a double-edged effect on his strategic defense objectives. US handling of the crisis intensified his disenchantment with NATO. His perception of US unilateralism and mismanagement confirmed his plans for additional withdrawals of French air and naval forces from NATO's integrated command structure and reinforced his determination to equip France with nuclear weapons. In the wake of the Berlin crisis in January 1963, de Gaulle issued his infamous *double non* of vetoing Britain's Common Market candidacy and his rejection of the US offer of Polaris missiles for a multilateral NATO nuclear force. Those blows to the Atlantic alliance notions of economic and military integration would be followed by the 1963 Franco-German Treaty of Friendship. Historically, the United States had regarded European integration as a vehicle for the containment both of a resurgent Germany and the Soviet Union. The Franco-German Treaty of Friendship potentially disrupted that strategy. US policymakers questioned whether Adenauer intended to follow de Gaulle's lead in altering the integrated command structure of NATO. They also worried about possible policies that a Franco-German bloc might pursue toward the Soviet Union. Although Adenauer never planned or spoke of the substitution of a Franco-German entente for US protection under NATO, the Kennedy administration misread the treaty as a Faustian bargain.

The ongoing Berlin crisis of the 1960s brought into stark relief the challenges of deterrence for the Atlantic alliance. The Berlin problem raised the question of the city's defense and the credibility of the American position in the context of flexible response. Due in no small measure to the never-ending Berlin problem, mistrust permeated NATO and East-West relations. Kennedy believed that if the West probed the Soviets for arrangements over Berlin and the security of central Europe, then the Allies could create an atmosphere for resolving Cold War disputes. Yet those very contentious issues—Berlin and the overall German question—polarized the NATO alliance and generated perpetual East-West enmity.[44]

NOTES

1. Andreas W. Daum, "Berlin," in *A Companion to John F. Kennedy*, ed. Marc J. Selverstone (Oxford: Wiley and Blackwell, 2014), 209.
2. The general parameters of the Berlin crisis are outlined in numerous accounts. For a superb scholarly work that discusses Berlin as a protracted problem, see

Marc Trachtenberg, *A Constructed Peace: The Making of the European Settlement,
1945–1963* (Princeton, NJ: Princeton University Press, 1999). For an accessible
account of crisis diplomacy, see Michael Beschloss, *The Crisis Years: Kennedy and
Khrushchev, 1961–1963* (New York: Edward Burlingame Books, 1991).

3. For a comprehensive and recent historiographical essay on the Berlin crises, see
Daum, "Berlin" 209–27. For the standard works about de Gaulle's ultimate stead-
fast support of the NATO position, see, for example, Maurice Vaïsse, *La grandeur:
Politique étrangère du Général de Gaulle* (Paris: Fayard, 1998); Andrew Knapp,
Charles de Gaulle (New York: Routledge, 2020), or Cyril Buffet, "De Gaulle, the
Bomb and Berlin: How to use a political Weapon," in *The Berlin Wall Crisis,* ed.
P. S. Gearson and Kori Schake (New York: Palgrave Macmillan, 2002).

4. See, generally, Ronald Granieri, *The Ambivalent Alliance: Konrad Adenauer, the
CDU/CSU, and the West, 1946–1966* (New York: Berghahn Books, 2003), 116,
136. For specific documentary references, see, for example, François Seydoux
to Ministry of Foreign Affairs, February 2, 1961, File series: Europe 1961–65,
République Fédérale d'Allemagne, dossier 1571 (janvier 1961–mars 1962),
Ministry of Foreign Affairs, Archives Diplomatiques [hereafter MAE], Paris,
France; and Courson to Ministry of Foreign Affairs, February 8, 1961, File
series: Europe 1961–65, République Fédérale d'Allemagne, dossier 1571 (janvier
1961–mars 1962), Ministry of Foreign Affairs, MAE.

5. Theodore White, *The Making of the President: 1960* (New York: Atheneum
House, 1962), 145.

6. Meeting minutes, "NATO Strategy and Berlin Contingency Planning Meeting," June 13, 1961, RG 59, Bureau of European Affairs, Office of German
Affairs, Records Relating to Berlin, 1957–1963, box 6, folder: NSC discussion
of Berlin, June–July 1961, NARA II.

7. Gregory W. Pedlow, "Allied Crisis Management for Berlin: The LIVE OAK
Organization, 1959–1963," in *International Cold War Military Records and History: Proceedings of the International Conference on Cold War Military Records
and History Held in Washington, D.C., 21–26 March 1994,* ed. William W. Epley
(Washington, DC: Office of the Secretary of Defense, 1996), 87–116.

8. Christian Nuenlist, "Into the 1960s: NATO's Role in East-West Relations,
1958–1963," in *Transforming NATO in the Cold War: Challenges Beyond Deterrence,* ed. Andreas Wenger, Christian Nuenlist, and Anna Locher (New York:
Routledge, 2007), 74.

9. Nuenlist, 74–75.

10. Report by Dean Acheson, June 28, 1961, *FRUS, 1961–1963,* 14: 128–59.

11. Walt Rostow, Memorandum for the President, July 7, 1961, JFK Presidential
Office Files: Countries, box 117, folder: Germany Security, 7/61, JFK Presi-
dential Library (hereafter JFKL), Boston; McGeorge Bundy, "Proposed Use of
Substantial Non-Nuclear Ground Forces in Europe," undated, JFK National
Security Files: Countries, box 82, folder: Germany, General, 7/23/61–7/26/61,

JFKL; Charles Bohlen, memorandum for the files, July 17, 1961, RG 59, Central Files, 762.00/6–2861, box 1743, National Archives and Records Administration [hereafter NARA], College Park, MD.

12. For Adenauer quote characterizing his consistently articulated sentiment toward increased conventional weapons, see Roland Jacquin de Margerie to Ministry, telegram, January 5, 1963, File: Europe, 1961–65, République Fédérale d'Allemagne, dossier 1565 (relations avec les États-Unis, 1963), MAE. See, generally, Lawrence Kaplan, *NATO and the United States: The Enduring Alliance* (Woodbridge, CT: Twayne International Publishers, 1988), 89; and Douglas Brinkley, *Dean Acheson: The Cold War Years, 1953–1971* (New Haven, CT: Yale University Press, 1992), 128–29.

13. Walter S. Poole, *The Joint Chiefs of Staff and National Policy, 1961–1964* (Washington, DC: Office of Joint History, 2011), 147. See also, Lawrence Kaplan, *The McNamara Ascendancy, 1961–1965* (Washington, DC: Government Printing Office, 2006), 155.

14. "Radio and Television Report to the American People on the Berlin Crisis," July 25, 1961, *Public Papers of the Presidents of the United States: John F. Kennedy, 1961* (Washington, DC: Government Printing Office, 1962), 533.

15. "Radio and Television Report," 535–37; For McNamara's testimony before Congress, see Kaplan, *The McNamara Ascendancy*, 158.

16. Conclusions of Cabinet Meeting, July 28, 1961, CAB 128/35 Part II[C.C. 45(61)], Public Records Office [PRO], Kew, UK. For a well-written, nuanced perspective on the British position, see John Gearson, *Harold Macmillan and the Berlin Wall Crisis* (New York: St. Martin's Press, 1998).

17. Macmillan to Secretary of State for Foreign Affairs, June 20, 1961, DEFE 7/2265, PRO; A. W. Ramsbotham (Foreign Office) to A. W. France (Treasury), July 7, 1961, DEFE 7/2265, PRO; France to Ramsbotham, July 7, 1961, DEFE 7/2265, PRO.

18. Bernard Ledwidge, "La crise de Berlin 1958–1961: Stratégie et tactique du general de Gaulle," *De Gaulle en son siècle*, 4 (1992): 380; Hervé Alphand, *L'Étonnement d'etre: Journal* (1939–1973) (Paris: Fayard, 1977), 352.

19. De Gaulle, *Memoirs of Hope*, 260. Alphand to C. de Murville, June 22, 1961, Amérique, États-Unis, dossier 381 (Allemagne), MAE.

20. Inspection general de l'armée de terre, "Les forms de la guerre et de l'armée future," no. 412, undated, Cabinet du minister de la defense, politique de defense, carton 1R58, dossier 2, Ministère de la Défense, Service Historique de l'Armée [SHAT], Paris; De Gaulle, undated note, January 5, 1962, Papers of Couve de Murville, tome II, CM 7, dossier 1962.

21. Many Gaullist contemporaries noted his rhetorical ploy. See, for example, Horst Osterheld, "Adenauer and de Gaulle: Portraits compares," in *Espoir: Revue d'Institut Charles de Gaulle* 79 (March 1992): 4–9.

22. Laloy to Ministry of Foreign Affairs, telegram, July 5, 1961, Pactes, Politique de l'OTAN, carton 408, dossier: Berlin, réponse au note sovietique du 2 juin 1961, MAE. Unable to agree on a common reply to the Soviet aide-mémoire, the French government issued its own reply on July 12, which reiterated almost verbatim Couve's comments to Soviet Foreign Minister Andrei Gromyko on July 5. See: texte de la note francais sur Berlin, July 12, 1961, Pactes, Politique de l'OTAN, carton 408, dossier: Berlin, réponse au note sovietique du 2 juin 1961, MAE.

23. Kaplan, *The McNamara Ascendancy*, 156–57.

24. See generally Berlin conversations, the Miller Center of Public Affairs, University of Virginia, Charlottesville (hereafter MCPA), *The Presidential Recordings: John F. Kennedy; The Great Crisis,* ed. Philip Zelikow and Ernest May, vols. 1 and 2 (the author transcribed all conversations related to Berlin). For Rusk's statement, see US Department of State, *American Foreign Policy: Documents on Germany, 1944–1985* (Washington, DC: GPO, no date), 776.

25. Granieri, *The Ambivalent Alliance*, 135.

26. Kaplan, *The McNamara Ascendancy*, 159; and Poole, *The JCS and National Security*, 149.

27. Quoted in Poole, *The JCS and National Security*,148.

28. Alphand, *L'Étonnement d'etre*, 364.

29. Martin Hillenbrand oral history, 37, JFKL; John Duffield, *Power Rules: The Evolution of NATO's Conventional Force Posture* (Stanford, CA: Stanford University Press, 1995), 154, 158.

30. Author's telephone interview with Hillenbrand, September 19, 1997.

31. Memorandum of Conversation, July 27, 1961, RG 218, Records of Joint Chiefs of Staff, Records of General Maxwell Taylor, box 34, folder: Memos for President, 1961, NARA II; Francis Gavin, "The Myth of Flexible Response: United States Strategy in Europe during the 1960s," *International History Review* 23 (December 2001): 858–59.

32. Kennedy to Adenauer, July 20, 1961, *The Berlin Crisis, 1958–1961* (Washington, DC: The National Security Archives and Chadwyck-Healy, 1996), no. 2198. Memorandum on Berlin, Inter-departmental coordinating group on Berlin, July 21, 1961, 9 Berlin Crisis Collection, box 30, National Security Archive.

33. Memorandum of Conversation, July 27, 1961, RG 218, Records of Joint Chiefs of Staff, Records of General Maxwell Taylor, box 34, folder: Memos for President, 1961, NARA II.

34. Grandes unites revenant d'Algérie en Metropole, Commission de la Défense à l'issue d'un voyage aux F.F.A., July 1961, Cabinet du minister de la Défense, Forces françaises en Allemagne, carton 1R179, dossier 12/B8, SHAT; Laloy à de Rose, fiche, compte rendu de reunion relative au memorandum U.S. sur Berlin, July 26, 1961, Pactes 1961–1970, Politique de l'OTAN, carton 408,

dossier: Conférence des ministers des Affaires étrangères, July 28 and August 4 1961, MAE.

35. Inspection Géneral de l'Armée de terre, "Les forms de la guerre et de l'armée future," no. 412, July 1961, Cabinet du minister de la Défense, Politique de defense, carton 1R58, dossier 2, SHAT.

36. For de Gaulle's evolving views on NATO, see, for example, Vaïsse, *La Grandeur*, 111–61.

37. Memorandum of Conversation between Paul Spaak and Kennedy, May 28, 1963, *FRUS, 1961–1963*, 13: 95–110.

38. Francois Seydoux, *Mémoires d'outre-rhin* (Paris: B. Grasset, 1975), 224.

39. Kennedy to de Gaulle, June 30, 1961, Cabinet du minister, Couve de Murville, dossier 346 (échange de messages et notes), MAE.

40. États-Major Général de la Défense nationale to Prime Minister Michel Débre, July 7, 1961, État-Major des Armees, OTAN: conseil de l'atlantique nord, 1961–63, carton 12S75, dossier: Commandement unique à Berlin, 1960–63, SHAT.

41. Notes by de Gaulle: September 18, 1961, October 4, 1961, October 26, 1961—all in Fondation nationale des sciences politiques, Paris (FNSP), Archives de Couve de Murville, vol. II, CM7. Oral history interview with General George Buis, Institut Charles de Gaulle, Paris (ICG), Archives orales. The scholarly literature on de Gaulle's management of the Berlin crisis and its effects on his overall European strategy is limited. For exceptions that were published before the opening of French documents on the crisis, see Cyril Buffet, "La politique nucléaire de la France et la seconde crise de Berlin, 1958–1962," *Rélations internationals* 59 (Fall 1989): 347–58; Bernard Ledwidge, "La crise de Berlin, 1958–1961: Stratégie et tactique du Général de Gaulle," in ICG, *De Gaulle en son siècle*, vol. 4, *La securité et l'indépendance de la France* (Paris: Plon, 1992), 366–80. For one book published after French documentation opened but that speaks in generalities, see Frédéric Bozo, *Deux strategies pour l'Europe: De Gaulle, les États-Unis et l'alliance atlantique, 1958–1969* (Paris: Plon, 1996), 77–82.

42. Kennedy talked about his discussion with Alphand of September 10, 1962, in "Meeting with Dwight Eisenhower," The MCPA, *The Presidential Recordings*, 129. Transcribed by author.

43. For quote, see "Meeting with Dwight Eisenhower," 129. For NATO contribution levels, see John S. Duffield, *Power Rules: The Evolution of NATO's Conventional Force Posture* (Stanford, CA: Stanford University Press, 1995), 123–30.

44. See Erin R. Mahan, *Kennedy, De Gaulle, and Western Europe* (New York: Palgrave, 2002).

1. The SPD sought to position itself as a nationally conscious party with election posters such as this one from the 1949 Bundestag elections, which reads: "With the SPD from Bonn over Berlin for a free, social, and united Germany." Archiv der sozialen Demokratie

2. Gen. Dwight D. Eisenhower and Lt. Gen. Lucius D. Clay, with Gen. Omar N. Bradley in the background, speak in Berlin, July 20, 1945. The three officers were instrumental in forming military policy regarding Berlin and Germany. Truman Library, Image 63-1455-73

3. By the time Dwight D. Eisenhower became US president in 1953, he had four years' experience with Berlin issues as a military officer. This familiarity and his national security strategy led him to view the city as an integral part of the wider Cold War. Dwight D. Eisenhower Presidential Library

Berliner seid wachsam Macht Schluß mit den Menschenräubern!

Eigenbericht „Der Abend"

Zusammenfassung aller Kräfte im Kampf gegen die Menschenräuber aus dem Osten – diese Forderung aller freiheitlichen Berliner verstummt seit dem niederträchtigen Verbrechen an Dr. Truchnowitsch nicht mehr. Mit grausamer Deutlichkeit hat diese Schandtat gezeigt, wie leicht es das Regime der Unmenschlichkeit noch immer hat, seine Gegner aus Westberlin in die Keller des NKWD und des SSD zu verschleppen. Berlin fragt: Ist wirklich schon alles geschehen, um Westberliner Bürger vor dem Terror des Ostens zu schützen? Herrscht bei allen verantwortlichen Stellen, deutschen wie alliierten, endlich die gesammelte Entschlossenheit, um den Menschenräubern das Handwerk zu legen?

DER ABEND fragt: Warum gibt es noch immer keine einheitliche Zusammenfassung aller Stellen, deren Aufgabe die Bekämpfung des kommunistischen Terrors ist? Warum verhindern noch immer Finanzschwierigkeiten und „Zuständigkeitsfragen" den geschlossenen Einsatz aller Mittel zum Schutz freiheitliebender Menschen?

4. "Berliners be vigilant. Put an end to the people snatchers!" Headline in the West Berlin daily newspaper *Der Abend* after a violent kidnapping, April 21, 1954. *Der Abend*

5. President John F. Kennedy meets with French minister of foreign affairs Maurice Couve de Murville (*middle*) and French ambassador to the United States Hervé Alphand (*left*) in the Oval Office, May 25, 1963. John F. Kennedy Presidential Library and Museum, Image AR7939-A

6. Three East German Volkspolizei peer into West Berlin over the wall of the Sophienkirche cemetery, 1961. USIS image

7. President Lyndon Johnson and Chancellor Kurt Georg Kiesinger on the South Lawn of the White House, August 16, 1967. LBJ Library, Image C6311–8

8. President Gerald R. Ford and Secretary of State Henry Kissinger meet with West German chancellor Helmut Schmidt in the Oval Office, December 5, 1974. Ford Library, Image A2298–23

9. President George H. W. Bush, with Chancellor Helmut Kohl at his side, delivers a speech in Mainz, West Germany, May 31, 1989. George H. W. Bush Library, Image 41-AV-P03639-018-05311089

10. Alexander Scheer as Ivan Karamazov on the roof of the Volksbühne Berlin in Frank Castorf's *Die Brüder Karamasow* (*The Brothers Karamazov*, 2016). Photograph by Thomas Aurin

11. Johanna Freiburg (*second from the right*) with the Chorus of Local Delegates in She She Pop's *Oratorium* (Oratorio, 2018). Photograph by Benjamin Krieg

12. The cast of Frank Castorf's *Hauptmanns Weber* (Hauptmann's weavers, 1997, at the Volksbühne Berlin). Costumes and set by Bert Neumann. © Fieguth / drama-berlin.de

CHAPTER 6

The Berlin Wall in History and Memory

HOPE M. HARRISON

More than thirty years after the fall of the Berlin Wall and amid Russia's brutal war on his country, Ukrainian president Volodymyr Zelensky warned German leaders of a new wall in Europe between countries under Russia's domineering influence and those free of it. In a speech to the Bundestag on March 17, 2022, delivered via video feed from his bunker somewhere in Kyiv, Zelensky criticized the Germans for not doing enough to help Ukraine against Russia's assault and for prioritizing their economic ties with Russia, particularly in fossil fuels, over the lives of Ukrainians and the principles of peace and freedom. He evoked President Ronald Reagan's speech at the Berlin Wall in 1987 and appealed to the German leader, "Dear Chancellor Scholz! Tear down this wall."[1] Zelensky argued that it was essential not just for Ukrainians that Germans do more to prevent Ukraine from being trapped behind a Russian wall, but also for the Germans themselves so they would not in the future again face "a long process of coming to terms with their past behavior"—as they did for decades with regard to Nazi policies in the Holocaust and World War II and Communist policies behind the Berlin Wall. Zelensky, or his speechwriters, knew exactly how to appeal to the Germans.

For a country that for decades has been committed to openly confronting, remembering, teaching about, and learning from negative aspects of its past, being told that they would regret it if they didn't do everything possible to help Ukraine against Russia packed a powerful moralistic punch. To hammer the point home, Zelensky referred to Germany's "historical responsibility" and called upon the German leaders to "give Germany the leadership you deserve. And what your descendants will be proud of."

The Berlin Wall marked and symbolized an era in German and global history. The Germans themselves played a fundamental role in erecting what became a lethal border zone between the East and the West, and they have been grappling with that part of their history since the country united in 1990. The Berlin Wall and the Communist regime behind it have joined the Holocaust and World War II as central parts of a German commitment to facing up to and learning from dark parts of the past.[2] It was no surprise that Zelensky utilized the image of the wall as the thread tying his address together. This essay will examine the German role in constructing the Berlin Wall and in remembering the edifice and all it meant after its fall.

BUILDING THE BERLIN WALL

While in recent years Ukraine has been at the forefront of the struggle between those favoring closer ties with the Russians and those preferring the West, during the Cold War it was Berlin that was on the front line of this battle. Between the end of World War II and the erection of the Berlin Wall in 1961, more than three million people fled from the German Communist East to the democratic, capitalist West, and East German leader Walter Ulbricht had long sought to persuade the Soviets to shut down this escape hatch.[3] Although the Soviet dictator Joseph Stalin had directed the closure of the nearly nine-hundred-mile-long border between the Communist German Democratic Republic (GDR) and the democratic Federal Republic of Germany (FRG) in 1952, his successors rejected Ulbricht's request to seal the border in Berlin in 1953.[4]

West Berlin was an island of freedom, capitalism and democracy located 110 miles inside of and surrounded by the Communist GDR. World War II agreements had granted the US, USSR, UK, and France occupation zones in both Germany as a whole and in the city of Berlin, with the Soviet sector forming East Berlin and the Western sectors forming West Berlin. The city was closer to East Germany's border with Poland than it was to West Germany. With the bigger (or longer) inner-German border closed, increasing numbers of East German refugees made their way to West Berlin. Even for East Germans who visited West Berlin but did not seek to remain there permanently, seeing the shops full of goods, reading uncensored newspapers, and getting a whiff of freedom in West Berlin made many more critical of life in the GDR. Ulbricht wanted to close this "loophole" in Berlin.

Since the city was under Four Power control after World War II, however, Stalin's successors did not want to risk alienating the Western powers (to say nothing of all Berliners) by sealing off that border. Instead, they repeatedly instructed Ulbricht to do more to attract East Germans to stay instead of leave, to moderate his hard-line policies. In seeking to bring the Soviets around to his way of thinking, the GDR leader employed three strategies: resisting or ignoring Soviet calls for moderation; using popular dissatisfaction (domestic weakness) to persuade Moscow to give the GDR more economic aid so it could compete better with the FRG; and undertaking unilateral action at the border in Berlin.

In 1953 with the so-called Soviet "New Course"[5] and in 1956 with Khrushchev's policies championing "peaceful coexistence" with the West and an end to Stalin-like "cults of personality,"[6] the Soviets called for wide-ranging reforms in the GDR and throughout the Soviet bloc, believing that Stalin's form of Communist control had been too harsh and had alienated a large group of citizens. In the case of the GDR, popular dissatisfaction fueled an ongoing exodus to the West, particularly via West Berlin. Throughout the 1950s, including after the 1953 Soviet refusal to close the border in Berlin, the Soviets expressed frustration that Ulbricht was not doing more to examine the reasons people were leaving and to devise policies that would succeed in enticing them to stay. Ulbricht's preferred method of dealing with the problem, however, was to block their escape route, not moderate his policies so they would stay. He asserted that "the struggle for the protection [of the GDR] and socialism must be carried out not only with means of persuasion but also with the means of state power."[7]

The GDR leader felt that any moderation of his hard-line policies would ultimately lead to him losing control and the West taking over, particularly in the wake of the June 1953 East German uprising. Three years later, when Poland and Hungary emulated the reforms Khrushchev inaugurated at the Twentieth Party Congress, Ulbricht declared, "We are on the frontline. We are the western-most country of the socialist camp. We cannot allow such things. I do not mean to say by this that this cannot be done elsewhere. But we certainly cannot do this."[8]

Soviet military intervention to put down the uprisings in the GDR in 1953 and in Hungary in 1956 made Ulbricht feel vindicated in his hard-line approach. Both uprisings ultimately persuaded the Soviets to augment their support for Ulbricht as the leader as well as to provide more economic aid to the GDR.

In the aftermath of these uprisings, Ulbricht increasingly used his domestic vulnerability as leverage over the Soviets. He could credibly claim that Communism in the GDR would fail if the Soviets did not give him the aid he requested—both in terms of economic support and control over the border in Berlin. Khrushchev significantly increased economic aid to the GDR. Although he was exasperated by Ulbricht's regular requests for economic bailout, the Kremlin leader reluctantly observed: "We must understand that the GDR's needs are our needs."[9] He knew that the collapse of the GDR would pose an extreme threat to his own personal reputation and to that of the Soviet Union. Nonetheless, he continued to drag his feet on Ulbricht's calls to close the border. As Khrushchev noted later in his memoirs, "It was my dream to create such conditions in Germany that the GDR would become a showcase of moral, political, and material achievement—all attractively displayed for the Western world to see and admire."[10] Closing the border in Berlin would make that much more difficult and might risk war with the West.

While Ulbricht could not act on his own to prevent East Germans from visiting or escaping to the alluring "show window of the West" in West Berlin, he could do more to protect his own regime from popular unrest. During the Hungarian revolution in the fall of 1956, the GDR leader had been extremely worried by the violence perpetrated in Budapest by angry crowds who killed Hungarian and Soviet officials. Accordingly, he ordered his secret police, the Stasi, to oversee construction of a walled compound north of Berlin for the East German rulers. The leaders moved into the Wandlitz enclave in 1960. Located in a forest and not marked on any map, it was surrounded by a wire-mesh fence with signs saying it was a "wild game research zone." Inside the fence was a cement wall, six and a half feet high and painted green, with guard towers, spotlights, and trip wires for additional security. An even more fortified barrier would be erected in Berlin the following year to "protect" East Germans from West Berlin.

When Khrushchev had launched a crisis in 1958 over Berlin, insisting that the West withdraw from West Berlin and sign a peace treaty with both German states or a united Germany within six months, he hoped to resolve the refugee exodus this way.[11] With Western troops gone from the "free city" of West Berlin, it would be much easier for the Communists to gain influence and ultimately take over the city, shutting it down as an escape hatch. In the wake of Khrushchev's ultimatum, the Four Powers held a series of meetings among the foreign ministers and the leaders, which made Khrushchev believe he was making progress. Accordingly, to Ulbricht's chagrin, the Kremlin ruler let his initial six-month deadline lapse and kept holding out hope for agreement.

Meanwhile, the East German refugee exodus was continuing, and it included significant numbers of highly skilled workers, such as doctors and teachers.[12] By 1960 there were whole towns lacking doctors. While Khrushchev was enjoying the international limelight accorded him in meetings with the Western leaders, including the first trip by a Soviet leader to the United States in September of 1959, Ulbricht was losing patience, and in the fall of 1960 he began to take unilateral action at the border in Berlin.

Ulbricht was relentless in his efforts to wear the Soviets down and sanction the closing of the Berlin border. As Oleg Troyanovsky, adviser to Soviet leader Nikita Khrushchev, put it, "There were periods when Moscow was literally bombarded by messages and phone calls from East Berlin."[13] This was increasingly the case in late 1960 and in 1961.

In September 1960, contrary to Four Power agreements about officials from all Four Powers having unfettered access throughout Berlin, the GDR announced that Western officials accredited to the FRG needed to secure permission from the GDR foreign ministry to enter the GDR and East Berlin. Ulbricht had not informed the Soviets about this and certainly had not received Soviet permission to violate the Four Power agreements. The US ambassador to Bonn, Walter Dowling, flew to West Berlin to test the new regulation. When he arrived at Checkpoint Charlie on September 22 to enter East Berlin, East German border officials declared at first that since he had no permission from the GDR foreign ministry, they could not let him through. Dowling refused to leave the checkpoint. The East Germans then demanded that he show his documents, even though he was in an official car with the American flag. Dowling complied and was let through.[14]

In the wake of this East German–US confrontation, Soviet diplomat Oleg Selianinov met with GDR deputy foreign minister Johannes König twice over three days to question him over what happened. Selianinov was "astounded" to learn about the new regulation from Western media.[15] Then, in late October, Khrushchev directed Ulbricht "not to carry out any measures that would change the situation on the border of West Berlin."[16] A few days earlier, a Soviet diplomat in East Berlin had warned Moscow that the East Germans "are studying the possibility of taking measures directed toward . . . stopping the exodus of the population of the GDR through West Berlin. One of such measures . . . could be the cessation of free movement through the sectoral border."[17]

Meeting with Ulbricht in November, Khrushchev pledged significant additional economic aid and informed the GDR leader that he was waiting for word from the newly elected US president John F. Kennedy about a possible summit concerning Berlin and Germany. The Kremlin leader reiterated that the GDR should "not unilaterally take steps" to change "the control regime for the crossing of the sectoral border in Berlin." He hoped that the economic aid would be enough to pacify Ulbricht for the time being.[18]

In January 1961, however, Ulbricht established the Politburo Working Group to examine options to halt the refugee exodus. The focus was particularly on West Berlin, which was the exit path for 90 percent of the refugees. The plans would ultimately involve measures first to stop East Germans from working in West Berlin and then to seal off West Berlin from East Berlin and the surrounding East German countryside. Ulbricht and his colleagues regularly spoke of the complications of "the open border," and they kept up the pressure on the Soviets to agree to close it.

Khrushchev and Kennedy agreed to meet at an early-June summit in Vienna, where they would discuss the future of Germany and Berlin, as well as other pressing matters. Two weeks beforehand, however, precisely when Khrushchev was eager to avoid anything that might hinder a productive meeting with Kennedy, the Soviet ambassador in East Berlin, Mikhail Pervukhin, sent an urgent message to Soviet foreign minister Gromyko in Moscow:

> Our friends would like to establish now such control on the
> sectoral border between Democratic [East] and West Berlin
> which would allow them to, as they say, close "the door to
> the West," reduce the exodus of the population from the

Republic. . . . Our German friends sometimes exercise impatience and a somewhat unilateral approach to this problem, not always studying the interests of the entire socialist camp or the international situation at the given moment. Evidence of this, for example, is their effort to stop free movement between the GDR and West Berlin as soon as possible by any means.[19]

As far as the Soviets were concerned, "the interests of the entire socialist camp" dictated that Khrushchev, not Ulbricht, should be the one to use Berlin to pressure Kennedy. And "at the given moment," Khrushchev was not interested in doing that.

In Vienna, the US president pushed back firmly against the demands Khrushchev had been making since 1958, insisting that the West withdraw from West Berlin, leaving it as a neutral "free city," and sign a peace treaty with both German states or a united Germany. Kennedy stated in no uncertain terms that the US would not withdraw its troops from West Berlin and that a peace treaty could only be concluded with a democratically elected government. Khrushchev responded that he would go ahead and sign a treaty with Ulbricht and give the East German leader "sovereignty" over all of GDR territory, including the borders in Berlin. The US and others would then have to come to agreements with the GDR on all matters concerning West Berlin.[20] The summit ended in stalemate, which stimulated even more East Germans to flee to the West.

By July, more than a thousand East Germans were arriving in West Berlin every day.[21] Ulbricht told Ambassador Pervukhin to inform Khrushchev that "if the present situation of open borders remains, collapse is inevitable."[22] With the reputation of the Soviet Union and the Communist bloc on the line if the GDR imploded, the Kremlin leader finally relented and agreed to allow Ulbricht to seal the border in the way the East Germans had been urging.

For months Ulbricht and his colleagues had been preparing what the Stasi called "Operation Rose," and at the end of July Soviet military officials joined them in finalizing the plans to close off the "escape hatch."[23] As Gen. Anatoly Grigorevitsch Mereshchko, deputy director of the operational department of the Group of Soviet Forces in Germany and one of the officials in charge of the final coordinated plan to close the border, later recalled: "Carrying out the job was facilitated by the fact that Ulbricht had already asked Khrushchev many times to seal the border. But for a long time Khrushchev didn't want to do this. The preparations on the part of the GDR authorities, however, were clearly in full swing."[24]

On August 13, 1961, East German soldiers and construction workers, using barbed wire, began to close the border to West Berlin. When this did not stop people from continuing to escape to West Berlin, Ulbricht directed his military chiefs to replace the barbed wire with a wall. They tried to dissuade him, arguing that a wall would "cast shadows at night and provide favorable opportunities for the enemy to approach it" and escape.[25] But Ulbricht overruled them, wanting something more solid.

What the West called the Berlin Wall and the East German Communist regime called "the antifascist protective barrier" was in fact a death strip directed against East Germans seeking to escape. The ninety-six-mile lethal border zone cut through city streets, forests, rivers, lakes, sewers, and subways lines. The fortifications grew over time into a death strip that consisted of multiple obstacles to escape. These included armed border soldiers who were ordered to stop so-called "border violators" by any means necessary, including use of their Kalashnikov rifles.[26] Unauthorized entry into the border area was a criminal offense.

The GDR continually expanded and "improved" the border fortifications to make them more impenetrable, and by the 1970s the East Germans had constructed a border strip ranging from 16 to 165 yards in depth and consisting of not just the outer wall but also an inner wall or fence, floodlights, concrete guard towers, signal wires, guard dogs, metal spikes, sand strips for seeing footprints, antitank barriers, and other obstacles. The external wall was 11 to 13 feet tall and the internal wall or fence was 6½ to 10 feet tall.

Millions of Germans were cut off from family and friends on the other side of the border. The wall became a symbol of both the Cold War and the repressive nature of Communism. In the twenty-eight years the Berlin Wall stood, more than 140 people were killed at the wall[27] and hundreds more were killed along the East-West German border.[28] Tens of thousands of East Germans were imprisoned for trying to escape, being suspected of trying to escape, helping others escape, or allegedly helping others escape.[29]

Not surprisingly, these events were depicted very differently in the East and the West. Banner headlines in the West told stories of a brutal regime killing German citizens and of dramatic escapes. West Germans compared the wall to a concentration camp. They publicly mourned those killed trying to escape and criticized the "killers" for their deaths. The East German regime, on the other hand, declared that it was necessary to defend against the hostile West. People who left were "traitors," and the border soldiers who prevented escapes were "heroes." The regime rewarded soldiers who stopped escapes with a monetary bonus, a nice watch, and extra vacation time. Border soldiers killed in the line of duty were held up as role models and had barracks and streets named after them.[30]

When the wall was unexpectedly opened in 1989, East German military designers were in the midst of planning for a fifth generation of high-tech wall that they called "Wall 2000." This was to be augmented by infrared sensors, laser tripwires, high-frequency cables, microprocessors, and seismic sensors, including underwater microwave and vibration detectors. Military planners were frustrated, however, that they lacked sufficient expertise to produce—or money to buy—the necessary technology to make this fifth generation of wall a reality.[31]

The Berlin Wall was a significant drain on East Germany's struggling finances. While the personnel and materials comprising the death strip cost 610 million East German marks in 1970, the annual costs rose to nearly one billion marks in 1983 and 1.2 billion marks in 1989. In 1989, by dividing the costs to maintain the border by the number of would-be escapees stopped at the border, East German economists calculated that each apprehension cost about 2.1 million marks.[32] Yet for Ulbricht and his successor, Erich Honecker, the closed border was essential to maintaining their power.

Between 1961 and 1989, hundreds of thousands of East Germans were involved in supporting the Berlin Wall, from the political, military, and Stasi leaders who gave the orders to stop anyone trying to escape to the border soldiers who implemented them, the military R&D experts, and the Stasi officials who oversaw posts at the border. Also involved were the construction workers tasked with fixing and "improving" the wall, as were the Stasi doctors, morticians, and lawyers employed to cover up evidence about those who were wounded or killed at there—and, finally, the local informants who watched for and reported on suspicious activity near the border.[33] The Berlin Wall was the most infamous product created by East Germany.

After twenty-eight years of living with the wall, and spurred on by Soviet leader Mikhail Gorbachev's reforms, people in East Germany and elsewhere in the Soviet bloc took to the streets en masse in the fall of 1989, calling for change, including freedom of travel. A combination of factors contributed to the unplanned opening of the wall on November 9, 1989: popular protests; an unprepared senior East German official mistakenly announcing at a press conference that the Berlin Wall was open; and local officials at the border needing to make independent, spontaneous decisions in the face of crowds of people wanting to cross the border.[34] The border crossing at Bornholmer Straße was the first to open, and others soon followed.

Four months later, in March 1990, in the first and last free elections in the GDR, East Germans voted for the party favoring a fast track to unification. That track called for the fusion of the GDR into the FRG, instead of a slower path by which representatives of both Germanys would have devised a new constitution and new system. Germany united on October 3, 1990,[35] and if German history had been different, the leaders would have chosen November 9 as unification day, marking the anniversary of the fall of the Berlin Wall. However, the 1938 precedent of targeted Nazi attacks on Jews, their homes, synagogues, businesses, and cemeteries on November 9—Kristallnacht, or the Night of Broken Glass—made it impossible to choose November 9 as a day to celebrate German unification.[36]

REMEMBERING THE WALL

Following the fall of the wall and German unification, Germans set their sights on removing all remnants of the wall and reuniting the city and country. Berliners and Germans wanted to get on with their lives and remove what had been a symbol of Communist repression and the Cold War. Although tourists flocked to the city to see the wall and take or purchase a piece of it to bring home,[37] most Germans wanted nothing to do with it. In the more than thirty years since its fall and German unification, Germany approaches to the history of the wall have evolved from not giving it much to attention to anchoring it in official memory. The remainder of this chapter will examine this process; the focal points of German memory policy have shifted over time among victims, perpetrators, and heroes of the Berlin Wall.

The night after the wall fell, Willy Brandt, former West German chancellor and mayor of West Berlin when the wall went up, publicly urged

Germans to "leave standing a piece of this abominable edifice" to show future generations what they had lived through.[38] He found a strong ally in Pastor Manfred Fischer of the Protestant Reconciliation parish, which had been divided by the wall. Fischer believed passionately that a section of the wall should be preserved as a memorial to its victims. His West Berlin parish house on Bernauer Straße had long been located just across the street from it, and in the summer of 1990, the pastor went so far as to stand in front of a bulldozer to prevent the removal of the wall there. In the following years, Fischer fought tirelessly against critics and ultimately succeeded in preserving nearly two blocks of the original wall. Fischer was also the driving force behind the creation of a memorial to the victims, a museum about the history of the wall, an outdoor exhibit along eight blocks of what used to be the death strip, and a chapel, the Chapel of Reconciliation. All of this now comprises the national Berlin Wall Memorial, a site where German leaders have commemorated anniversaries of the construction and the toppling of the wall since the late 2000s.[39]

Like Pastor Fischer, those who had lost a loved one killed at the wall did not want to just move on and forget it. They worked with state prosecutors to bring border soldiers and their military and political superiors to justice. Between 1991 and 2004, there were trials of more than five hundred individuals up and down the chain of command. While the first trials were of border soldiers who had pulled the trigger to stop people from escaping, their defense of their actions (generally: "Yes, I shot him, but I was just following orders") and broader public sentiment led to trials of their superiors. The builder of the wall, Walter Ulbricht, had passed away in 1973, but his successors Erich Honecker and Egon Krenz, along with their senior political and military colleagues, were brought to trial for their orders that had resulted in deaths at the border.

Since there had been no independent judiciary in the GDR, West German judges and prosecutors dominated the trials. In this sense, Germany has occupied a unique place in grappling with the Communist past. Other countries of the former Soviet bloc could control the process of whether, when, and how to deal with their own Communist past. But as we have seen, the GDR ceased to exist and was fused into the (formerly western) Federal Republic of Germany. Thus, although it was generally East German family members of those who had been killed at the wall who initiated the manslaughter charges, the fact that Western prosecutors took on the cases, and Western judges were the ones to decide on the verdict and sentencing, led Ulbricht's successors, Honecker and Krenz, to denounce the trials as "victor's justice."[40] They also tried to blame Moscow and the general Cold War as much as possible for the Berlin Wall.

Given that, as demonstrated in the first part of this chapter, the East German regime had been the main initiator and advocate of the decision to build the Berlin Wall as well as the force that carried out the brutal measures there, this defense was problematic. Indeed, some of those called to testify at the trial presented evidence that the GDR had control over the level of lethality practiced at the border. This was particularly clear in Honecker's 1984 decision, taken without initial consultation with the Soviets, to remove the SM-70 splinter mines from the inner-German border as a gesture to get more economic aid from West Germany.[41] It was also clear when GDR leaders suspended the order to shoot during state visits, holidays, and other significant events so as not to face any potential uproar if someone was killed at the wall while a foreign leader or an important international group was visiting East or West Berlin. As Judge Friedrich-Karl Föhrig concluded in his verdict in the Border Troops trial, "If it was politically opportune, soldiers were prohibited from shooting."[42]

Senior political and military leaders were given sentences ranging from three to seven and a half years in prison. Border soldiers generally received sentences ranging from one to ten years, with the vast majority of those sentences suspended, since the soldiers were at the bottom of the command chain. In the one case of a border soldier who was sentenced to ten years in prison, he had fired thirty shots at a would-be escapee who had already surrendered.[43]

The high point of public attention to these trials came in the mid to late 1990s, particularly with the Politburo trial of Egon Krenz and others. After this, however, most Germans lost interest or grew disillusioned and wanted to move on from thinking about the wall. Some felt the Western rule-of-law system allowed defendants too many rights and that perpetrators had not been punished enough; others felt that the trials made the perpetrators scapegoats, standing in for the whole East German past, for which some, in the midst of the new capitalistic world where many East Germans had lost their jobs, now felt nostalgic.[44] Those who believed there should be active remembrance of victims of the wall did not find widespread support until the mid-2000s.

The director of the Checkpoint Charlie Museum, Alexandra Hildebrandt, played an important role in directing public attention to the memory of people who had been killed at the wall. In fall 2004, for the fifteenth anniversary of the wall's fall, Hildebrandt unveiled more than a thousand wooden crosses in an outdoor installation at the historic Checkpoint Charlie, attracting much attention from media and tourists as well as many Germans.[45] The crosses had names and faces of victims Hildebrandt said were killed at the wall, declaring that the federal and municipal governments had not done enough to commemorate these victims, so she was taking matters into her own hands. At that point, neither government had yet seriously invested in Fischer's Berlin Wall Memorial on Bernauer Straße (which Hildebrandt disparaged as being too far from the center of the city) or devoted significant, consistent attention to commemorating victims of the wall.

Hildebrandt's crosses changed that, albeit not in the way she had hoped, since her action resulted in more attention to and investment in Bernauer Straße than in Checkpoint Charlie. In 2006 the Berlin Senate passed a "Masterplan for Remembering the Berlin Wall," devoting 40 million euros to preserve sections of it, highlight its history around the city, and especially to commemorate its individual victims.[46] The plan made Bernauer Straße the central site among several, including Checkpoint Charlie. In 2007 the federal government provided funds for researchers at Bernauer Straße to conduct the research necessary to ascertain biographical details about people who were killed at the wall, information that would later be used for the creation of a "Window of Commemoration" at the Berlin Wall Memorial, giving the victims' names and faces, and for special memorial services for these victims in Pastor Fischer's Chapel of Reconciliation. In 2008 the federal government passed an updated "Memorial Plan," which provided increased funding for sites connected to the East German regime, such as the Berlin Wall and Stasi headquarters and prisons.[47] As a result, by the mid-2000s the main focus of collective memory of the wall and government history policy was on the wall's victims. This had not been an easy process, since it involved a certain competition for attention and funding with those representing Jewish victims of the Holocaust. The federal government tried to resolve this with careful wording, declaring that "any remembrance of the dictatorial past in Germany must take it as a given that national socialist crimes should not be relativized nor should the injustice practiced by the SED dictatorship be minimized."[48]

With the commemoration of victims of the Berlin Wall anchored in public policy, a new focus of memory policy turned to those viewed as heroes of the wall: those who helped bring it down in 1989. Several steps paved the way for the Germans to adapt a more "positive" approach to the wall's history. The dedication of the Monument to the Murdered Jews of Europe in 2005 on the fiftieth anniversary of Germany's surrender in World War II played an essential role. The massive Holocaust Memorial in the heart of Berlin, a symbol of German acknowledgment of and contrition for the Holocaust, made it more acceptable to devote attention to another part of contemporary German history, one centered around the fall of the wall and German unification.

A second development fostering a more "positive" approach to German history occurred the following year when Germany hosted the World Cup. Many German soccer fans waved flags and enthusiastically cheered on their team, "Deutschland, Deutschland!" By demonstrating that peaceful expressions of patriotism were permissible, the fans indirectly facilitated a willingness to look at a "good" moment in national history.[49]

The Bundestag took a key step in support of a more positive narrative of the wall when it voted on November 9, 2007, to create a monument to freedom and unity to celebrate the peaceful fall of the wall and the GDR regime as well as German unification. Bundestag vice president Wolfgang Thierse observed, "Of course, we Germans will remain obligated to remember our shameful actions, above all the crimes of the Nazi regime. . . . But a people cannot really gain orientation solely from their failures. We Germans can also tolerate some encouragement, for example, by remembering the nice side of our history, the aspirations for freedom and unity, the breakthroughs and beginnings, the successes."[50] The Bundestag viewed the peaceful fall of the wall and unification as clear successes that should be marked and indeed celebrated.[51]

While sports fans, Bundestag members, and others played their own roles, it was the actions of one particular memory activist[52] that significantly impacted the changing memory culture for the twentieth anniversary of the fall of the wall in 2009. Former East German civil rights activist Tom Sello believed that the story of the East Germans who took part in what he and others were increasingly calling the "Peaceful Revolution" (capital P, capital R) of 1989–90, including the toppling of the wall, was insufficiently understood and respected in united Germany.[53] The fact that an East German activist, Joachim Gauck, was invited only at the last minute to be one of the speakers at the official tenth-anniversary commemoration in the Bundestag in 1999 was a good indication that Sello was right. Sello sought to make more people aware of the role of East German citizens in bringing down the Berlin Wall. There were others who shared this goal and worked with Sello or on their own, but his role was unique.

In 2003 Sello had been inspired by the broad public attention given to the fiftieth anniversary of the June 1953 East German uprising, with the Germans commemorating the uprising with ceremonies, films, books, and conferences. For the first time since unification, politicians and the media were devoting great attention to East Germans who had opposed the SED regime.[54] Sello, who believed that the same sort of attention and respect should be devoted to the East German opposition in 1989, realized that the twentieth anniversary of the fall of the wall in 2009 could be the perfect opportunity.

While there had been much public discussion of the victims of the wall and the perpetrators, in Sello's view there had not been sufficient discussion of the wall's heroes, the people he felt had been instrumental in bringing down the wall as part of the Peaceful Revolution. He had been stunned in 2003 when he met with a group of high school teachers who told him that they taught about heroes who resisted the Nazis but that "there were no such heroes in the GDR."[55]

Sello set out to show that this impression was wrong and to highlight the role of courageous East German dissidents in the Peaceful Revolution and the events surrounding the wall's fall and German unification. In 2008 he received government funding to install a series of informational stelae at key sites of the Peaceful Revolution in Berlin and to mount an outdoor exhibit. The site of the exhibit, Alexanderplatz, had witnessed a demonstration of 500,000 East Germans on November 4, 1989, five days before the toppling of the wall. The stelae and exhibit were unveiled in 2009 as part of Berlin's twentieth-anniversary celebrations of the fall of the wall. The bilingual German-English exhibit was called "'We the People!' The Peaceful Revolution, 1989–90." Its main message was that the East Germans on the streets and working in opposition groups behind closed doors were the main historical actors pushing for change behind the Berlin Wall, even if they were helped at various moments by others, including similar groups in Eastern Europe, East Germans who fled the country, and Mikhail Gorbachev, whose reforms opened up a path for change.

This message was taken up by German politicians, including the federal minister of culture, Bernd Neumann, Foreign Minister Frank-Walter Steinmeier, and Berlin mayor Klaus Wowereit, all of whom joined Sello to open the exhibit at Alexanderplatz on May 7, 2009. The politicians praised the courageous East German citizens, "who risked life and limb" to protest against the SED regime and to call for freedom. Neumann spoke of the Peaceful Revolution as "the only lasting, successful revolution in German history." Germans should be "proud, because neither freedom in East Germany nor German unity would have been possible without the resistance and opposition of people in the GDR."[56] Neumann, Wowereit, and Steinmeier (all from the West) expressed deep gratitude to these East Germans, some of whom were present as honored guests at the opening ceremony.[57]

While the "negative" side of the wall—the brutality of the border regime and the people who were killed as a result—continued to be acknowledged, the "positive" side of the wall, its toppling, moved to the center of attention in 2009. The events surrounding the twentieth anniversary of the fall of the wall in Germany emphasized that there were heroes to laud and a much more positive way of looking at recent German history. Over the course of the year, it became increasingly common for German politicians to use the word "proud" in describing their sentiments about the fall of the wall.

The twentieth-anniversary commemorations produced a new official narrative, a new founding myth about the fall of the wall and the birth of the new united Germany out of the first successful, democratic, peaceful revolution in German history. As Bundestag member Eckart von Klaeden had argued in supporting a monument to freedom and unity, "With the Peaceful Revolution, the East Germans have freed us from the stigma of never having won our freedom on our own."[58] The Peaceful Revolution had thus (at least partially) salvaged Germany's reputation and identity. Yes, Germans had been perpetrators of the Holocaust, whose end was brought about not by the Germans but by the Allies in World War II, but (East) Germans had *also* been heroes in 1989–90, bringing down the Berlin Wall and the Communist regime with it. The latter by no means negated the former, but the 1989 example of civic activism for freedom and democracy has been used by German leaders ever since as a model and source of pride and has formed the core of a new historical narrative and identity.

This narrative has been adopted by German leaders ever since and was given prominent attention at the twentieth, twenty-fifth, and thirtieth anniversaries of the fall of the wall in 2009, 2014, and 2019 in ceremonies at the Berlin Wall Memorial, the Brandenburg Gate, and elsewhere. For the twentieth anniversary, Merkel invited prominent East German dissidents to a special celebration in their honor at Bornholmer Straße, the site of the first opening of the wall on November 9, 1989, and they were featured at the evening ceremony at the Brandenburg Gate.[59] EU, American, and Russian leaders were also present at the gate on that date.

Used to somber gatherings of leaders to mark anniversaries of the two world wars, it was a very different feeling for the Germans on November 9, 2009, when EU, American, and Russian leaders wanted to be in Berlin to mark the happy occasion. They joined Angela Merkel in walking from East to West Berlin through the Brandenburg Gate as part of grand festivities attended by a crowd of 250,000 and a live television audience of millions. There seemed to be a palpable sense of relief among German leaders that they had something to celebrate about their twentieth-century history, that Germany was where it had long wanted to be: in the community of nations with democratic revolutions as their founding moment. Beethoven's "Ode to Joy" and a finale of fireworks captured the feeling.

In Merkel's third term as chancellor beginning in 2013, the increased attention to the importance of the Peaceful Revolution and the fall of the Berlin Wall for German historical identity was reflected in the coalition treaty forming the new government of the Christian Democrats, Christian Socialists, and Social Democrats. The treaty noted that "our consciousness for liberty, justice, and democracy is marked by the memory of the Nazi regime of terror, Stalinism, and the SED dictatorship, *but also by positive experiences of Germany's history of democracy*" (emphasis added).[60] The latter part of this statement about "positive experiences" marked the first such appearance in a coalition treaty and clearly stemmed from the change of view about German history that took hold on the twentieth anniversary of the fall of the wall. The 2021 federal coalition treaty between the Social Democrats, Greens, and Free Democrats similarly stated: "We want to make the history and sites of democracy in Germany more visible. A particular concern of ours is also to support sites connected to the Peaceful Revolution."[61] Indeed, on the thirtieth anniversary of German unification in 2020, President Steinmeier called for establishing a specific site to commemorate the courage of the Peaceful Revolutionaries.[62] While "memory of the Holocaust," as Aleida Assmann has written, "was the negative founding myth of reunited Germany,"[63] as of 2009, this has been joined by a "positive founding myth" about the peaceful fall of the wall and East Germany and about German unification.

CHALLENGING THE DOMINANT NARRATIVE ABOUT THE BERLIN WALL

Not everyone, however, has bought into the narrative about the heroic East German Peaceful Revolutionaries being such an essential part of the fall of the wall and contemporary German history. Indeed, Germans themselves, in a poll in June 2009, indicated that they viewed the reforms in the Soviet Union, Poland, and Hungary[64] and the economic weakness of the GDR system as more important in leading to the opening of the wall and the collapse of the SED regime than the East German demonstrations in the fall of 1989.[65] In a July 2009 survey, when asked who contributed most to the success of the Peaceful Revolution, 62 percent of Germans said it was more Gorbachev than the actions of the East German citizens.[66] Indeed, at the twentieth-anniversary celebrations, as Berlin's *taz* newspaper observed, "The biggest star of the day [November 9, 2009] was . . . 'Gorbi.'"[67] However, a decade later the widespread focus by politicians and the media on the role of courageous East Germans seemed to be having an impact on German views of 1989–90. A survey in September 2019 found that 68.5 percent of Germans believed "that it was primarily the courage of East Germans in 1989 that enabled reunification."[68]

The main narrative about the peaceful nature of the path to the wall's fall focuses on the ordinary East German citizens on the streets and their widespread slogan of resistance, "Keine Gewalt!" (No violence!). But the fact that the revolution of 1989 was largely peaceful was not just due to the behavior of the demonstrators. Also essential was the reluctance to use force by many (but certainly not all) of the political and military officials from the top to the bottom of the hierarchy.[69] Much less public attention has been paid to this aspect of the Peaceful Revolution.

The actions of Harald Jäger, the senior officer on duty at the Bornholmer Straße crossing point at the Berlin Wall that night, resulted in the wall's first opening. A member of both the border police and the Stasi, Lieutenant Colonel Jäger had served for twenty-five years at Bornholmer Straße. As more and more East German citizens gathered at his crossing point after GDR press spokesman Günter Schabowski announced (erroneously) at a live press conference around 7 p.m. that the borders were open, Jäger kept trying to reach his superiors in the Stasi for guidance on how to handle the growing crowds. He was told he could allow the loudest, most aggressive people to cross into West Berlin, but this only made all the others more angry and impatient. Hundreds and then thousands of peaceful citizens continued to gather at the checkpoint. Jäger still received no guidance about what to do. Eventually, around 11:30 p.m., Jäger decided to open the border. Officials at other checkpoints followed his lead.

Jäger is not part of the dominant narrative of the fall of the wall, and he was not invited to the twentieth-anniversary celebrations in 2009. His personal history is too closely tied to the East German regime to fit comfortably into the main narrative of the brave East German citizens demanding change. Jäger has been much more popular with journalists than with politicians commemorating the fall of the wall.[70] His story was turned into a TV movie, "Bornholmer Straße," and its premiere on ARD in November 2014 was seen by nearly seven million viewers. The film won the most prestigious German media awards: the Bambi for the "TV hit event of the year" in 2014 and the Grimme prize for fiction in 2015. Commentators and the juries for the awards noted the groundbreaking nature of the film, which told the story of the fall of the wall, not from the usual perspective of East German citizens on the street, but from the perspective of GDR border officials.

One interesting exception to political silence about Jäger's role in the opening of the wall came in 2011, when Thomas de Maizière, then minister of defense, gave an address in Dresden on the occasion of the opening of the Military History Museum of the Bundeswehr. De Maizière ruminated aloud about which traditions in German military history were worthy of emulation and asked: "Was . . . Jäger's disobedience . . . an exemplary individual act? Left to his own devices by his superiors, listening only to his conscience, he decided on his own to do away with the border controls and to open the official border crossing point at Bornholmer Straße."[71] De Maizière did not answer his own question, but raising it was a rare example of a German official recognizing Jäger's important role in opening the Berlin Wall.

De Maizière also addressed the role of the East German army more generally in the Peaceful Revolution. He asked rhetorically, "Can it be called exemplary when some soldiers in the NVA [National People's Army]—seeing its imminent dissolution before their eyes—reliably and with discipline protected their weapons and ammunition from misuse?" Their holding fire was essential in keeping the Peaceful Revolution peaceful. This part of the history, however, has not received much public attention. As one author observed critically in *Neues Deutschland,* Chancellor Merkel regularly thanked "communists abroad" for their role in 1989, particularly Gorbachev, but expressed no such gratitude for how the East German Communists allowed things to unfold in the fall of 1989.[72]

In 2020 President Steinmeier took a step toward acknowledging the role of the East German armed forces in keeping things peaceful. In his speech marking the thirtieth anniversary of unification, Steinmeier remembered images of the wall's fall: "People celebrating on top of the Wall, tears of joy, hugs, soldiers and members of the People's Police who dropped their weapons. Fear changed sides. A state was powerless, because the people wouldn't follow it anymore."[73] It was not just the people on the streets who helped end the system that had existed in the GDR; people who were part of that system, including those with arms at the Berlin Wall, did as well.

Just as the main official narrative of 1989–90 has downplayed the role of the East German authorities, it has also tended to overlook the fact that not all of the East Germans calling for change wanted a Western-style system of democracy and capitalism or sought unification. In fact, some of the leaders of the opposition movement, such as Bärbel Bohley and others in *Neues Forum,* were eager to create a new socialist democratic regime in the GDR. They felt that just when they had finally gained the freedom to organize as they wanted and to plan for reforming socialism, most of their countrymen voted with their feet or at the ballot box for leaving the GDR behind and joining the FRG.[74]

Among East Germans who took part in the Peaceful Revolution, a passionate debate was carried out thirty years later in the pages of the *Frankfurter Allgemeine Zeitung* about who was more important: the many people who took to the streets in demonstrations or the few civil rights activists who for years had been engaged in oppositional activities at great personal risk.[75] That debate also referred to another group of East Germans who until recently have not figured prominently in the historical memory of the fall of the wall: those who fled the country in the weeks and months before November 9, 1989, adding another form of pressure on the GDR leaders. Escape routes included Hungary's border with Austria and West German embassies in Prague and Warsaw or the Permanent Representation in East Berlin. Only in recent years have these people been mentioned as playing a role in the fall of the wall, as was the case with Merkel's speech on November 9, 2019, for the thirtieth anniversary of the fall.[76]

There are also problems with how West Germany is portrayed, whether directly or indirectly, in the 2009 narrative of the fall of the wall and the unification of Germany. First, the "happy" narrative about the Peaceful Revolution and the fall of the wall has scant resonance with some in the West. Many in western Germany, particularly older generations, felt little connection to the fall of the wall, since it did not result in much change in their lives. They often do not see that event as part of their own history. To the extent that they think about 1989–90, they tend to believe that the strength and attractiveness of the West and its system as well as the role of Chancellor Kohl were more important than anything the East Germans did.

Second, the 2009 narrative's focus on the heroes of the Peaceful Revolution and the villains of the East German state generally ignores the extent to which West Germans and West Berliners, including their leaders, had long been bystanders who accepted the wall. At a discussion in Berlin in 2009 between high school students and former West Berlin Mayor Eberhard Diepgen, one student asked Diepgen, "Did you do something against the wall? Did you protest?" The former mayor dodged the question by answering generally that "everyone" in West Berlin protested against the wall.[77] Several years later, the writer Claudia Rusch enjoined, "Why does no one speak about the role the West Germans played with the Wall? Why didn't tens of thousands of West Germans go to the Wall to try to tear it down? This question still bothers me. We speak of people who didn't do anything against atrocities in Rwanda, etc., but no one raises this question about the FRG and the Wall."[78] Eastern Germans are directly or indirectly asked why they did not stand up more and earlier against the SED and its wall, but that question is not directed toward Western Germans.

The artist and architect Yadegar Asisi captured the passivity of the West vis-à-vis the Berlin Wall in his panorama *The Wall*, erected at Checkpoint Charlie in 2012. Asisi's massive 270-degree panorama depicts the section of Kreuzberg where he lived. It shows houses next to the wall, people strolling along the street, children playing, and West Berliners going about their normal lives without any regard for the wall, while the death strip was just on the other side of it.[79] Like Rusch, Asisi was long struck by this Western passivity in the face of the wall, and this ultimately led him to create the panorama: to remind people how accustomed West Berliners became to the wall instead of fighting against it—an attitude that, in retrospect, he felt shocked by.

A new form of challenge to the positive narrative about the fall of the wall and unification has developed in recent years. When Germany was inundated in 2015–16 by over one million refugees from Syria, Afghanistan, Iraq, and elsewhere, a relatively new political party, the Alternative for Germany (Alternative für Deutschland, AfD) saw a chance to expand its voter base by tapping into xenophobia, racism, and anti-Muslim attitudes, all of which were stronger in East than in West Germany. The AfD and its supporters argued that Germany should do more to help its own people, particularly those in the East, than to help others. By the thirtieth anniversaries of the fall of the wall in 2019 and unification in 2020, a vocal minority made the case that unification had in fact produced a new set of German victims: those in the East who had been treated as second-class citizens by those in the West and who had not been able to find their footing in the new system.

Angry citizens in the East asserted that their interests and voices had been ignored since German unification. In the 2017 federal elections, the AfD earned 12.6 percent of the vote, with parts of the East voting for them at rates of 25 percent. This pattern continued in state elections two years later. Speaking at the Brandenburg Gate in November 2019, on the thirtieth anniversary of the wall's fall, President Steinmeier lamented the divisions in German society and referred to the East German leader who was responsible for cementing the division in Berlin in 1961: "The Berlin Wall, this was built by Ulbricht. . . . But the new walls in our country, these we have built ourselves. And we are the only ones who can tear them down."[80] While Berlin mayor Klaus Wowereit had declared in 2009 that the experience in Berlin that "Walls can fall" should inspire Germans to help "tear down the walls that still stand" in the world,[81] ten years later, Steinmeier and others directed Germans' attention to the renewed need to tear down their own domestic walls "of frustration, anger and hate, walls of silence and alienation. Walls that are invisible, but still divide."[82] The German president was clearly chagrined that some of the old feeling of division had returned in Germany. Indeed, an East-West German division in attitudes toward Russia's war on Ukraine is a further manifestation of this.[83]

German leaders have repeatedly spoken of lessons from both the history of the Berlin Wall and the Holocaust, highlighting that democracy and freedom cannot be taken for granted and must be fought for every day. Speaking on August 13, 2021, at the sixtieth anniversary of the erection of the wall, Steinmeier declared: "Remembrance of the Berlin Wall must not stop at recollection. It is a continuing challenge for us, both today and tomorrow. Freedom and democracy are never nature's gift, never achieved once and for all. Freedom and democracy must be fought for, but subsequently also protected, defended and preserved."[84] This was precisely the message Ukrainian president Zelensky delivered to German leaders in March 2022: that if Germans are really guided by these lessons, they must help prevent Ukraine from being cut off from Europe and the world by a new wall in Europe, a Russian wall.[85]

NOTES

1. "Address by President of Ukraine Volodymyr Zelensky to the Bundestag," President of Ukraine, March 17, 2022, https://www.president.gov.ua/en/news /promova-prezidenta-ukrayini-volodimira-zelenskogo-u-bundesta-73621.

2. Hope M. Harrison, *After the Berlin Wall: Memory and the Making of the New Germany, 1989 to the Present* (New York: Cambridge University Press, 2019).

3. For a more comprehensive account of the process leading to the building of the Berlin Wall, see Hope M. Harrison, *Driving the Soviets up the Wall: Soviet-East German Relations, 1953–1961* (Princeton, NJ: Princeton University Press, 2004).

4. "Draft Instructions for General Vasilii Chuikov and Vladimir Semyonov regarding GDR Control of Borders," March 18, 1953, History and Public Policy Program Digital Archive, Foreign Ministry Archive, Russian Federation (AVP RF), RF, Fond 06, Opis 12, Papka 18, Portfel' 283, https://digitalarchive .wilsoncenter.org/.

5. USSR Council of Ministers Order "On Measures to Improve the Health of the Political Situation in the GDR," June 2, 1953, https://digitalarchive.wilsoncenter .org/document/110023.pdf?v=44aac637074df62f3b7fb11f2ac90805.

6. Khrushchev's Secret Speech at the 20th Congress of the Communist Party of the Soviet Union, Moscow, February 24–25, 1956, https://www.marxists.org/ archive/khrushchev/1956/02/24.htm.

7. Ulbricht, "Zwischenrede," 33. ZK-Plenum, October 19, 1957. Bundesarchiv, Stiftung Archiv der Parteien und Massenorganisationen (SAPMO), DY 30/IV 2/1/186.

8. Bundesarchiv, SAPMO, DY 30/IV 2/1/163.

9. Bundesarchiv, SAPMO, DY 30/IV 2/1/163.

10. Nikita S. Khrushchev, *Khrushchev Remembers,* with introduction, commentary, and notes by Edward Crankshaw, trans. and ed. Strobe Talbott (Boston: Little, Brown, 1970), 456.

11. The ultimatum Khrushchev sent to the Western Powers on November 27, 1958, launched the Berlin crisis. See, for example, "Text of Soviet Government's Note to the US Urging Free-City Status for West Berlin," *New York Times,* November 28, 1958.

12. Refugee movement from the GDR and the Eastern Sector of Berlin, 1949–61, https://www.chronik-der-mauer.de/material/178761/fluchtbewegung-aus-der -ddr-und-dem-ostsektor-von-berlin-1949-1961.

13. Oleg Troyanovsky, *Cherez Gody i Rasstoianiia: Istoriia Odnoi Sem'i* (Moscow: Vagrius, 1997), 209.

14. Sydney Gruson, "German Reds Fail in Bid to Bar Envoy of U.S. from East Berlin," *New York Times,* September 23, 1960.

15. Descriptions of the September 23 and 26, 1960, meetings between Ambassador Johannes König and Oleg Selianinov of the Soviet Foreign Ministry are found in letters from König to Ulbricht on September 23 and 27, 1960, Bundesarchiv, SAPMO, DY 30/3497.

16. Letter from Khrushchev to Ulbricht, October 24, 1960, Bundesarchiv, SAPMO, DY 30/3682.

17. "Zapis' besedy s sekretarem Berlinskogo okruzhkoma SEPG G. Daneliisom," October 17, 1960, from the diary of A. P. Kazennov, second secretary of the Soviet embassy in the GDR, October 24, 1960, Russian State Archive of Contemporary History (RGANI), Rolik 8948, Fond 5, Opis 49, Delo 288, 5.

18. "Record of Meeting of Comrade N. S. Khrushchev with Comrade W. Ulbricht," November 30, 1960, History and Public Policy Program Digital Archive, AVP RF, Fond 0742, Opis 6, Por 4, Papka 43. Published in CWIHP Working Paper no. 5 by Hope M. Harrison, "Ulbricht and the Concrete 'Rose,'" https://digitalarchive.wilsoncenter.org/document/112352.

19. "Letter from Ambassador Pervukhin to Foreign Minister Gromyko on the German Problem," May 19, 1961, History and Public Policy Program Digital Archive, AVP RF, Referentyra po GDR, Opis 6, Por 34, Inv. 193/3, v. 1, Papka 46. Published in Harrison, "Ulbricht and the Concrete 'Rose,'" https:// digitalarchive.wilsoncenter.org/document/116209.

20. Memorandum of Conversation between Kennedy and Khrushchev, Vienna, June 4, 1961, 10:15 a.m., in *Foreign Relations of the United States, 1961–1963, Volume XIV, Berlin Crisis, 1961–1962,* ed. Charles S. Sampson (Washington, DC: United States Government Printing Office, 1993), https://history.state .gov/historicaldocuments/frus1961-63v14/d32.

21. For an analysis of the reasons people fled in July 1961, see "Auslösende Fluchtgründe von 2.810 Flüchtlingen im Juli 1961, 31. Juli 1961," Chronik der Mauer,

accessed December 7, 2023, https://www.chronik-der-mauer.de/material/178776/ausloesende-fluchtgruende-von-2-810-fluechtlingen-im-juli-1961-31-juli-1961.

22. Julij A. Kwizinskij, *Vor dem Sturm: Erinnerungen eines Diplomaten* (Berlin: Siedler Verlag, 1993), 179, 175.

23. Manfred Wilke and Alexander J. Vatlin, "Interview mit Generaloberst Anatolij Grigorjewitsch Mereschko, 'Arbeiten Sie einen Plan zur Grenzordnung zwischen beiden Teilen Berlins aus!,'" *Deutschland Archiv* (2/2011), https://www.bpb.de/themen/deutschlandarchiv/54123/arbeiten-sie-einen-plan-zur-grenzordnung-zwischen-beiden-teilen-berlins-aus/. See also the planning meeting between Khrushchev and Ulbricht in Moscow, August 1, 1961, https://www.wilsoncenter.org/publication/new-evidence-the-building-the-berlin-wall.

24. Wilke and Vatlin, "Interview."

25. General Staff Discussion of the Situation at the Border, September 20, 1961, as cited in Matthias Uhl und Armin Wagner, eds., *Ulbricht, Chruschtschow und die Mauer: Eine Dokumentation* (Munich: Oldenbourg Verlag, 2003), 49.

26. For a description of the four generations of the Berlin Wall, see Axel Klausmeier and Leo Schmidt, *Wall Remnants, Wall Traces: The Comprehensive Guide to the Berlin Wall* (Berlin: Westkreuz Verlag, 2004), 14–17; and Hans-Hermann Hertle, *The Berlin Wall: Monument of the Cold War* (Bonn: Bundeszentrale für politische Bildung, 2007), 91–96.

27. For a list of their names, backgrounds, and the circumstances of their death, see "Todesopfer an der Berliner Mauer," Chronik der Mauer, accessed December 7, 2023, https://www.chronik-der-mauer.de/180126/todesopfer-an-der-berliner-mauer.

28. "Muss die Zahl der Mauertoten korrigiert werden?," MDR, June 24, 2021, https://www.mdr.de/geschichte/ddr/mauer-grenze/richtige-zahlen-mauertote-102.html.

29. For some stories of people who escaped or were imprisoned for trying to escape as well as for more information on the Berlin Wall, see Hope M. Harrison, *The Berlin Wall: A World Divided* (Newark, NJ: Audible, 2021).

30. On contrasting portrayals of the wall and people who escaped or were killed there, see Pertti Ahonen, *Death at the Berlin Wall* (New York: Oxford University Press, 2011); and Cyril Buffet, "The Cold War as a Visual Conflict: Photographic Representations of the Berlin Wall," *Brolly: Journal of Social Sciences* 2, no. 3 (2019): 69–82.

31. Wolfgang Rathje, *"Mauer-Marketing" unter Erich Honecker: Schwierigkeiten der DDR bei der technischen Modernisierung, der volkswirtschaftlichen Kalkulation und der politischen Akzeptanz der Berliner "Staatsgrenze" von 1971–1990*, 2 vols. (Berlin: Ralf Gründer Verlag), 2006.

32. Rathje. See also Hertle, *Berlin Wall,* 97.

33. Jochen Maurer and Gerhard Sälter, "The Double Task of the East German Border Guards: Policing the Border and Military Functions," *German Politics and Society* 29, no. 2 (Summer 2011): 23–39; Hans-Hermann Hertle and Maria Nooke, eds., *The Victims at the Berlin Wall, 1961–1989,* trans. Miriamne Fields (Berlin: Ch. Links, 2011), 23–25.

34. For a comprehensive account of the fall of the wall, see Mary Elise Sarotte, *The Collapse: The Accidental Opening of the Berlin Wall* (New York: Basic Books, 2014).

35. For some of the German documentary record of the process leading to German unification, see Hanns Jürgen Küsters und Daniel Hofman, eds., *Dokumente zur Deutschlandpolitik: Deutsche Einheit: Sonderedition aus den Akten des Bundeskanzleramtes 1989/90* (Munich: R Oldenbourg Verlag, 1998).

36. The coincidence of this date in German history has required some finesse in the commemoration of two very different parts of German history, *Traum und Trauma* (dream and trauma), as longtime chancellor Angela Merkel put it in 2009. "Rede von Bundeskanzlerin Angela Merkel anlässlich der Eröffnung des Freiheitsmuseums 'Villa Schöningen,'" Potsdam, November 8, 2019, https://www .bundeskanzlerin.de/bkin-de/aktuelles/rede-von-bundeskanzlerin-angela-merkel -anlaesslich-der-eroeffnung-des-freiheitsmuseums-villa-schoeningen--367944.

37. Ronny Heidenreich, "From Concrete to Cash: Turning the Berlin Wall into a Business," in *Where in the World Is the Berlin Wall?,* ed. Anna Kaminsky (Berlin: Berlin Story Verlag, 2014), 268–81.

38. Willy Brandt's speech, Rathaus Schöneberg, November 10, 1989, https://www .willy-brandt-biografie.de/quellen/bedeutende-reden/rede-vor-dem-rathaus -schoeneberg-zum-fall-der-berliner-mauer-10-november-1989/.

39. For a thorough investigation of the path to the creation of the national Berlin Wall Memorial and more generally how united Germany has dealt with the history and legacy of the Berlin Wall, see Harrison, *After the Berlin Wall.*

40. For statements during the trials to this effect, see Border Guards Chief Klaus-Dieter Baumgarten's statement during the Border Troops trial on November 3, 1995, in Roman Grafe, *Deutsche Gerechtigkeit: Prozesse gegen DDR-Grenzschützen und ihre Gefehlsgeber* (Munich: Siedler, 2004), 59–60. See also the testimony by Egon Krenz in the Politburo trial, February 19, 1996, in Grafe, 110; and the testimony of Defense Minister Heinz Kessler in the trial of the National Defense Council, September 14, 1993, in Grafe, 29.

41. Grafe, 33–35; and testimony by Fritz Streletz, deputy defense minister and chief of the National Defense Council, at the Politburo trial, July 11, 1996, in Grafe, 151.

42. Judge Föhrig's verdict, Border Troops trial, September 10, 1996, in Grafe, 328.

43. Hertle and Nooke, *Victims at the Berlin Wall,* 197–99.

44. Aline Sierp, "Nostalgie for Times Past: On the Uses and Abuses of the Ostalgie Phenomenon in Eastern Germany," *Contemporary European Studies* 2 (2009): 47–60.

45. Sybille Frank, *Wall Memorial and Heritage: The Heritage Industry of Berlin's Checkpoint Charlie* (New York: Routledge, 2016).

46. Thomas Flierl, ed., *Gesamtkonzept zur Erinnerung an die Berliner Mauer* (N.p.: Gesamtkonzept, 2006), https://www.parlament-berlin.de/ados/iiiplen /vorgang/d15-5308.pdf.

47. Deutscher Bundestag, Unterrichtung durch den Beauftragten der Bundesregierung für Kultur und Medien, "Fortschreibung der Gedenkstättenkonzeption des Bundes," Drucksache 16/9875, June 19, 2008, https://www.bundesregierung .de/resource/blob/973862/414660/5c88e4e4ecb3ac4bf259c90d5cc54f05/ 2008-06-18-fortschreibung-gedenkstaettenkonzepion-barrierefrei-data.pdf ?download=1.

48. Deutscher Bundestag, 2.

49. Richard Bernstein, "In World Cup Surprise, Flags Fly with German Pride," *New York Times,* June 18, 2006. See also the speech by Bundestag president Norbert Lammert, "Rede zum Tag der Deutschen Einheit," Schwerin, October 3, 2007, https://www.bundestag.de/parlament/praesidium/reden/2007/ 014-246452.

50. Wolfgang Thierse, Deutscher Bundestag, Plenarprotokoll 16/124, November 9, 2007, 12965, https://dipbt.bundestag.de/dip21/btp/16/16124.pdf.

51. Only in May 2020 did construction begin of the Monument to Freedom and Unity in front of of the rebuilt Prussian palace (rechristened the Humboldt Forum) in the heart of Berlin. The monument is slated to be completed in 2024. Political disagreements about the need for the monument and its location, combined with construction complications, account for the delay in carrying out the 2007 Bundestag resolution. Jon Olsen, "Monument(s) to Freedom and Unity: Berlin and Leipzig," *German Politics and Society* 3 (September 2019): 111–31.

52. For more on memory activists, see Harrison, *After the Berlin Wall,* 16–17.

53. Author's interview with Tom Sello, Berlin, February 10, 2010.

54. For articles discussing the widespread coverage of the fiftieth anniversary of 1953, see Edgar Wolfrum, "Die Massenmedialisierung des 17. Juni 1953," *Aus Politik und Zeitgeschichte* 40–41 (October 1, 2003); and Christoph Klessmann, "Gedenken und Erinnern," *Deutschland Archiv,* June 13, 2013.

55. Author's interview with Sello, Berlin, February 10, 2010.

56. Speech of Minister of Culture Bernd Neumann at the opening of the exhibit *Friedliche Revolution 1989/90* on May 7, 2009 at Berlin's Alexanderplatz. While Neumann's speech is not available online, some of his comments on the exhibit are contained in the exhibit catalog: *"Wir sind das Volk!" Magazin*

zur Ausstellung Friedliche Revolution 1989/90 (Kulturprojekte Berlin GmbH, 2009), 8–9, https://revolution89.de/fileadmin/user_upload/pdf/Ausstellung/Katalog_FR_dt_Web.pdf.

57. In addition to Wowereit's speech, see also the speech by Foreign Minister Frank-Walter Steinmeier at the opening of the exhibit on May 7, 2009, "Rede von Außenminister Frank-Walter Steinmeier anlässlich der Eröffnung der Ausstellung 'Friedliche Revolution 1989/90,'" Auswärtiges Amt, https://www.auswaertiges-amt.de/de/newsroom/090507-bm-1989/218110; and comments by Minister of Culture Bernd Neumann in *"Wir sind das Volk!"*

58. Eckart von Klaeden, Deutscher Bundestag, Plenarprotokoll 14/199, November 9, 2001, 19511, http://dip21.bundestag.de/dip21/btp/14/14199.pdf.

59. German presidents Joachim Gauck and Frank-Walter Steinmeier highlighted the role of activists in Central and Eastern Europe in the commemorations in 2014 and 2019, respectively.

60. *Deutschlands Zukunft gestalten: Koalitionsvertrag zwischen CDU, CSU und SPD. 18. Legislaturperiode* (Rheinsbach, Germany: Union Betriebs-GmbH, December 14, 2013), 91, https://archiv.cdu.de/sites/default/files/media/dokumente/koalitionsvertrag.pdf.

61. "Koalitionsvertrag zwischen SPD, Bündnis 90/die Grünen und FDP, 2021–2025," 125, https://www.bundesregierung.de/breg-de/service/gesetzesvorhaben/koalitionsvertrag-2021-1990800.

62. Speech by President Steinmeier on Unity Day, Potsdam, October 3, 2020, https://www.bundespraesident.de/SharedDocs/Reden/EN/Frank-Walter-Steinmeier/Reden/2020/10/201003-Ceremony-German-Unity.html. The federal government will fund the Center for the Future of German Unity and European Transformation in Halle on the Saale, one of the more successful cities of the former East Germany. The center is expected to open in 2028. "Ein Ort für die deutsche und europäische Einheit," Bundesregierung.de, March 1, 2023, https://www.bundesregierung.de/breg-de/themen/deutsche-einheit/zukunftszentrum-deutsche-einheit-2165268.

63. Aleida Assmann, *Das neue Unbehagen an der Erinnerungskultur* (Munich: C. H. Beck, 2013), 67.

64. The Poles and Hungarians have been very frustrated with the global focus on the fall of the wall as the key moment signaling the downfall of the Iron Curtain and Communism in Europe and have sought to highlight the roles of Solidarity and of the Hungarian opening of its border with Austria as key milestones. Jacek Stawaski, "Berlin Wall: Lest We Forget Poland . . . ," *Polska Times* (Warsaw), November 9, 2009; Bronislaw Geremek, remarks during the debate over a Constitution Treaty for the European Parliament, Strasbourg, January 11, 2005, https://www.europarl.europa.eu/doceo/document/CRE-6-2005-01-11-ITM-005_EN.html; Andreas Oplatka, *Der erste Riss in der Mauer: September 1989—Ungarn öffnet die Grenze* (Vienna: Szolnay, 2009); Gyula

Horn, *Freiheit, die ich meine: Erinnerungen des ungarischen Aussenministers, der den eisernen Vorhang öffnete* (Hamburg: Hoffmann und Campe, 1991).

65. "Welcher der folgenden Faktoren war Ihrer Meinung nach für das Ende der SED-Herrschaft ausschlaggebend?," BVMBS, June 2009, https://de.statista .com/statistik/daten/studie/13022/umfrage/wichtigste-faktoren-fuer-ende-der -sed-herrschaft/.

66. "Wird die historische Leistung der friedlichen Revolution im Herbst 1989 heute in der Öffentlichkeit gesehen als Leistung der . . . ," Volkssolidarität Bundesverband, July 2009, https://de.statista.com/statistik/daten/studie/ 30263/umfrage/meinung-zu-verantwortung-fuer-revolution-von-1989/.

67. G. Asmuth and P. Gessler, "Die Geschichte weitergeben: 20. Jahrestag der Maueröffnung," *taz*, November 10, 2009. See also Nicholas Kulish and Judy Dempsey, "Leaders in Berlin Retrace the Walk West," *New York Times*, November 10, 1989.

68. "Umfrage: Mehrheit halt Mut von DDR-Bürgern für essenziell für Einheit," *Der Newsburger*, October 1, 2019, https://newsburger.de/umfrage-mehrheit -haelt-mut-von-ddr-buergern-fuer-essenziell-fuer-einheit-117676.html.

69. See the chapters by Sabrow, Bergien, Gieseke, and Bröckermann in Martin Sabrow, ed., *1989 und die Rolle der Gewalt*, (Göttingen: Wallstein Verlag, 2012).

70. Gerhard Haase-Hindenberg, *Der Mann, der die Mauer öffnete* (Munich: Wilhelm Heyne Verlag, 2007); and interviews conducted by Cordt Schnibben for *Spiegel* magazine, "The Soldier Who Opened the Berlin Wall: 'I Gave My People the Order—Raise the Barrier,'" *Spiegel Online*, November 9, 2009; and by Anne Haeming, "Der Grenzer, der die Mauer öffnete: 'Ich habe nur das Menschliche getan,'" *taz.de*, November 5, 2014.

71. Rede des Bundesministers der Verteidigung, Dr. Thomas de Maizière, anlässlich der Neueröffnung des Militärhistorischen Museums der Bundeswehr, October 14, 2011, in Dresden, Presse-und Informationsstab BMVg.

72. Jürgen Reents, "Der nötige Schlussstrich," *Neues Deutschland*, November 11, 2009.

73. "Festakt zum Tag der Deutschen Einheit," Der Bundespräsident, October 3, 2020, Potsdam, https://www.bundespraesident.de/SharedDocs/Reden/DE/ Frank-Walter-Steinmeier/Reden/2020/10/201003-TdDE-Potsdam.html.

74. Charles Maier, *Dissolution: The Crisis of Communism and the End of East Germany* (Princeton, NJ: Princeton University Press, 1997), 192–200.

75. Detlef Pollack, "Es war ein Aufstand der Normalbürger," *Frankfurter Allgemeine Zeitung*, July 12, 2019; Ilko-Sascha Kowalczuk, "Eine Minderheit bahnte den Weg," *Frankfurter Allgemeine Zeitung*, July 15, 2019; and Detlef Pollack, "Die Abwanderung bestärkte den Protest," *Frankfurter Allgemeine Zeitung*, July 29, 2019.

76. "Rede von Bundeskanzlerin Merkel bei der Andacht zum 30. Jahrestag

des Mauerfalls in der 'Kapelle der Versöhnung,'" Bundeskanzler.de, November 9, 2019, Berlin, https://www.bundeskanzlerin.de/bkin-de/aktuelles /rede-von-bundeskanzlerin-merkel-bei-der-andacht-zum-30-jahrestag-des -mauerfalls-in-der-kapelle-der-versoehnung-am-9-november-2019-in-berlin -1690432.

77. Commemorative ceremony and dialogue sponsored by the Robert Havemann Gesellschaft, Gethsemane Church, Berlin, October 7, 2009.

78. Claudia Rusch, comments at panel discussion, "Zwischen Aufarbeitung und Nostalgie: Die DDR in der Erinnerungskultur," sponsored by Stiftung Aufarbeitung, Berlin Landeszentrale für Stasi Unterlagen, and the Deutsche Gesellschaft, April 8, 2014.

79. Yadegar Asisi, *Die Mauer: Das Asisi Panorama zum geteilten Berlin* (Berlin: Asisi Edition, 2012); and author's interview with Asisi, February 9, 2010.

80. "Rede von Bundespräsident Dr. Frank-Walter Steinmeier bei den Feierlichkeiten zu 30 Jahren Friedlicher Revolution und Mauerfall," Bundesregierung .de, November 9, 2019, Berlin, https://www.bundesregierung.de/breg-de /service/bulletin/rede-von-bundespraesident-dr-frank-walter-steinmeier -1691136.

81. Jens Anker and Birgit Haas, "Die Welt feiert Deutschlands Einheit in Berlin," *Berliner Morgenpost*, November 7, 2009.

82. "Rede von Bundespräsident Dr. Frank-Walter Steinmeier."

83. Hope M. Harrison, "Russia, the United States, Germany, and the War in Ukraine: A New Cold War but with a Dangerous Twist?," *Cold War History*, 23, no. 1 (2023): 34–47.

84. "Federal President Frank-Walter Steinmeier at an Event to Mark the 60th Anniversary of the Construction of the Berlin Wall," Bundespräsidialamt, August 13, 2021, Berlin, https://www.bundespraesident.de/SharedDocs/ Downloads/DE/Reden/2021/08/210813-Gedenken-Mauerbau-Englisch.pdf? __blob=publicationFile.

85. "Address by President of Ukraine Volodymyr Zelensky."

CHAPTER 7

Between Freedom's Symbol and Casus Belli

Berlin in the Johnson and Nixon Years

THOMAS SCHWARTZ

> In the eyes of many Americans, the defense of Berlin was a glowing
> example of the country fulfilling its mission to advance freedom worldwide.
>
> —Andreas W. Daum, *Kennedy in Berlin*

> Europeans were not innocent bystanders in the Cold War. They were
> the issue. The United States was not going to fight the Soviet Union
> about polar bears in the Arctic; it would go to war over Europe.
>
> —Dean Rusk, quoted in Thomas Zeiler, *Dean Rusk: Defending the
> American Mission Abroad*

The city of Berlin, located deep within the Communist territory that
became East Germany, was the most profound symbol of the ideological
divide of the Cold War. From the Russian blockade and Western airlift to
the building of the wall and Soviet and American tanks facing each other
near Checkpoint Charlie, there was no more dangerous yet inspiring place
for Americans in the superpower struggle over the future of Europe. When
President John F. Kennedy proclaimed *Ich bin ein Berliner*, his Boston-
accented German stirred tumultuous cheers from a massive crowd in the
former German capital city. But it also connected emotionally with his own
countrymen as well, clarifying the distinction between the free world and
a Communist system that required a wall to keep its people in. The great

irony in this was that Kennedy's administration had been trying to find a formula to defuse the crisis status of the city, a negotiating process that only came to an end after the Cuban Missile Crisis led the superpowers to pull back from the brink of nuclear war. Even during that crisis, President Kennedy had speculated at first that Nikita Khrushchev's purpose in Cuba was to trade the Caribbean country for Berlin.[1]

This essay argues that both the Johnson and Nixon administrations faced an acute dilemma over Berlin. On the one hand, they wished to preserve the freedom of the Western half of the city as the symbolic capital of the West in the Cold War, a city whose separation by an ugly wall perfectly represented the ideological struggle in a clear "good vs. evil" manner. As Kennedy himself had put it, when describing how some had talked about Communism as the progressive wave of the future or described the great progress made under Communism, "Let them come to Berlin." For the West German political elite as well as the broader population, standing firm in Berlin also represented the ultimate hope of Germany's reunification rather than the dreaded idea of permanent division. American leaders feared that any abandonment of Berlin would result in losing German support for the Western alliance.

On the other hand, both Lyndon Johnson and Richard Nixon wanted to lower the temperature of the Cold War and move toward some type of détente, a complex process in which the de facto division of Germany and Berlin would have to be recognized and in which the national interests of the United States and its German ally might not coincide, but in which West Germany remained committed to the West. Central to that process would be some type of arrangement over Berlin, an arrangement that would regulate its status and maintain the freedom of its Western sector but would prevent it from again becoming a possible source of direct military conflict between the superpowers. The solution to this dilemma would be the Quadripartite Agreement of September 1971, whose fiftieth anniversary was recently noted and is one of the least heralded but most important international agreements of the Cold War.

THE JOHNSON ADMINISTRATION AND BERLIN

As vice president, Lyndon Johnson had traveled to Berlin shortly after the wall was built and told some 300,000 Berliners at City Hall that America's commitment to Berlin was the same that "our ancestors pledged in forming the United States: 'our lives, our fortunes, and our sacred honor.'"[2] However, by the time he became president after Kennedy's assassination, the Cold War had changed, and such stirring rhetoric seemed out of place. The Cuban Missile Crisis brought the United States and the Soviet Union closer to nuclear war than they had ever been, and in the aftermath of the crisis President Kennedy had taken steps to decrease the risk of conflict. Johnson observed how Kennedy's Limited Nuclear Test Ban Treaty, signed in August 1963, had boosted the president's popularity, and he was determined to continue Kennedy's attempt to reach agreements with the Soviet Union.[3] Although he pledged to keep faith with existing treaty commitments, "from South Vietnam to West Berlin," Johnson also told the United Nations General Assembly in December 1963 that "the United States of America wants to see the Cold War end," and one of Johnson's first successes in Congress came with the Christmas Eve passage of a bill allowing the sale of wheat to the Soviet Union.[4]

Christmas 1963 also brought with it one of the first openings in the Berlin Wall, as the pass program allowed thousands of West Germans to visit relatives in East Berlin. Over the holidays Johnson also hosted German chancellor Ludwig Erhard at his ranch in Texas and told Erhard that the United States was "going down the road to peace, with or without others," and asked the chancellor to be more flexible than his predecessor in dealings with the Soviet Union. Johnson made a point of emphasizing how Konrad Adenauer had repeatedly warned him about trusting the Russians, but that Adenauer's position was too "rigid," and that he didn't want the rest of the world to think that only the Russians wanted peace.[5] Johnson's approach acquired the name of "bridge building," a term he used in a May 1964 speech that spoke of the need to "build bridges across the Gulf which has divided us from Eastern Europe." One target of Johnson's approach was the Hallstein Doctrine, which compelled the German government to break relations with any nation that recognized East Germany. Erhard pushed back on the Hallstein Doctrine, but he and his foreign minister Gerhard Schröder pursued what they termed the "policy of movement," aimed at reducing suspicions about Germany in Eastern Europe and focused on trade agreements. Erhard also courted Soviet leader Nikita Khrushchev, whose son-in-law, Alexei Adzhubei, visited Bonn in July 1964 for talks. This paved the way for Erhard to announce that Khrushchev himself would visit the

Federal Republic, but the Soviet leader was ousted in October 1964 before the visit took place.

Lyndon Johnson genuinely liked Ludwig Erhard and considered him his favorite European leader. (There was not much to choose from on that front.) He met frequently with Erhard over the first three years of his presidency, though their discussions increasingly focused on Vietnam and what the Germans could do to help the United States with the expensive costs of its escalating war in Southeast Asia as well as its continuing commitment in Europe. Erhard deflected such requests based on Germany's recent history, although allowing for such gestures as deploying a hospital ship and providing other forms of economic aid to the struggling South Vietnamese government. Johnson also pressured Erhard to spend more to offset the costs of American troops in Germany. In one memorable exchange in December 1965, recorded by the American ambassador to Germany, George McGhee, Johnson's "tall rangy figure towered over the comparatively small figure of the chancellor. Gesticulating and speaking in a strong strident voice, Johnson alternately wheedled and threatened," frightening the chancellor with his outburst.[6] Erhard's subsequent failure to get a reduction in offset costs from the United States was one factor in his downfall in October 1966.

What is striking is that Berlin rarely rated a mention in any of the Johnson-Erhard talks after their first meeting. The divided city no longer preoccupied decision makers in Washington, and the status quo seemed to suit both countries. As part of its attempt to lower the temperature of the Cold War, the Johnson Administration deliberately decided to downplay the observance of the fifth anniversary of the building of the wall in August 1966.[7]

In October 1966 Johnson gave a major speech on European policy entitled "Making Europe Whole: An Unfinished Task." The speech was timed to two anniversaries, the end of the Berlin Airlift and the ratification of the Partial Test Ban Treaty, symbolically representing deterrence and détente. Johnson emphasized that "we want the Soviet Union and the nations of Eastern Europe to know that we and our allies shall go step by step with them as far as they are willing to advance."[8] Ironically enough, the speech came shortly before the grand coalition government of Kurt Kiesinger and Willy Brandt would take office and signal a new direction in German foreign policy. Although Brandt's *Ostpolitik* began cautiously in the coalition, it reflected a willingness on the part of the German government to move in the direction of better relations with the East and Soviet Union that the United States had been pursuing.

By the late 1960s Berlin itself was changing, as its demographics and political coloring shifted from Cold War fundamentalism to New Left radicalism. It became a haven for young German men avoiding military service, and as Andreas Daum noted, the city offered "the New Left and critics of the United States more room for maneuver than anywhere else in West Germany."[9] Vice President Hubert Humphrey's visit to the city in April 1967 encountered a "militantly anti-American protest" from the extra-parliamentary opposition. Shouts of "Johnson-Murderer," and "Washington go home," echoed through the streets.[10] Even more famously, the violence that greeted the shah of Iran during his visit to Berlin in June 1967, which led to the shooting of a German student, also seemed to indicate that the city was changing dramatically from the one that had greeted President Kennedy only four years earlier.

In fact, while the majority of West Berliners still supported the Atlantic alliance, the close emotional ties of the city to the United States were fraying. In June 1968, after the assassination of Senator Robert Kennedy, student organizations refused to participate in any memorial services, a striking contrast to their role five years earlier. The polarization of the city did not substantially dissipate even after the Soviet Union invaded Czechoslovakia and put an end to the hope that the Cold War in Europe was coming to a quick end and that the superpowers' hold over their part of Europe was dissolving.

THE NIXON ADMINISTRATION AND BERLIN

When Richard Nixon was inaugurated as president in January 1969, he proclaimed that "after a period of confrontation, we are now entering into a period of negotiations." Nixon's reputation as a tough and unreconstructed Cold Warrior led to considerable skepticism about this assertion, but the president understood the mood of the American people and the transformation of the international scene. He was elected, he believed, to end the Vietnam War, and scale back America's commitments, especially those involving the military and the possible deployment of American troops. He also recognized that the rapid growth of Soviet nuclear capabilities over the course of the 1960s had changed the dynamic of the Cold War, creating a genuine "balance of terror" and instilling doubt about America's commitment to defend Western Europe. Along with his foreign policy adviser, Dr. Henry Kissinger, a German-born Jewish immigrant, Nixon wanted to implement a less expansive and more realistic foreign policy that secured America's national interests but limited her sacrifice in blood and treasure.[11] Kissinger, who played the key role in explaining foreign policy to journalists, argued that "we have no permanent enemies, and that we will judge other countries . . . on the basis of their actions and not on the basis of their domestic ideology." This "new realism" was also the theme of the administration's "First Annual Report on United States Foreign Policy," issued in February 1970 and designed to convey Nixon and Kissinger's "new approach to foreign policy to match a new era in international relations."[12]

Almost immediately on entering office, Nixon and Kissinger faced a potential crisis in West Berlin, where the Federal Assembly to elect the Republic's new president was to be held. Given the contested status of West Berlin as a sovereign part of West Germany, the decision to hold the assembly there was a strong policy statement and potential provocation by the Kiesinger government. Even though the presidency was a largely ceremonial office with little power, the East German government protested vehemently, and the Soviet Union supported its position. The East Germans began harassing traffic between West Germany and West Berlin.

Nixon wanted his first trip abroad to be to Western Europe, an area he regarded as "blue chip" compared to the rest of the world. A trip by an American president to Europe at this point in the Cold War would be incomplete without a trip to West Berlin, and even though Nixon worried about comparisons with his charismatic predecessor, he arrived in Berlin only a few days before the scheduled election on February 27, 1969. Prior to his arrival, Nixon had used Kissinger's "backchannel" with Soviet ambassador Anatoly Dobrynin to make it clear to the Soviets that a new crisis over Berlin, or anything approaching another blockade, would have a serious impact on his willingness to enter into arms control negotiations or otherwise improve US-Soviet relations. While in Berlin, Nixon made it a point to stress his commitment to the city. "No unilateral move, no illegal act, no form of pressure from any source will shake the resolve of the Western nations to defend their rightful status as protectors of the people of free Berlin." In words less eloquent than Kennedy's but also less dangerous, Nixon argued that "if this is an age of symbols, one of the great symbols of the age is this city." However, Nixon also pleaded to his listeners to "set behind us the stereotype of Berlin as a 'provocation,'" and that the "question now is how best to end the challenge and clear the way for a peaceful solution to the problem of a divided Germany." Taking a cue from Kennedy, but changing the words in an important fashion, Nixon closed his speech by saying, "In the sense that the people of Berlin stand for freedom and peace, all the people of the world are truly Berliners."[13]

Nixon's speech was an early indication that while he and Kissinger were theoretically willing to negotiate new arrangements on Berlin, this was not an urgent priority. The administration was dealing with Vietnam, nuclear weapons talks with the Soviets, and trying to open a channel to Communist China. It would take the German elections of September 1969 to force Nixon and Kissinger to reconsider their approach to Berlin and Germany. Germany's Social Democrats narrowly prevailed in the election and came to power in coalition with the Liberal Democrats for the first time in postwar history. Willy Brandt, the famous and charismatic mayor of West Berlin, took office as chancellor with a determination to accelerate the Ostpolitik he had begun as foreign minister in the previous government. Brandt's key adviser, Egon Bahr, visited the United States and told Kissinger that Germany would now be "more self-reliant and not always compliant toward [the US]," signaling, in effect, that the Germans would practice their own form of informing, rather than consulting, with the United States.[14] Kissinger later remarked that "though Bahr was a man of the left, I considered him above all a German nationalist who wanted to exploit Germany's central position to bargain with both sides." Kissinger doubted that Bahr was "as unquestioningly dedicated to Western unity as the people we had known in the previous government," as well as being "free of any sentimental attachment to the United States."[15] Kissinger told Bahr that America wanted to "deal with Germany as partner, not a client," but these words belied the real concerns about Brandt taking the leadership of Europe and unleashing a "detente-euphoria," at a time when the United States, frustrated by the lack of success in its attempts to get Soviet help on Vietnam, found its own movement toward better relations with the Russians bogged down. Nixon's deep distaste for Brandt, a figure who reminded him of the Kennedys, and whose "socialist" policies he despised, only complicated matters for Kissinger, as he found himself explaining his former countrymen's policies to his unsympathetic boss.

Over the next several months, despite private misgivings, frequent predictions of failure, and constant appeals from Germany's political opposition to intervene, the United States found itself essentially led by its West German ally. Brandt's determination to move in directions which earlier American administrations had suggested, including the recognition of Oder-Neisse border with Poland, exchanges with East Germany, talks with Moscow—accelerated the movement toward European détente far more quickly than the Nixon administration planned. For achieving treaties with Moscow and Poland, Willy Brandt was *Time's* Man of the Year in 1970, a designation which greatly irritated Nixon. Kissinger's own analysis of the process reflected an acute and pessimistic understanding of the dynamics of German domestic politics, which found Brandt facing enormous pressures to produce results in a very short period of time. Not surprising given his personal experience with Germany, Kissinger also feared that Brandt's efforts might rekindle a "debate about Germany's basic position" within the West, "not only inflaming German domestic affairs but generating suspicions among Germany's western associates as to its reliability as a partner." He also feared a resurgence of German nationalism, a fear that he would express often to associates, even though Brandt seemed anything but a nationalist. But Kissinger feared the unintended results of Brandt's policies, especially if they might lead to greater demands for reunification outside of the Western European framework. As he concluded in one memo to Nixon, "[Brandt's] problem is to control a process which, if it results in failure could jeopardize their political lives and if it succeeds could create a momentum that may shake Germany's domestic stability and unhinge its international position."[16]

Kissinger's mistrust of Brandt and the direction of Ostpolitik found a sympathetic listener in Nixon. When Brandt traveled to East Germany and Kissinger wrote of the "dim prospects" for the success of his talks, Nixon wrote in the margins of the memo, "If Brandt continues in this soft headed line, this would be in our interest,' and the president hoped Brandt's government would collapse.[17] Kissinger considered Brandt 'not the brightest man in the world" and spoke disdainfully of the "reptile Bahr."[18] Despite his personal feelings—no doubt intensified by his family's experience with German nationalism—Kissinger approached German policy with great care and made sure that Nixon's frequent emotional outbursts had no real effect on policy.[19] Kissinger urged Nixon "to along with Brandt's policy and to use our influence to embed it in a wider framework than German nationalism." He cautioned that such encouragement "should be no more than general support for the improvement of the FRG [Federal Republic of Germany] relations with the East—without approving specific FRG moves."[20]

Consistent with his realpolitik approach and complimented by his deep knowledge of Germany's political realities, Kissinger was certain that "no German leader could afford to conduct a policy of which we strongly disapproved. His domestic position would not sustain it; his own convictions belied it; no rational calculations of benefits would encourage it." This assessment led Kissinger to a conclusion that would become clear over the next two years:

> Berlin became the key to the whole puzzle, for one simple reason. Whatever treaties Brandt negotiated with the USSR and East Germany would have to be ratified by the West German parliament, in which his coalition had the slimmest of majorities. . . . It became clear that only with a Berlin agreement would Brandt's eastern treaties be ratified. A Berlin agreement required the concurrence of all four wartime powers. . . . Thus our active cooperation was crucial; we alone had the strength to counterbalance the reality of Berlin's isolation; in time we would achieve thereby a major voice in the process, however it was started.[21]

Nixon and Kissinger did make various attempts to slow down the momentum of Brandt's Ostpolitik. In December 1970 Kissinger secretly organized a group of Cold War American senior diplomats with close ties to Germany, including Dean Acheson, Lucius Clay, and John McCloy, to visit Nixon in the White House and complain publicly about the "mad race to Moscow" that Brandt's government seemed engaged in. Kissinger told Acheson beforehand that he hoped "they could make some concrete suggestions about leadership we could exercise in Europe right now in respect to Ost-Politik which I think is a disaster. Brandt is sincere but there are a lot of sincere fools in the world."[22]

The fact that Kissinger's role in the Acheson visit remained hidden allowed him to distance himself from the critique Acheson had made, and to meet with German state secretary Horst Ehmke two weeks later. Ehmke wanted the Americans to intensify the Berlin talks, which had been underway since earlier in the year. Kissinger was now receptive to this offer, for a number of interconnected reasons. His bureaucratic battles with Secretary of State William Rogers were increasingly successful, and Kissinger had become Nixon's key adviser on the most important foreign policy issues. Berlin could now be added to that list. In addition, Kissinger interpreted food riots, which had broken out in Poland after the signing of the Warsaw Treaty, as an event that might push the Soviets toward détente with the United States. He was also aware that China had signaled its own interest in a possible meeting with the Americans. Kissinger believed now, as he told Ehmke, that "the Germans could not jeopardize our interests in Europe without jeopardizing their own."[23]

In January 1971 the Soviet Ambassador, Anatoly Dobrynin, made it clear to Kissinger that the Soviets were interested in a summit with the United States, and that they hoped to make "an objective improvement" in the Berlin situation. The fact that the Soviets were willing to use the secret backchannel with Kissinger to help hammer out an agreement on Berlin appealed to the national security adviser, who knew how much Nixon wanted foreign policy successes for his domestic political situation. To Kissinger, it seemed as though he could now control the negotiations. He told Dobrynin, "Bahr would tell me what the German government might be willing to consider; I would discuss it with Dobrynin; if the three of us agreed, we would introduce it first in the Four Power Western group and subsequently in the Four Power talks in Berlin."[24]

Over the next months the Berlin negotiations proceeded on these two levels, officially on the ambassadorial level with the four major powers, and secretly during meetings of the US ambassador Kenneth Rush, the Soviet ambassador Valentin Falin, and Brandt's aide Egon Bahr. (They referred to themselves as "the three musketeers.") Rush was the one participant in both sets of talks—and, as Kissinger called him, the "linchpin." Rush, Kissinger wrote, "kept me briefed for my negotiations with Dobrynin; he kept in close touch with the other Western Allies to make sure that the allied positions remained compatible; he also had to curb Bahr's propensity for solitary efforts and for claiming credit with the Soviets for all concessions made." Although Kissinger would also connect Berlin with other parts of his own complicated diplomacy during this period, on Berlin he acknowledged that the process worked, "due in large measure to Rush's unflappable skill."[25] (Kissinger's willingness to give so much credit to Rush for a foreign policy achievement in the Nixon administration is noteworthy, largely because it is so out of character.)

Ironically enough, the Berlin negotiations proceeded rapidly, as the Brandt government, facing a continual challenge from the conservative opposition, was desperate to speed up the acceptance of the Moscow and Warsaw treaties. The only way to do that was to push ahead for a Berlin agreement, and Egon Bahr wanted to focus on practicalities rather than legal issues. As Bahr told Kissinger, "The way to break the deadlock was to get away from judicial arguments and stress only the obligations and undertakings of each side."[26] The negotiations accelerated as the fruits of the Nixon and Kissinger triangular diplomacy were starting to become apparent. At the end of April, the US received the official word that the Chinese government would receive an envoy from the United States for negotiations, and in May, the US and the Soviet Union agreed to the start of a negotiation over a Strategic Arms Limitation treaty, the SALT talks, which would culminate in a summit. For his part, Kissinger quite deliberately slowed the pace of the Berlin negotiations before his trip to China, telling Rush on June 28, 1971, that it "was imperative that you do not come to a final agreement until after July 15 for reasons that will become apparent to you."[27] Nixon's announcement on July 15 of his trip to China shocked the nation but was greeted with an overwhelmingly favorable response. Although it did unsettle the Soviets, there is no compelling evidence that it altered in any fundamental way the Quadripartite Agreement, which was signed September 3, 1971.

The Quadripartite Agreement was not signed in a vacuum, and its final approval would only come months later, after various crises rocked both US-Soviet and US-European relations and threatened to prevent the onset of détente between the superpowers. One of the first was what the Japanese called "the Nixon shock," the August 15, 1971, announcement that the United States was ending the link between the price of gold and the dollar, and effectively terminating the Bretton Woods system.[28] This unilateral policy step, although originating from the underlying fact of European and Japanese economic recovery after World War II, caused deep consternation among the Allies, especially since it was connected to the imposition of a punishing tariff as well. The "New Economic Policy," which also involved wage and price controls at home and a rhetorical blast at "unfair" foreign competition, initially proved popular at home, and Nixon relished the favorable stories about his bold leadership. His treasury secretary, the outspoken Texan John Connally, spoke of "screwing foreigners before they screwed you," and his style caused further problems, especially for the Europeans. Yet Nixon did not want to weaken the Western alliance in any meaningful way, and he quickly dispatched various aides, including Henry Kissinger, who had not been involved in the original decision, to soothe hurt feelings among the Allies. However, Nixon did believe that the negotiation of the Berlin Agreement gave him some special leverage over the Germans, who had resisted the devaluation of the dollar relative to their strong currency, the D-Mark. He told Arthur Burns, the chair of the Federal Reserve, that the "Berlin Agreement was as important or even more important to Brandt and his political future as [repatriating] Okinawa was to [Japanese prime minister] Sato. At this point, with them, they owe us one."[29]

Whether or not the Germans shared the feeling that they "owed" the Americans, the end of Bretton Woods ultimately did not lead to a rupture in the alliance that might have affected the finalization of the Berlin Agreement. Negotiations ensued that gradually brought a realignment of currencies and a lifting of the tariffs. Oddly enough, it was a war half a world away that almost torpedoed the US-Russia summit and the possibility of moving ahead with the Quadripartite Agreement. The India-Pakistan war of November–December 1971 had deep roots, and subsequent historians have blasted the American decision to "tilt" toward Pakistan as an acceptance of that country's genocidal policies toward its Bengali population.[30] In realpolitik terms, Nixon and Kissinger saw the war as a battle between a Soviet proxy, in this case India, and an American—and Chinese—ally, Pakistan. Their desire to support Pakistan flowed in large measure from this desire to reassure China and preserve their new relationship with the Beijing government. The two men's dangerous—and very strange—discussions about the possibility of nuclear war over the issue seemed to have stemmed largely from this concern over China's possible change of heart about the Nixon visit.[31] At one point late in the crisis, Nixon believed that the Soviet failure to restrain India from what was rapidly shaping up to be its overwhelming military victory put into question the value of the scheduled US-Soviet summit meeting. He encouraged Kissinger to leak to the press this threat to superpower détente. The resulting public furor found Nixon quickly disassociating himself from the threat and putting the blame on Kissinger, leaving Kissinger to feel like Nixon was "letting me twist slowly, slowly in the wind," a phrase later used during the Watergate scandal about FBI Director Patrick Gray.[32] Nixon came close to firing Kissinger over the incident, and Kissinger came close to resigning.

However, one key reason why Nixon pulled back from his threat to cancel the summit was that 1972 was an election year, and Nixon hoped to enhance his image as a peacemaker through his summitry with both the Soviets and the Chinese. This image as a peacemaker would offset the fact that he had not yet settled the Vietnam War. It was that ongoing and seemingly unsolvable conflict that energized the opposition Democrats and would be their main issue against him. To try to defuse that opposition, Nixon announced in January that he had been sending Henry Kissinger to negotiate secretly with the North Vietnamese and had offered terms for withdrawal not unlike those being put forth by the antiwar Democrats. This announcement temporarily quieted the opposition, but the lull was short lived.

In February Nixon began his historic trip to China, which received extraordinary coverage within the American media and enhanced his image as a peacemaker. At the same time as Nixon was heading to China, debate began in the Bundestag on the ratification of the Moscow and Warsaw treaties that Willy Brandt had negotiated. As historian Mary Sarotte noted, "The outcome was far from certain." The opposition Christian Democrats, led by Rainer Barzel, and their allies in the Bundestag, "were vehemently opposed to ratification" and had decided to seek a vote of no confidence in Brandt for April 1972.[33] Although the Berlin Treaty was not at stake directly, it was unlikely that Moscow would agree to put the agreement into force if Brandt was deposed and the other treaties were not approved. Indeed, as Sarotte makes clear, the Soviet leadership and their East German allies launched a concerted campaign to save Brandt's chancellorship, a campaign that included bribing some Bundestag deputies. For their part, the German conservatives continually asked Nixon and Kissinger for some sign of support in their desire to depose Brandt and block the treaties, but the Americans resisted.

Once again, however, international events interfered. On March 31, 1972, the North Vietnamese launched their Easter Offensive, an all-out invasion of the South that threatened to inflict a humiliating defeat on the United States. Shortly before the offensive began, the Soviet leader Leonid Brezhnev had asked Nixon directly to "actively facilitate [ratification] with all means at [his] disposal."[34] Brezhnev's personal prestige was connected to his German policy, and the Soviets knew that the West also linked their long-sought proposal for a "European Security Conference" with the conclusion of the Quadripartite Agreement. Kissinger himself seemed to signal White House support for the ratification of the treaties by receiving Egon Bahr for a meeting, while declining to meet with a representative of the CDU. Bahr certainly thought that Kissinger was indicating his support, and he reported to Chancellor Brandt that the atmosphere of his talks was the warmest it had been and that Kissinger suggested regular meetings in the future.

The Vietnamese attack changed the atmosphere in Washington. Largely for domestic political reasons—Nixon's belief that defeat in Vietnam would lead to his defeat in the November elections—Nixon was determined to use overwhelming American military force to stop a North Vietnamese conquest of the South. Nixon now authorized an unprecedented level of bombing in South Vietnam as well as renewed raids against the North. Nixon was also angry at the obvious Soviet role in the invasion, particularly the armor and supplies they had provided the North Vietnamese. On April 3, 1972, he told Kissinger to tell Soviet ambassador Anatoly Dobrynin that the Soviets "are risking the summit, that they are risking Berlin—the German treaties—and our whole relationship."[35] On April 9 Nixon repeated to Kissinger to tell Soviet ambassador Anatoly Dobrynin that "the Summit is on the line now." Kissinger told Nixon that both the Soviets and Germans had requested a letter from the United States endorsing the ratification of the Moscow and Warsaw treaties. Kissinger refused, telling Dobrynin that "under the circumstances—since this is the second time Soviet arms are engaged in an offensive—we are reassessing the whole policy."[36] A few days later an exasperated Kissinger responded to Dobrynin's concern about the bombing by saying, "You are responsible for this conflict . . . and as a result have put yourself into the position where a miserable little country can jeopardize everything that has been striven for for four years." Kissinger went on to tell the Soviet ambassador that the United States would offer no support for ratification of the German treaties as long as the Soviets continued their support for Hanoi.[37]

Ironically enough, the United States came to reverse this policy. When on May 1, 1972, the North Vietnamese captured the city of Quang Tri, and there were real concerns about a possible collapse of South Vietnamese resistance, Nixon decided to escalate his use of force to include B-52 bombings of the North as well as the mining of Haiphong harbor. These military steps, which President Lyndon Johnson had avoided because of a fear of hitting Soviet ships and bringing the Soviets into the war, created immediate concern that Brezhnev would cancel the summit meeting with

Nixon. Kissinger now found himself reassuring Dobrynin that the United States was using its influence in West Germany to ensure the ratification of the Eastern treaties and the survival of the Brandt government, On May 9, the day after Nixon announced the new military escalation, Kissinger called Dobrynin to tell him that the CDU leader Barzel had reached agreement with Brandt on a parliamentary resolution that would allow the Eastern treaties to pass. Kissinger used the call to assure Dobrynin that the United States wanted to continue to work with the Soviets cooperatively on issues of mutual importance, and to imply that the conflict in Vietnam should not prevent them from doing so. Although the issue seems to have received heated debate among Soviet leaders, Brezhnev's pro-détente position prevailed, assisted in no small measure by the superpower agreement on Germany.[38] Nixon and Brezhnev clinked their glasses of vodka, and for a time, détente was the name of the game.

* * *

In her important study of the diplomacy of German détente, Mary Sarotte concluded that "the Quadripartite Agreement must be judged a success. After its signing, it had the desired effect of making Berlin much less of a flashpoint than it had previously been." Sarotte goes on to note that even harsh critics of the Nixon and Kissinger foreign policy, like the journalist Seymour Hersh, found the agreement "remarkable." Most importantly, as historian Peter Pulzer wrote, the Quadripartite Agreement showed that détente "could operate in a number of arenas—in Southeast Asia, in the Middle East, or in arms limitations. But unless it also operated in Germany . . . the remainder would be no more than a series of partial and peripheral deals." Sarotte adds that the negotiators of the Dayton Accord in 1995, which settled the Bosnian conflict, looked to the Quadripartite Agreement as a template for their own work.[39]

The dilemma that had faced American leaders, to maintain Berlin's symbolic value while reducing its potential to trigger a conflict with the Soviet Union, seemed at first to be decided largely in favor of the latter objective. Many in Washington began to forget the significance of the American position in Berlin. In the spring of 1975, the State Department organized a seminar to brief former senator John Sherman Cooper, who had been nominated to be the first US ambassador to East Germany. Among the distinguished experts it invited was Hans Morgenthau, the University of Chicago's international relations theorist. Cooper posed this question to the assembled diplomats and experts: "Why are we still in Berlin anyway?" Surprisingly enough, the Washington officials struggled to answer, and even Morgenthau could not explain the American position. The American embassy official who finally spoke up, John Kornblum, gave the traditional geopolitical reasons.[40] Kornblum subsequently made it his mission to keep the purpose of America's position in Berlin salient to Washington leaders. When he became a political adviser to the secretary of state in the 1980s, Kornblum found a particularly receptive listener in George Schultz. Schultz's support for Kornblum's Berlin advocacy would later play a key role in approving Ronald Reagan's "Tear Down This Wall" speech of June 1987.

Even though the Quadripartite Agreement never actually mentioned the city of Berlin by name, it did serve to stabilize West Berlin's position and guarantee practical improvements in the lives of its residents. While it did increase a Soviet presence in the city and decrease West Germany's political presence, the legal rights of the Western Allies remained, and the city survived, albeit with a substantial subsidy from Bonn. Critics at the time did focus on the increased Soviet presence in West Berlin as well as the Allies failure to gain any concessions on East Berlin. However, eighteen years later, when East Berlin party leader Günter Schabowski announced that travel restrictions were being lifted, it would be in Berlin where the Cold War came to its symbolic end. To this extent, Western leaders had managed to resolve the dilemma of Berlin as a symbol and possible trigger to war in a way that preserved the peace and brought an advance of freedom. Such achievements are relatively rare in history, and this one deserves its recognition and praise.

NOTES

1. Ernest R. May and Philip D. Zelikow, *The Kennedy Tapes: Inside the White House during the Cuban Missile Crisis* (Cambridge, MA: Belknap Press of Harvard University Press, 1997), 38–39.

2. Quoted in Robert Dallek, *Flawed Giant: Lyndon Johnson and His Times, 1961–1973* (New York: Oxford University Press, 1998), 20.

3. I have drawn heavily from my *Lyndon Johnson and Europe: In the Shadow of Vietnam* (Cambridge, MA: Harvard University Press, 2003), 17ff.

4. Jon Margolis, *The Last Innocent Year: America in 1964* (New York: Morrow, 1999), 53.

5. *Foreign Relations of the United States [FRUS] 1961–1963,* vol. 15, *Berlin Crisis 1962–1963* (Washington: GPO, 1994), 672.

6. George McGhee, *At the Creation of a New Germany* (New Haven, CT: Yale University Press, 1989), 184.

7. Schwartz, *Lyndon Johnson and Europe,* 211.

8. Lyndon B. Johnson, "Remarks in New York City Before the National Conference of Editorial Writers," the American Presidency Project, October 7, 1966, https://www.presidency.ucsb.edu/documents/remarks-new-york-city-before-the-national-conference-editorial-writers.

9. Andreas W. Daum, *Kennedy in Berlin,* trans. Dona Geyer (Washington, DC: Cambridge University Press, 2008), 204.

10. Daum, 205–6.

11. Thomas A. Schwartz, *Henry Kissinger and American Power: A Political Biography* (New York: Hill and Wang, 2020), 67–68.

12. *Foreign Relations of the United States [FRUS] 1969–1976,* vol. 1, *Foundations of Foreign Policy 1969–1972* (Washington: GPO, 2003), 153 58, 195–203.

13. Richard Nixon, "Remarks at the Siemens Factory, West Berlin," the American Presidency Project, February 27, 1969, https://www.presidency.ucsb.edu/documents/remarks-the-siemens-factory-west-berlin.

14. Memo, Kissinger to Nixon, 10/20/69, *FRUS 1969–1976* 40: 103–5.

15. Henry Kissinger, *White House Years* (Boston: Little, Brown, 1979), 410–11.

16. Memo, Kissinger to Nixon, 2/16/70, *FRUS 1969–1976* 40: 153.

17. Memo, Kissinger to Nixon, 3/10/70, *FRUS 1969–1976* 40: 172.

18. Holger Klitzing, *The Nemesis of Stability: Henry A. Kissinger's Ambivalent Relationship with Germany* (Trier: Wissenschaftler Verlag, 2007), 259.

19. Klitzing, 262.

20. Kissinger, *White House Years,* 530.

21. Kissinger, 530–31.

22. Klitzing, *Nemesis of Stability,* 282.

23. *FRUS 1969–1976* 40: 455.

24. Klitzing, *Nemesis of Stability,* 294.

25. Kissinger, *White House Years,* 825.

26. *FRUS 1969–1976* 40: 676.

27. *FRUS 1969–1976* 40: 764.

28. The Bretton Woods system was a collective currency international exchange regime that was created in the aftermath of World War II. It required countries to peg their currency's value to the US dollar, which was in turn pegged to the price of gold.

29. Nichter, *Nixon and Europe,* 73.

30. Gary J. Bass, *The Blood Telegram: Nixon, Kissinger, and a Forgotten Genocide* (New York: Knopf, 2013).

31. There is an extended discussion of this in Thomas A. Schwartz, *Henry Kissinger and American Power: A Political Biography* (New York: Hill and Wang, 2020), 144–60.

32. Henry Kissinger, *White House Years* (Boston: Little, Brown, 1979), 918.

33. M. E. Sarotte, *Dealing with the Devil: East Germany, Détente, and Ostpolitik, 1969–1973* (Chapel Hill: University of North Carolina Press, 2001), 130.

34. Klitzing, *Nemesis of Stability*, 326.

35. WHT conversation, Nixon and Kissinger, April 3, 1972, Nixon Tapes, 022–69, Richard Nixon Presidential Library, https://www.nixonlibrary.gov/white-house-tapes.

36. Richard A. Moss, *Nixon's Back Channel to Moscow: Confidential Diplomacy and Détente* (Lexington: University Press of Kentucky, 2017), 233.

37. Klitzing, *Nemesis of Stability*, 329.

38. Klitzing, 332–33.

39. Sarotte, *Dealing with the Devil*, 122.

40. Correspondence with John Kornblum, March 15, 2022.

PART III

BEYOND THE COLD WAR IN BERLIN,
1972-1990S

CHAPTER 8

Trade and Energy Diplomacy as Catalysts for Détente

Berlin and the Schmidt and Kohl Governments

STEPHAN KIENINGER

LONG DÉTENTE AND NO SECOND COLD WAR

This chapter has something important to say that is often missed: it argues that, during the 1970s and 1980s, détente in Europe was sustainable—and it included Berlin.[1] This is a point often neglected regarding the key year 1983. When asked about their impressions of 1983, people might recall it as the year of the missiles, the year when NATO began deploying Pershing II and cruise missiles. Or they may refer to it as a dangerous year of multiple crises, including antinuclear protests in the US and Western Europe, NATO's Able Archer maneuver, and the Soviet shoot-down of a civilian Korean airliner.[2] All of this is on display in the TV series *Germany 1983,* including the sensation and the danger—and all of this is not inaccurate.

In terms of Berlin and inner-German relations, 1983 did not see a crisis. Rather, the year brought tremendous progress. In 1983 there was agreement that West Berlin would soon be connected to the newly constructed Siberian gas pipeline, the largest pipeline for the transport of natural gas supplying twenty million households in Western Europe. This was a key project for meeting rising energy demands in West Berlin, and both Germanys and the Soviets found consensus on the construction of a stub pipeline from the Czechoslovakian border to Berlin, including 250 kilometers in the German Democratic Republic's territory—for which transit the GDR received handsome fees. All of this happened in the shadow of the Euromissile crisis and against the backdrop of the above-mentioned international tensions.[3] The project materialized without any kind of legal haggling. All sides were able to reap economic benefits.

Economically, Berlin turned into a hub for joint East-West projects, which had been unthinkable before. The Quadripartite Agreement of 1971 and the inner–German Basic Treaty of 1972 turned Berlin into a cornerstone of détente.[4] The Germans could do all of this without interference from the Four Powers, as Henry Kissinger's adviser Helmut Sonnenfeldt had already predicted in 1972, when he wrote that

> the [basic] treaty in effect fully Germanizes the German question, with the Allied role even in West Berlin being relegated to minor importance. It is astonishing in how many areas the East Germans have agreed to open themselves up to dealings with the FRG. Brandt has gone a long way toward achieving the Annaeherung which Bahr set as a policy objective a decade ago. The East German regime has decided to take the risk that this will cause some Wandel in its internal structure too and in its relations with West Germany.[5]

It goes without saying that Berlin was still a cause for continued diplomatic battles. Détente did not imply that both sides kissed and made friends. But it did imply pragmatism and search for a more attainable peace, as John F. Kennedy had once put it, and that included Berlin. All of this this was entirely different from the Cold War confrontation of the 1950s.[6]

Moreover, in 1983 the two Germanies revived the negotiations on a cultural agreement, they concluded an environmental agreement, and the GDR's Reichsbahn and the West Berlin Senate agreed on the takeover of the S-Bahn in the West Berlin urban area by the Senate. In 1982 both sides opened a new superhighway linking Hamburg and Berlin, the two largest cities in divided Germany. West Germans with transit visas were allowed to use the road for jaunts to Berlin, and even border controls were less harassing for some time in 1983.[7] All of this was possible because the West Germans bailed out the East German regime in 1983: the West German billion Deutschmark credit (*Milliardenkredit*) saved the GDR from bankruptcy. In return, the East Germans allowed for more contacts and more cooperation; the deal was more contacts in return for cash. The Kohl government continued the *Deutschlandpolitik* that the Brandt and Schmidt governments had initiated, and in times of international crisis, Chancellor Kohl pursued it with even more vigor.[8] One key for the success of this was the personal diplomacy between Bavaria's leader Franz-Josef Strauß and GDR hard-currency fundraiser Alexander Schalck-Golodkowski. They liked each other instantly and negotiated the Milliardenkredit on behalf of Kohl and Honecker. Strauß and Schalck-Golodkowski had their own backchannel and met thirteen times in 1983 and 1984. They exchanged hundreds of backchannel messages and in 1984 were able to conclude yet another billion DM credit for the GDR. Financial interdependence and joint infrastructure projects were essential for long détente and the perforation of the Iron Curtain.[9]

Ostpolitik was not just about facilitating contacts as a way to alleviate the situation in divided Germany. It had a deeper purpose, whose aim was to bring about societal changes.[10] The long-term objective was to work for Germany's unification in a new Europe whole and free. Ostpolitik was not focused on the "classical reunification approach," however. Rather, unification was conceived as a distant objective. For the present, it was decisive to retain a sense of "Germanness" and to expand human contacts. The concept being that both Germanies would come closer and closer to each other in economic, cultural, and social ways, and in the movement of people.[11] In 1963 Willy Brandt made no bones that the objective was "the transformation of the other side."[12] The difficult task was to balance power and mission in inner-German relations. How much stability did one need? How much change was possible? In 1969 Egon Bahr said that the crucial question was how one could "disengage the Soviets from Eastern Europe step-by-step." Bahr argued that "the only way is beginning projects that link Eastern and Western Europe in ways the Soviets don't consider dangerous." Bahr emphasized that "you bring this about only if you don't put Soviet domination into question." He reiterated that "this is a long procedure with its own contradictions, but it is the only way unless you give up the objective of liberating Europe."[13]

This rationale was successful. Prior to the conclusion of the Basic Treaty between the two Germanys in November 1972, the number of annual visits from the Federal Republic and West Berlin to the GDR and East Berlin was about 2.5 million. As a result of détente, the number rose to more than 8 million in the mid-1970s. Helmut Schmidt reiterated that Ostpolitik brought "practical humanitarian improvement so that the effects of détente can be felt immediately by the people in Europe themselves."[14] In the 1980s, trade and credits were essential to maintain détente as a transformative process: Ostpolitik brought changes and these changes were intended.[15] The Helsinki Final Act (1975) codified the premises of the dynamic détente policies. The East German and Soviet leadership knew about the dangers, but they decided that economic benefits were more important. The assumption was that they could cope with the multiplication of societal contacts.[16]

During the late 1970s and early 1980s, the Schmidt government fought hard to maintain the benefits of détente during the crisis of US-Soviet relations and against the backdrop of the Soviet invasion in Afghanistan and the declaration of martial law in Poland. In July 1980 Schmidt went to Moscow in order to maintain dialogue. This ran very much against the Carter administration's efforts to freeze contacts with the Soviet Union. Prior to his Moscow visit, Schmidt used the World Economic Summit in Venice as a way to explain his policy, emphasizing the human benefits of détente and his responsibility for the 16 million Germans in East Germany, the 2 million in Berlin, and the 2 million scattered through Eastern Europe. He reiterated that "the German Government had a difficult task in managing a divided nation and persuading the German people not to rebel against that division." His main objectives were "a) to make it possible for as many Germans as possible to come to Germany; and b) to build as good a human relationship as possible between East and West." Schmidt emphasized that "the Federal Government, without any publicity, were succeeding in getting 30 to 40 thousand Germans out of Poland each year. The price, paid within the Helsinki framework and the framework of various bilateral agreements, was to have economic exchanges with Eastern European countries." Finally, Schmidt went on to explain that "these exchanges were, therefore, far more than a mere matter of trade. They made it possible for the German Government to get 'their own people out.'"[17]

BERLIN'S ROLE IN SCHMIDT'S DIPLOMACY: THE SOVIET NUCLEAR
POWER PLANT PROJECT, 1974–76

The East German regime was dependent on West Germany money. Starting in 1974 at the outset of his chancellorship, Helmut Schmidt instantly
utilized trade initiatives in his contacts with the Soviet leadership as a way
for Berlin's integration in large-scale infrastructure projects across the Iron
Curtain. West Berlin needed electricity in vast amounts, and Schmidt's idea
was to supply West Berlin with electricity from a 1,200-megawatt nuclear
power plant in the Soviet Union, more precisely in Kaliningrad, which was
to be purchased by the West German Kraftwerk Union. Both sides had
a compensation deal in mind. The Soviet authorities suggested supplying
Berlin with electricity as part of the payment for the construction costs of
the plant.[18] Such a large-scale energy project had been unthinkable before
Ostpolitik; the project being envisaged as a win for all sides involved: a win
for the Germans, as Berlin's supply would be secured; a win for the Soviets,
as they would get credits from the Germans to do this and the latest state
of the art technology as well; and a win for Poland and the GDR, as they
would obtain transit fees, as the route would go through their territories.
Perhaps it was seen as less of a win for the East Germans, as they thought
they could provide electricity from their old coal power plants in return for
hard currency.[19]

Schmidt's economic statecraft was conceived as a new way to keep Ostpolitik going resembling his pragmatic and hard-nosed style. At the time,
Ostpolitik's bust-and-boom phase was over. In previous years the Brandt
government had achieved bold changes in inner-German relations. The
East German regime had begun to accept millions of Western visitors in
return for recognition and economic benefits. Over time, the Communist
rulers feared the societal effects of détente as a threat to the very existence
of Communism. From the vantage point of the Honecker regime, détente
made it imperative to highlight ideological delimitation.

In November 1973 the GDR doubled the minimum exchange requirement for hard currency on entering East Germany territory; this was accompanied by the withdrawal of the exemptions for pensioners.[20] In turn,
the number of West German visitors plummeted by half. Willy Brandt was
furious and saw the move as an assault on the heart of Ostpolitik.[21] In
addition, domestic critics of Ostpolitik began to criticize its achievements.

In July 1974 Karl Carstens, the floor leader of the German conservatives, made the case that there "is a great disappointment with Brandt's Ostpolitik because people feel they were cheated as far as Menschliche Erleichterungen [human alleviations] is concerned."[22]

Ostpolitik ran into the kind of problems that had already been anticipated by its architects during the planning phase in the 1960s: Egon Bahr noted that the Soviet side could only make "partial concessions" in the field of human contacts, as "granting liberty of expression was tantamount to the disintegration of communism."[23] The decisive question was this: What number of contacts could a Warsaw Pact country afford without endangering its inner system of power? Schmidt initiated economic incentives to keep the Warsaw Pact states engaged in détente, seeing trade as an invaluable means for soothing the underlying East-West disagreements over the meaning and the aims of détente. Economic diplomacy helped to lessen tensions to the point, ultimately, where they could no longer recover their power to divide nations.

East Germany's thirst for Western money provided the lever for new initiatives. The reduction in the compulsory exchange quota in November 1974 was an important proof for the success of Schmidt's approach. In return, Honecker seized a substantial expansion of the overdraft credit agreement for inner-German trade, the so-called SWING, amounting to 850 million deutsche marks. Schmidt's and Honecker's first personal encounters at the Helsinki Summit in 1975 furthered the inner-German rapprochement. The two German leaders struck a deal over the so-called *Transitpauschale*—the handsome annual compensation for Western transport to Berlin. The new agreement secured the GDR annual revenues worth 400 million DM.[24] The GDR was in urgent need of fresh money, and the Federal Republic had the financial means to buy more contacts across the Iron Curtain.

In 1974 Schmidt's idea was to finalize the Kaliningrad nuclear power plant deal at his first summit in Moscow in October. Yet there were debates about the appropriate routes of the power lines transporting electricity to West Berlin. The West German argument was that the route for the power line had to touch base in Berlin so as to avoid an electrical switch on East German territory. The Soviet side wanted a separate stub line to Berlin. Schmidt proposed a compromise solution, suggesting a power line running through West Berlin as well as the construction of an electrical transfer station right at the border between West Berlin and East Germany. Each side could obtain energy without dependence on the other.[25] Brezhnev accepted

Schmidt's scheme. At the October 1974 summit, the economic elements of the deal were in place, and Schmidt went public praising the compensation business as an important sign of West Berlin's integration into the emerging pan-European energy infrastructure.[26]

Bold political objections remained, however. The Kaliningrad power plant project ran counter to the new and stricter US nonproliferation policy: after India's first nuclear test in May 1974, the Ford administration policy was to curb nuclear exports.[27] In order to be on the safe side, the Schmidt government applied for approval under the rules of the Coordinating Committee for Multilateral Export Controls (COCOM).[28] Ford and Kissinger indicated their consent to the COCOM exception, provided that the Soviets accepted on-site inspections and safety checks by the International Atomic Energy Organization. The Germans pointed out that the Soviets had hitherto continuously refused to be bound by IAEA safeguards and that they had previously rejected any commitment to such regulations.[29] Schmidt did not hear back from Brezhnev, however. In the summer of 1975, Schmidt thought about additional economic incentives to foster the power plant project. He used his meetings with Brezhnev at the Helsinki Summit to undertake a rescue operation.

Schmidt met Brezhnev for a private discussion.: He brought up the idea to donate to the Soviet Central Bank an amount of 400 million DM from the Federal Republic's foreign currency savings. The money would be drawn away from the USA, and it would be placed in the Soviet Union for five years: Schmidt encouraged Brezhnev to use the money as a loan to start the long-envisaged purchase of the nuclear power plant. Schmidt's plan was top secret; he had only consulted his trusted economic adviser, Karl Klasen, president of West Germany's Central Bank. In fact, as Schmidt confided in a top-secret note, he had thought about a considerable increase in the loan, assuming that Brezhnev would give his final consent to the project. Now he proposed the following plan to implement the scheme: he urged Brezhnev to instruct Mefody N. Sveshnikov, the president of the USSR's Central Bank, to meet with Klasen and to negotiate the technical details, while the amount of the investment would be determined by Schmidt and Brezhnev themselves. Thus Brezhnev would be in a position to claim the loan as his personal success.[30]

The power plant project was also discussed during the official meetings in Helsinki. Schmidt had the impression that Brezhnev did not appreciate the fact that the project would result in the first direct transfer of electricity across the blocs. Indeed, Brezhnev remained noncommittal and criticized Schmidt's "explosive mood."[31] But in September 1975 Schmidt started yet another initiative to facilitate the project. He wrote Brezhnev a letter of reassurance, reiterating that "he was determined to display a willingness to jump over his shadow if necessary";[32] he emphasized his readiness for an expansion of the loan in the spring of 1976. However, the Soviet response ruined the transaction. In January 1976 Brezhnev told Schmidt he was eager to go after the loan right away, but he wanted to postpone the power plant deal until after the CPSU's XXV party convention, to take place in February and March 1976.[33] Brezhnev obviously wanted to have his cake and eat it, too. Schmidt used a conversation with Soviet ambassador Valentin Falin in January 1976 to complain about the unpredictability of Soviet policies, and his line was clear: no power plant, no loan for the Soviet Union.[34] So the power plant project failed, after which it was obvious that both Schmidt and Brezhnev were eager to avoid a public blame game.[35]

The failure of the power plant deal underscored the limits of Eastern trade: the nuclear aspects eventually foreclosed the project, the game plan having presupposed US-Soviet concurrence over a package of American consent to COCOM exceptions in return for Soviet acceptance of IAEA safeguards. In effect, the crisis in US-Soviet relations stood in the way. As Werner Lippert put it, "The deal failed because neither superpower was willing to budge."[36] Schmidt and Brezhnev, trying to avoid a lasting impasse, now sought to limit the damage.[37] The plan for another Brezhnev visit in Bonn in 1976 was canceled, and Schmidt took the time to calm down the legal arguments over the status of West Berlin.

A NEW PROJECT: SCHMIDT AND WEST BERLIN'S CONNECTION TO THE SIBERIAN PIPELINE, 1978–82

In 1978 Schmidt and Honecker managed to conclude a comprehensive accord to improve the conditions for Western transit traffic to Berlin. The GDR agreed to finish up the construction of a motorway from Berlin to Hamburg until 1982. The agreement guaranteed the East German regime revenues worth 6.5 billion DM during the following decade.[38] In return, the Honecker regime was willing to accept additional societal links to the Federal Republic: the annual number of West German visits to Berlin and the GDR amounted to 8 million. East and West Germany were still divided, yet increasingly connected, and the intensifying people-to-people détente between the two Germanys concerned the Soviet leadership. Soviet foreign minister Andrei Gromyko warned Honecker that the GDR sought détente at the expense of socialism, making itself dependent on the West. Gromyko's concern was that the enormous expansion of human contacts might cause "unhealthy and nationalist moods."[39]

Schmidt envisaged trade as the most promising means of long-term cooperation with the Soviet Union, despite the USSR's buildup in SS-20 nuclear missiles. He argued that "the Russians would not reduce their armaments, but the goal should be to engage them in a joint perspective of trade, industry and technology over the next twenty years within which would emerge a greater Soviet dependence upon European or Western supplies. This would result in more European influence on their policies."[40] Schmidt and Brezhnev used their 1978 summit as a platform to reiterate the mutual interest in the expansion of natural gas trade. The real significance of their meeting was the conclusion of an economic framework agreement with a duration of twenty-five years.[41] In his dinner speech on the occasion of Brezhnev's visit, Schmidt reiterated that "the economic agreement extends far beyond the range of economic affairs. It provides an orientation for the development of political relations in general, for long-term peaceful development which presupposes that the people in both countries acquire a permanent interest in one another's economic welfare."[42] Schmidt believed that freer trade and more investments had inherent value in building stronger economies and, hence, more secure, reliable, and predictable diplomatic partners.

Energy trade was still the most promising field for new initiatives. Both sides envisaged an increase of West Germany's natural gas imports from 12 to 20 billion cubic meters (BCM). The 1978 talks were the starting point for the construction of the largest pipeline for the transport of natural gas from the Soviet Union to Western Europe (Urengoy–Pomary–Uzhgorod) in the first half of the 1980s.[43] The strategic energy partnership between the GDR and the Soviet Union continued even after the Soviet invasion of Afghanistan. Schmidt's and Brezhnev's Moscow summit in June 1980 signaled that the Schmidt administration would provide the kind of flank protection that West German companies needed to put the Urengoy project on track despite intermittent US sanctions.[44] Eventually, the framework agreement for the construction of the Urengoy pipeline was signed on the occasion of Leonid

Brezhnev's last visit to the Federal Republic in November 1981.[45] The contracts between Ruhrgas and Soyusgasneft stipulated gas supplies over twenty-five years, starting in 1984 and reaching into the twenty-first century (2008).[46]

In 1979 the Schmidt administration revived its long-cherished plans for West Berlin's inclusion in the emerging pan-European gas trade structure. The Urengoy gas project offered a most welcome chance to achieve a stabilization of West Berlin's energy supplies. Ideally, the plan was to supply West Berlin with Soviet gas by connecting it to the gas pipeline running from Siberia and Ukraine via Czechoslovakia to Bavaria. Eventually, the East German regime endorsed the plan for the construction of a transit pipeline running from Czechoslovakia through the GDR and connecting West Berlin to the pan-European gas infrastructure. In return, the GDR received handsome transit fees. Thus Berlin remained a crucial factor in the political economy of the triangular relations between Bonn, East Berlin, and Moscow. Berlin benefited from Schmidt's economic engagement with the Soviet Union, proving that the fruits of détente in Europe could be maintained in times of crisis.

Gas supplies had a peculiar relevance for West Berlin. So far, its gas consisted of petrol (*Leichtbenzin*), and fuel prices were bound to increase. Since an extension of Berlin's gas production was not possible, there was enormous pressure for an increase in gas imports by about 1 BCM per year. Hence, West Berlin's policymakers were eager for the city's inclusion in the Urengoy project.[47] In August 1980 West Berlin's governing mayor Dietrich Stobbe had a chance to discuss the issue with Schmidt, and ten days later the Schmidt administration seized the initiative for the start of official talks on West Berlin's inclusion in the Urengoy project. On September 1, 1980, Undersecretary of Economics Dieter von Würzen handed his East German counterpart Horst Sölle a first proposal at the Leipzig trade fare.[48]

The pipeline was an issue for Honecker and his trusted negotiator, Alexander Schalck-Golodkowski, who became involved in the summer of 1981. Schalck discussed the issue with Klaus Bölling, the head of the Federal Republic's Permanent Representation in East Berlin, arguing that "gas transport routes were a hot political topic and could thus be discussed at the highest level."[49] Indeed, in September 1981 Honecker informed Schmidt of his readiness to start official negotiations in the channel between Schalck and Bölling.[50] The Soviet side acknowledged the importance of West Berlin's inclusion, and in October 1981 Soyusgasneft offered Ruhrgas deliveries to West Berlin. Further, in November 1981 there was agreement over the start of negotiations among Soyusgasneft, the GDR, and Ruhrgas, as well as West Berlin's GASAG.[51] All sides had a shared interest in the speedy conclusion of the contracts against the background of the upcoming Schmidt-Brezhnev meeting in November 1981. The last obstacle was overcome in the spring of 1983 when all parties involved eventually found agreement over the terms of West Berlin's inclusion. Ruhrgas managed to conclude satisfactory contracts with Soyuzsgas and the GDR's Verbundnetze Energie.[52] All the pieces were in place. The annual gas deliveries to West Germany would amount to 10.5 BCM, and the Soviet side gave its consent to provide an additional 700 million BCM of gas for the supply of West Berlin.

THE MILLIARDENKREDIT, BERLIN, AND INNER-GERMAN RELATIONS IN THE LAST YEARS OF THE COLD WAR

The Euromissiles crisis did not stand in the way of inner-German cooperation. The fruits of détente could be maintained despite the deployment of Pershing II and cruise missiles in the Federal Republic starting in 1983. Helmut Kohl and Erich Honecker had a shared interest in avoiding a "relapse into the times of the Cold War."[53] In October 1983 Honecker offered Kohl "a coalition of reason."[54] Kohl himself referred to the term *Verantwortungsgemeinschaft* (common bond of responsibility).[55] Indeed, Kohl and Honecker were eager to dispense the two Germanys from the crisis in East-West relations as far as they could. The Milliardenkredit of 1983 signaled that they had managed to keep détente alive.[56] There was a convergence of interests: the GDR was in urgent need of fresh money, and the FRG had the money to buy more contacts across the Iron Curtain. The Milliardenkredit (loans over billions of DM), an advance payment, was an investment to perforate the Iron Curtain. The GDR received the money in July 1983 but made no move in response until September 1983, when the minimum exchange requirement for adult visitors and children visitors under the age of fifteen was abolished.[57] Moreover, the GDR authorities began to dismantle the automatic shooting devices along the inner-German border. Although these moves fell short of the response that public opinion in West Germany had been hoping for, the rapprochement nevertheless continued. Granting the Milliardenkredit made possible an agreement on environmental questions.[58]

Moreover, in November 1983 both sides managed to conclude a new postal agreement improving the flow of communication between the two Germanys.[59] The Kohl government's aim was to build sustainable agreements and durable institutions in an effort to transcend Germany's division. In 1983 Kohl defended the Milliardenkredit against internal party criticism, arguing that "the belief in the unity of the nation is impossible without contacts between people from both sides."[60]

The link between the money and the improvement in contacts was obvious. But there was no contract that would have stipulated freer movement in return for cash. There were assurances and non-papers, but there was no formal linkage. The GDR rejected a binding commitment and a deadline to fulfill its part of the deal. Erich Honecker needed the money, but he was eager to claim, vis-à-vis the Soviet leadership, that the deal did not impair the GDR's sovereignty. The advance payment required trust in the reliability of the GDR. And the backchannel between Strauß and Schalck was essential to building confidence.

The credit did not cost the West German taxpayer a single penny. Neither the Kohl government nor the involved banks had a financial risk. The GDR mortgaged its revenues from the fees that it received from the FRG in order to facilitate traffic to West Berlin. In the case of a default in payment, the federal government could deny the GDR these payments and redirect the money directly to the banks.[61] The Milliardenkredit was a novelty in inner-German relations. The Brandt and Schmidt administrations had followed the iron rule that the transfer of money was bound to specific infrastructure projects, such as the construction of motorways from West Germany to Berlin through GDR territory. Kohl, however, abandoned this principle: the one billion DM loan was not bound to specific purposes.

It was a private credit agreement between the GDR's Deutsche Außenhandelsbank and a consortium of West German banks under the leadership of the Bayerische Landesbank. The interest rate was 7.75 percent.[62] The interest rate was quite usual at the time. In effect, the deal was signed by foreign subsidiaries of the involved banks. The parent corporations were not allowed to conclude the credit agreement, as the direct inner-German transfer of money was prohibited according to the so-called Militärregierungsgesetz 53 (MRG 53)—a law by the Allies and a relic of the occupation era that was still in place.[63]

Strauß and Schalck were able to find attainable agreements on these issues. At the same time, it was essential for them to know their limits, and both had their maximum demands. So far, only senior GDR citizens were permitted to travel to West Germany. Time and again Strauß told Schalck that the GDR could afford a reduction of the travel age. On Kohl's behalf, Strauß reiterated that it should be manageable for the GDR to reduce the age limit for men from sixty-five to sixty and from sixty to fifty-five for women. But when Strauß mentioned the issue, Schalck countered with demands for the recognition of the GDR's citizenship.[64]

Honecker calculated that the majority of people would not return. He estimated that a reduction of the travel age might cost the GDR about 20 billion DM.[65] So it was in vain when Helmut Schmidt tried to convince him that most GDR citizens considered improved travel opportunities more important than a higher number of exit permissions to leave the GDR forever. That was in September 1983, when Schmidt privately visited the GDR.[66] But the events of 1984 underpinned the fact that the SED regime could not withstand more freedom of movement from East to West, as dissent was growing rapidly.

Starting in January 1984, more and more East Germans sought asylum in Western embassies, trying to force their way to exit permissions for leaving the GDR for the Federal Republic. The FRG's permanent representation in East Berlin did not force their fellow countrymen to leave. The asylum seekers stayed—and the Kohl government bought them out.[67] Following the first embassy sit-in came the *Ausreisewelle*. In 1984 the GDR authorities gave permission for 40,000 citizens to emigrate to the Federal Republic on a legal basis. The intention was to weed out dissidents and malcontents. If the easing up was meant to improve domestic morale, it failed. It had the opposite effect: an increasing number of people felt encouraged to apply for exit visas. The Ausreisewelle signaled that the GDR's leadership lacked a recipe for coping with dissent and the apparent lack of its legitimacy, and the Soviet leadership grew increasingly alarmed. Honecker intended to visit the FRG in autumn 1984 for a summit meeting with Kohl. He met Soviet secretary general Konstantin Chernenko in June and from this unreasonably assumed he had got Soviet acquiescence for the visit.[68] Finally, in August 1984, Honecker and his colleagues from the SED's Politburo were ordered to Moscow, where they were forced to cancel the summit. Honecker was heavily attacked for his close relations with the Kohl administration and in addition was accused of selling out socialism in the GDR in return for economic assistance from the West Germans. For the time being, the Soviets did not tolerate further political concessions in return for money.[69]

Yet in the second half of the 1980s the inner-German rapprochement continued. The Honecker regime let an increasing number of its citizens travel to the Federal Republic—mostly pensioners or just single family members who would be bound to return.[70] In 1987 the number of East German visitors was two million—the highest figure since Germany had become divided. Gorbachev's policy had created pressure for reforms.[71] Moreover, the Kohl government wanted some concessions in return for Kohl's willingness to see Honecker for the long-awaited summit in 1987.[72] The visit was a win-win-situation for both Germanys—it brought short-term gains for the GDR and long-term benefits for the FRG. The flow of people nurtured the desire for unification, despite Honecker's energetic denials, and the plus in societal contacts spurred demands for domestic reforms in the GDR. In June 1987 Helmut Kohl told Ronald Reagan that "of the 2 million that visit the West, nearly half are relatively young, or at least not pensioners. Many are seeing the West for the first time in their lives."[73] The UK embassy in East Berlin noted that "while Honecker lasts, the inner-German tide will flow strongly irrespective of top-level manifestations. Chancellor Kohl may not come here in 1988, but it will be more important that another million active GDR citizens see the FRG for themselves. The policy is not yet irreversible, but could become very difficult to stop, short of a major crisis, in a few more years."[74]

Berlin had an important place in the inner-German rapprochement. It was a symbol for the relaxation of East-West tensions and a meeting point for the emerging inner-German epistemic communities in culture and science.[75] West Berlin's contacts with the GDR also improved over time. In January 1989 West Berlin's governing mayor, Eberhard Diepgen, told Margaret Thatcher that "there was better cultural cooperation, with cultural exhibitions from West Berlin permitted in various parts of the GDR. He had been allowed to open up some of them in his official capacity." Diepgen said that "Berlin's problems lay more with the Soviet Union than with the GDR." The Soviets still refused to accept Berlin's ties to the West. Hence, as Diepgen emphasized, "the solutions to Berlin's problems had to be sought in the context of wider East/West issues."[76] The Berlin Wall was, of course, the most obvious symbol of East-West tensions—a cruel reminder of Germany's division. Berlin's 750-year anniversary in 1987 was an important opportunity to strengthen the city for the future. The three

Western powers undertook a major effort to support the celebrations in West Berlin. Ronald Reagan, François Mitterrand, and Margaret Thatcher visited West Berlin to demonstrate their support for the city and its people. Their speeches combined a readiness for cooperation with the Warsaw Pact countries and appeals for more Soviet deeds and openness. President Reagan's tear-down-this-wall speech was the epitome of this approach.[77] It was important to emphasize the normative dissent between democracy and totalitarianism, while at the same time it was equally essential for the West to show a willingness for practical cooperation in an effort to perforate the Iron Curtain. "One had to start from the reality that the Wall divided Europe into two power blocs. We could not expect to dissolve the Eastern bloc. But in the long run we could loosen it up by demonstrating the superiority of the democratic system," Diepgen said.[78]

At the same time, there were limits in terms of the inner-German rapprochement. In 1987 East and West Berlin held separate celebrations to mark the city's 750th birthday. The GDR exploited the anniversary in an effort to promote the Soviet sector of the city as the "capital" and the authentic Berlin. To that end, the GDR authorities organized a major renovation of the Nikolaiviertel in the city center, where many of the district's old houses were restored. Chancellor Kohl attended the celebrations in West Berlin. Erich Honecker had been invited but did not show up, as a joint ceremony with West German leaders would have implicitly recognized the West German view of the status of West Berlin. When it became clear that the two sides still disagreed over Berlin's divided status, the East promptly retracted the invitation it had extended to Mayor Diepgen. Although both parts were increasingly connected, the city very much remained divided.[79]

The Berliners learned to cope with the wall and tried to establish a certain kind of normalcy under division and a special political status. The wall divided the city, cutting across streets and squares. In urban districts it would run directly on the streets or along rows of houses. The West Berliners developed a sort of an island mentality and a local patriotism that was found in the song "Der Insulaner verliert die Ruhe nicht" (The islanders don't want to give up their peaceful existence) on West Berlin radio station RIAS.[80] Later on, after the emergence of the student movement and the start of the Vietnam War, the younger generation of West Berliners grew increasingly critical toward the United States and the West in general, while the older generation mostly saw the Allies as friends and protectors.

Over time, the Berliners on both sides of the wall developed visions to escape the logic of the Cold War in the search for a more promising future. Arts, culture, and music were a key means to challenge the status quo and to end the existing order. In the 1960s and 1970s, all Berliners were able to tune into rock 'n' roll radio. The emerging youth counterculture began to transcend the wall and helped young people to channel their hopes and anxieties. Whereas the older generation of Berliners tended to see themselves as activists in the battle between the systems, the younger generation increasingly saw the existence of the wall as a semblance of normality. After the youth revolution of 1968, the generation born in the postwar began to turn West Berlin into a hub for new musical cultures, a hub that, during the second half of the 1970s, attracted the famous singer-songwriter David Bowie, who spent three of his most productive years there.[81] Last but not least, as the West German state subsidized people to remain there to keep the city alive, West Berlin was an attractive place. Residents were exempt from military service, which added an extra incentive, and unlike today, housing and rents were quite cheap. These cultural and economic trends, too, ran counter to the prevailing narrative about the crisis of 1983 and instead further illustrate how far contacts between the people and governments of the two German states had developed.

NOTES

1. See Oliver Bange and Poul Villaume, eds., *The Long Détente: Changing Concepts of Security and Cooperation in Europe, 1950s–1980s* (Budapest: Central European University Press, 2017).

2. See Stephan Kieninger, *The Diplomacy of Détente: Cooperative Security Policies from Helmut Schmidt to George Shultz* (London: Routledge, 2018); Simon Miles, *Engaging the Evil Empire: Washington, Moscow, and the Beginning of the End of the Cold War* (Ithaca, NY: Cornell University Press, 2020).

3. Leopoldo Nuti, Frédéric Bozo, Marie-Pierre Rey, and Bernd Rother, eds., *The Euromissile Crisis and the End of the Cold War* (Stanford, CA: Stanford University Press, 2015).

4. See Mary Sarotte, *Dealing with the Devil: East Germany, Détente, and Ostpolitik, 1969–1973* (Chapel Hill: University of North Carolina Press, 2001); Gottfried Niedhart, *Durch den Eisernen Vorhang: Die Ära Brandt und das Ende des Kalten Kriegs* (Wiesbaden: WBG Theiss, 2019).

5. Memo Sonnenfeldt to Kissinger: "Subject: FRG–GDR Treaty and our GDR NSSM," November 7, 1972, in *Foreign Relations of the United States* [*FRUS*],

vol. 40, *Germany and Berlin 1969–1972*, ed. David C. Geyer (Washington, DC: US Government Printing Office, 2007), 1090.

6. See Oliver Bange, "Keeping Détente Alive: Inner-German Relations under Helmut Schmidt and Erich Honecker, 1974–1982," in *The Crisis of Détente in Europe: From Helsinki to Gorbachev, 1975–1985*, ed. Leopoldo Nuti (London: Routledge, 2009), 230–43. For a recent account on the precursors of détente in the 1950s, see Christian F. Ostermann, *Between Containment and Rollback: The United States and the Cold War in Germany* (Stanford, CA: Stanford University Press, 2021).

7. For the context, see *Dokumente zur Deutschlandpolitik* (hereafter *DzD*), ser. VII, vol. 1, *October 1982–December 31, 1984* (Munich: De Gruyter, 2018).

8. See Karl-Rudolph Korte, *Deutschlandpolitik in Helmut Kohls Kanzlerschaft: Regierungsstil und Entscheidungen 1982–1989* (Munich: Deutsche Verlags-Anstalt, 1998).

9. See Stephan Kieninger, "Freer Movement in Return for Cash: Franz Josef Strauss, Alexander Schalck-Golodkowski and the Milliardenkredit for the GDR, 1983–1984," in *New Perspectives on the End of the Cold War: Unexpected Transformation?*, ed. Bernhard Blumenau, Jussi Hanhimäki and Barbara Zanchetta (London: Routledge, 2018), 117–37.

10. Oliver Bange and Gottfried Niedhart, eds., *Helsinki 1975 and the Transformation of Europe* (New York: Berghahn, 2008).

11. See "CSCE, the German Question, and the Eastern Bloc," *Journal of Cold War Studies* 18, no. 3 (summer 2016): 3–180.

12. See "Vortrag des Regierenden Bürgermeisters von Berlin, Brandt, in der Evangelischen Akademie Tutzing," July 15, 1963, *DzD,* ser. IV, vol. 9/2, 1963 (Frankfurt/Main: Alfred Metzner 1978): 565–71.

13. Remarks by Egon Bahr at the trilateral policy planning talks in Washington, April 18, 1969, in National Archives and Record Administration (NARA), College Park, MD; Records of the Department of State, Record Group 59 (RG 59,), Lot 73 D 363, Subject and Country Files of the Policy Planning Council and the Planning and Coordination Staff, 1967–73, box 401.

14. Helmut Schmidt, Address at the World Economic Summit in London, June 3, 1977, in Archiv Helmut Schmidt Hamburg (AHSH), Eigene Arbeiten, April 77–May 1977, Doc. 19.

15. See Thomas A. Schwartz, "Legacies of Détente: A Three-Way Discussion," *Cold War History* 8, no. 4 (November 2008): 513–25.

16. See Oliver Bange, "The GDR in the Era of Détente: Conflicting Perceptions and Strategies," in *Perforating the Iron Curtain: European Détente, Transatlantic Relations, and the Cold War 1965–1985*, ed. Poul Villaume, Poul and Odd Arne Westad (Copenhagen: Museum Tusculanum Press, 2010), 57–77.

17. Venice Summit, 2nd sess., June 22, 1980, 1515 Hours, "Discussion of Political Matters," in The National Archives (hereafter TNA), Prime Minister's Office

Files, (hereafter PREM) 19/189, accessed November 7, 2017, https://www.margaretthatcher.org/document/115755.

18. See Memcon Brandt and Novikov, January 18, 1974, in *AAPD 1974* (Munich: Oldenbourg Verlag, 2005), 64–72. Brezhnev had already discussed the idea at the German-Soviet summit in May 1973. See Memcon Brandt and Brezhnev, May 18, 1973, in *AAPD 1973* (Munich: Oldenbourg Verlag, 2004), 710–23.

19. For the context, see Helmut Schmidt, *Menschen und Mächte* (Berlin: Siedler Verlag, 1987).

20. For the context, see Hermann Wentker, *Außenpolitik in engen Grenzen: Die DDR im internationalen System* (Munich: Oldenbourg Verlag, 2007); *Heinrich Potthoff, Im Schatten der Mauer: Deutschlandpolitik 1961–1990* (Berlin: Propyläen Verlag, 1999).

21. Letter from Brandt to Wehner, December 18, 1973, in *DzD*, ser. 6, vol. 3, 1973–174 (Munich: Oldenbourg Verlag, 2005): 402.

22. Memcon Kissinger and Carstens, July 18, 1974, in NARA, RG 59, Records of the Office of the Counselor, Entry 5339, Helmut Sonnenfeldt, 1957–77, box 5.

23. Memcon Brandt, Bahr, and Belgium's Prime Minister Leburton, February 7, 1973, in *Akten zur Auswärtigen Politik der Bundesrepublik Deutschland* (hereafter *AAPD*) (Munich: Oldenbourg Verlag, 2005), 1973, 197.

24. See Minutes of a Meeting of Principals, November 26, 1974, in: *DzD*, ser. 6, vol. 3, 1973–74, 860–61.

25. See Memcon Schmidt and Kossygin, October 29, 1974, *AAPD 1974*, 1363–71.

26. Note by Hiss, director of the Division of Economic Affairs in the Chancellor's Office, on Schmidt's talks in Moscow (October 28–31, 1974), November 1, 1974, AHSH, Soviet Union Files (UdSSR), vol. 2, 1974–77, doc. 4.

27. See Jayita Sarkar, "US Policy to Curb West European Nuclear Exports, 1974–1978," *Journal of Cold War Studies* 21, no. 2 (spring 2019): 110–49.

28. See Letter from Schmidt to Kissinger, October 18, 1974, *AAPD 1974*, 1322–25. Schmidt also sent the letter to French President Giscard d'Estaing and British Prime Minister Wilson; see PA AA, Declassified Documents (Bestand 150), copies 1974, vol. 529. For COCOM's policy, see Michael Mastanduno, *Economic Containment: CoCom and the Politics of East-West-Trade* (Ithaca, NY: Cornell University Press, 1992), 220–33.

29. See Memcon Genscher, Kissinger, Callaghan and Sauvagnargues, December 11, 1974, *AAPD 1974*, 1612–16.

30. Note by Schmidt on his personal discussion with Brezhnev, July 31, 1975, AHSH, UdSSR, vol. 2, 1974–77, doc. 20. Schmidt wrote the note on his typewriter at his vacation refugee at the Brahmsee on August 12, 1975. See also Schmidt, *Menschen und Mächte,* 78.

31. Memcon Schmidt, Genscher, Brezhnev, Gromyko, July 31, 1975, *AAPD 1975* (Munich: Oldenbourg Verlag, 2006), 1106.

32. See letter Schmidt to Brezhnev, September 26, 1975, AHSH, UdSSR, vol. 2, 1974–77, doc. 21.

33. See letter Brezhnev to Schmidt, no date, January 1976, AHSH, UdSSR, vol. 2, 1974–77, doc. 25.

34. See Memcon Schmidt and Falin, January 30, 1976, in: AHSH, UdSSR, vol. 2, 1974–77, doc. 28.

35. See note from Bahr to Schmidt "Gespräch mit L[ednew]," March 18, 1976, AHSH, UdSSR, vol. 2, 1974–77, doc. 31.

36. Werner D. Lippert, *The Economic Diplomacy of Ostpolitik: Origins of NATO's Energy Dilemma* (New York: Berghahn Books, 2010), 134.

37. See letter from Schmidt to Brezhnev, July 7, 1976, AHSH, UdSSR, vol. 2, 1974–77, doc. 35.

38. See Michael Getler, "2 Germanys Agree On New Autobahn Linking Berlin, West," *Washington Post*, November 17, 1978. The agreement was finalized in negotiations between Schmidt's and Honecker's envoys Günter Gaus and Alexander Schalck-Golodkowski. See note by Schalck-Golodkowski on his talks with Gaus, November 13, 1978, *DzD*, ser. 6, vol. 5, 1977–78 (Munich: Oldenbourg Verlag, 2011): 956–58.

39. Memcon Honecker and Gromyko, May 12, 1978, *DzD*, ser. 6, vol. 5, 1977–78: 630.

40. Memcon Callaghan and Schmidt, April 24, 1978, TNA, PREM 16/1655, accessed 25 October 2017, http://www.margaretthatcher.org/document/111594.

41. See Memcon Schmidt, Genscher, Brezhnev, Gromyko, Tichonov, May 6, 1978, *AAPD 1978* (Munich: Oldenbourg Verlag, 2009), 685–91.

42. Handwritten notes by Schmidt, May 5, 1978, AHSH, UdSSR, vol. 3, 1977–78, doc. 17.

43. Per Högselius, *Red Gas: Russia and the Origins of European Energy Dependence* (Basingstoke, UK: Palgrave Macmillan, 2013); Jeronim Perovic, *Cold War Energy: A Transnational History of Soviet Oil and Gas* (Basingstoke, UK: Palgrave Macmillan, 2017).

44. For the context, see *Alan Dobson, US Economic Statecraft for Survival, 1933–1991: Of Sanctions, Embargoes and Economic Warfare* (London: Routledge, 2002); Werner Lippert, "The Economics of Ostpolitik: West Germany, the United States, and the Gas Pipeline Deal," in *The Strained Alliance: U.S.-European Relations from Nixon to Carter*, ed. Matthias Schulz and Thomas A. Schwartz (Cambridge: Cambridge University Press, 2009), 65–81; Tyler Esno, "Reagan's Economic War on the Soviet Union," *Diplomatic History* 42, no. 2 (April 2018): 281–304.

45. See Memcon Schmidt and Brezhnev, November 24, 1981, *AAPD 1981* (Munich: Oldenbourg, 2012): 1837–47.

46. See statement by Liesen, Press Conference Ruhrgas, November 20, 1981, Bundesarchiv Koblenz (BArch), Bundesministerium für Wirtschaft (B 102), vol. 270508.

47. See Minutes of Meeting of Principals, June 6, 1980, DzD, ser. VI, vol. 6, 1979–80 (Munich: Oldenbourg Verlag, 2014): 606–10. For further materials on West Berlin's inclusion in the Urengoy project, see BArch, B 102/234235, 270475–270482, 600275 and BArch, Records of the Federal Chancellor's Office, B 136/19231–19232.

48. See Minutes of Meeting of Ministers, August 22, 1980, DzD, ser. VI, vol. 6, 1979–80: 703–14.

49. Memcon Bölling and Schalck-Golodkowski, September 23, 1981, DzD, ser. VI, vol. 7, 1981–82 (Munich: De Gruyter Oldenbourg, 2016): 282–85.

50. See note from Bölling to Schmidt, "Botschaft von GS Honecker an den Herrn Bundeskanzler," September 25, 1981, DzD, ser. VI, vol. 7, 1981–82: 291–94.

51. See Memcon Schalck-Golodkowski and Bölling, November 17, 1981, DzD, ser. VI, vol. 7, 1981–82: 336–38.

52. See Memcon Schalck-Golodkowski and Bräutigam, February 8, 1983, DzD, ser. VII, vol. 1, 1982–84 (Munich: De Gruyter Oldenbourg, 2018): 140–43.

53. Memcon Jenninger and Fischer, December 2, 1982, DzD, ser. VII, vol. 1, 1982–84: 71.

54. Letter Honecker to Kohl, October 5, 1983, DzD, ser. VII, vol. 1, 1982–84: 354.

55. Letter Kohl to Honecker, December 14, 1983, DzD, ser. VII, vol. 1, 1982–84: 454.

56. See Stephan Kieninger, "'Niemand will einen Rückfall in den Kalten Krieg': Franz Josef Strauß, Alexander Schalck-Golodkowski und der Milliardenkredit für die DDR 1983," Zeitschrift für Geschichtswissenschaft 65, no. 4 (2017): 352–71.

57. See Schalck-Golodkowski to Strauß, November 15, 1983, DzD, ser. VI, vol. 1 (1982–84): 413–14.

58. See Astrid M. Eckert, "Geteilt, aber nicht unverbunden: Grenzgewässer als deutsch-deutsches Umweltproblem," Vierteljahrshefte für Zeitgeschichte 62, no. 1 (2014): 69–99; Astrid M. Eckert, West Germany and the Iron Curtain: Environment, Economy, and Culture in the Borderlands (Oxford: Oxford University Press, 2019).

59. For a comprehensive account of the Kohl's Administration's policy toward the GDR, see Karl-Rudolf Korte, Deutschlandpolitik in Helmut Kohls Kanzlerschaft: Regierungsstil und Entscheidungen 1982–1989 (Stuttgart: Deutsche Verlags-Anstalt, 1998).

60. Remarks by Kohl in a meeting of the CDU's federal party board, April 25, 1983, in Helmut Kohl, Berichte zur Lage 1982–1989: Der Kanzler und Parteivorsitzende im Bundesvorstand der CDU Deutschlands, ed. Günter Buchstab and Hans-Otto Kleinmann (Düsseldorf: Droste Verlag, 2014, 90).

61. The ministers of finance exchanged letters to seal the guarantee. See Letter from Höfner to Stoltenberg, June 4, 1983, DzD, ser. VII, vol. 3: 237–38.

62. The contract for the loan was concluded on July 1, 1983. See "Kreditvertrag zwischen der Deutschen Außenhandelsbank Aktiengesellschaft und der

Bayerischen Landesbank International S.A. (Federführer) sowie der West LB International S.A., der HELABA Luxemburg Hessische Landesbank International S.A., der Badischen Kommunalen Landesbank International S.A., der Deutschen Girozentrale International S.A. und der Landesbank Rheinland-Pfalz und Saar International S.A," July 1, 1983, BArch, B 126 (Ministry of Finance), vol. 88275.

63. The "Militärregierungsgesetz 53" (over the regulation of currencies and the traffic of goods) had initially been an occupation law regulating the entire foreign trade of the Western occupation zone and the Western sectors of Berlin. The GDR and East Berlin were treated as foreign currency areas. MRG 53 was kept in place even after the Allied occupation status was lifted. The GDR time and again raised demands to loosen or to lift it. For a summary in terms of its implications for inner-German relations in the late 1970s, see Memo, Stern to Wischnewski, July 4, 1977, *DzD*, ser. VI, vol. 5, January 1, 1977–31 December 1978 (Munich: Oldenbourg, 2011): 224–26.

64. Memcon Strauß and Schalck, November 2, 1983, *DzD*, ser. VII, vol. 1: 384–89.

65. Memcon Wischnewski and Honecker, September 13, 1982, *DzD*, ser. VI, vol. 7: 899–916.

66. See Memcon Schmidt and Honecker, September 5, 1983, *DzD*, ser. VII, vol. 3: 311–20.

67. See Ludwig A. Rehlinger, *Freikauf: Die Geschäfte der DDR mit politisch Verfolgten 1963–1989* (Halle: Mitteldeutscher Verlag, 2011). For a comprehensive study, see Jan-Philipp Wölbern, *Der Häftlingsfreikauf aus der DDR 1962/63–1989: Zwischen Menschenhandel und humanitären Aktionen* (Göttingen: Vandenhoeck & Ruprecht, 2013).

68. See Memcon Honecker and Chernenko, June 14, 1984, *DzD*, ser. VII, vol. 1 (1982–84): 670–80.

69. See Memcon Honecker and Chernenko, August 17, 1984, *DzD*, ser. VII, vol. 1 (1982–84): 763–87.

70. See Anja Hanisch, *Die DDR im KSZE-Prozess, 1972–1985: Zwischen Ostabhängigkeit, Westabgrenzung und Ausreisebewegung* (Munich: Oldenbourg Verlag, 2012).

71. See Oliver Bange, *Sicherheit und Staat, Die Bündnis-und Militärpolitik der DDR im internationalen Kontext 1969 bis 1990* (Berlin: Ch. Links Verlag, 2017).

72. See Andreas Wirsching, *Abschied vom Provisorium: Die Geschichte der Bundesrepublik Deutschland 1982–1989/90* (Munich: Deutsche Verlags-Anstalt, 2006); Hans-Peter Schwarz, *Helmut Kohl: Eine politische Biographie* (Munich: Deutsche Verlags-Anstalt, 2012).

73. Memcon Kohl and Reagan, June 12, 1987, Ronald Reagan Presidential Library, Peter Sommer Papers, box 7.

74. Memo, UK Embassy in East Berlin to FCO "German Democratic Republic: Annual Review for 1987," by T. J. Everard, January 14, 1988, https://www.margaretthatcher.org/document/111017.

75. See, e.g., Sabine Löwe-Hannatzsch, *Sicherheit denken: Entspannungspolitik auf der zweiten Ebene, 1969–1990* (Bern: Peter Lang Verlag, 2019).

76. Memcon Thatcher and Diepgen, January 12, 1989, TNA, PREM 19/2698.

77. See Ronald Reagan, "Remarks on East-West Relations at the Brandenburg Gate in West Berlin," Ronald Reagan Presidential Library and Museum, June 12, 1987, https://www.reaganlibrary.gov/research/speeches/061287d.

78. Memcon Thatcher and Diepgen, December 16, 1986, TNA, PREM 19/2698.

79. For the context, see Barny White-Spunner, *Berlin: The Story of a City* (New York: Simon & Schuster, 2021).

80. See Bryan T. van Sweringen, *Kabarettist an der Front des kalten Krieges: Günter Neumann und das politische Kabarett in der Programmgestaltung des RIAS 1948–1968* (Passau: Rothe, 1995).

81. See Thomas Jerome Seabrook, *Bowie in Berlin: A New Career in a New Town* (London: Publishers Group, 2008).

CHAPTER 9

Berlin 1989 and the New Atlanticism

US and West German Visions for the Post–Cold War Architecture of Europe

PETER RIDDER

In 1989 politicians in East and West presented competing concepts on how to overcome the division of Europe.[1] The fall of the Berlin Wall, on November 9, 1989, was thereby a decisive moment. Overnight the people of Berlin peacefully forced the German question back on the agenda of international politics. The reunification of Germany soon became inevitable, and one month later US secretary of state James A. Baker traveled to West Berlin to present his ideas for "A New Europe—a New Atlanticism." The US concept represented a "conservative approach"[2] that was built on "prefab structures"[3] developed after 1945 and that should now help to integrate the socialist countries into the Western-dominated international system of 1989. The West German administration in contrast propagated its vision of a "European peace order" after 1988. Its goal was to peacefully unite the capitalist and democratic countries of Western Europe with the socialist states in Eastern Europe. I argue that in 1989 these concepts merged and prevailed, whereas alternative ideas, like Mikhail Gorbachev's "common European home" or François Mitterrand's Gaullist dream of a "European confederation," failed to succeed. And while the process underlines the importance of US–West German relations in 1989, it also reveals that the US administration was not acting in a spirit of triumph but was driven by severe concerns of losing influence in Europe after the end of the Cold War.

To support my thesis, I will first analyze the development of the concept of a European peace order promoted by Hans-Dietrich Genscher and Helmut Kohl. Second, I will take a closer look at the emergence of the US concept of a "commonwealth of free nations" presented by George H. W. Bush in May 1989. Third, I will finally show how perceptions on both sides changed in November 1989 and how US and West German visions for the future political architecture of Europe converged within the concept of a "New Atlanticism."

Current debates concentrate on the question of NATO expansion and whether there was a "broken promise,"[4] or what intentions led to decisions made during the Two-Plus-Four negotiations, which were later presented as a reason for the outbreak of a new war in Europe in February 2022.[5] This chapter, in contrast, focuses on the different mindsets within the West German and US administrations during 1989 and how they formed the conceptual base for the decisions made in 1990.

A EUROPEAN PEACE ORDER

The idea of a European peace order goes back to the West German *Ostpolitik* created by the Social Democratic politicians Egon Bahr and Willy Brandt in the 1960s. They wanted to ease tensions between Eastern and Western countries in Europe, and make possible some kind of peaceful coexistence, through bilateral agreements and multilateral cooperation.[6] A European peace order should create a sphere of peace and stability in Europe that—in the long run—would lead to a dissolution of borders, barbed wire, and minefields between the Eastern and Western countries. In that future, socialist and capitalist states should live together peacefully.[7]

The concept of a European peace order shaped the détente policy of the West German governments beginning in the mid-1960s,[8] finding its expression not only in Ostpolitik but in international and multilateral agreements. The Harmel Report[9] of 1967, in which NATO members formulated the new strategy of flexible response combining détente and deterrence, stated: "The relaxation of tensions is not the final goal but is part of a long-term process to promote better relations and to foster a European settlement. The ultimate political purpose of the alliance is to achieve a just and lasting peaceful order in Europe accompanied by appropriate security guarantees."[10]

When Helmut Schmidt took office in 1974, the term disappeared from the political discourse within the Federal Republic of Germany (FRG), but its basic ideas were sustained. The new foreign minister, Hans-Dietrich Genscher, continued to adapt the concept by focusing on human rights and multilateral politics. This led to the Helsinki Final Act of 1975, and to intensify the cultural and political exchange between Eastern and Western European countries, it initiated the Conference on Security and Cooperation in Europe (CSCE).[11]

In 1987 the term "European peace order" reappeared in reaction to Gorbachev's idea of a "common European home." For the West German foreign minister concept of a European peace order was now equivalent to Gorbachev's vision, and he believed that Perestroika and Glasnost resulted from the social-liberal foreign policy of the 1960s and 1970s.[12] Genscher's approach reflected his adherence to the spirit of détente and was based on the presumption that a peaceful order in Europe could only be achieved through multilateral cooperation, the extension of open markets, and common values like human rights and democracy.[13]

Helmut Kohl also adopted the idea of a European peace order and made it his own in 1988. Two convictions shaped his interpretation of the concept. First was a commitment to the transatlantic partnership. Kohl was convinced that the United States and NATO not only ensured European security but were also important factors in the democratization of Western Europe after 1945 that stabilized its political unity. A future political peace order in Europe therefore needed a strong transatlantic link to sustain. Second was the process of European integration. For Kohl a European peace order could only be achieved within the framework of the European Community (EC). He wanted to incorporate the Eastern European countries into this process as members of a future European entity that was not only an economic affiliation but a political union.[14]

Both interpretations were not exclusive. They merged in 1989, and Kohl and Genscher acted closely together to promote their vision. They were focusing on three institutions: first, NATO, with its dual track strategy, laid out in the Harmel Report, to animate Western countries to continue the détente policy toward the Soviet Union; second, the CSCE, an instrument for stabilizing change and preventing turmoil within the Eastern European countries by supporting the implementation of human rights; third, the EC, in its securing of freedom, prosperity, and the rule of law and its appeal to Eastern European countries to adopt these principles. The final goal was to reunite Europe in a new entity where socialist and capitalist countries could peacefully live together with open borders, shared values, and economic and cultural exchange. The end of the Cold War was therefore achieved by overcoming the ideological and physical division of Europe. For both politicians the reunification of Germany was thereby still a vision that ought to be this process's outcome.[15]

But this concept was contested within the political discourse in West Germany. The Social Democrats and the Green Party still adhered to the ideal of "democratic socialism" seeking demilitarization and transformation of the political system in all of Europe. Conservatives, however, thought the idea of a European peace order was too moderate and that the Western alliance should instead reinforce political and military pressure on the Soviet Union.[16] Even within the Western alliance, Kohl and Genscher were unable to convince their partners in 1988. The US administration had no interest in changing its grand strategy in the last year of Ronald Reagan's presidency, and the British and French also rejected the concept. The government of Margaret Thatcher mistrusted the success of Gorbachev's domestic policies and didn't believe that the Soviet system could be reformed. Moreover, she rejected an overly dominant role for the EC, and in her view NATO should confine itself to defense and not to take on any political tasks. For the French the concept was too *dirigiste,* too strict, too German. In addition, they did not want a political order for Europe in which the US and the Soviet Union were given a firm place.[17] French president Mitterrand later formulated his own vision about the future of Europe and proposed a "European Confederation of East and West," free of influence from the superpowers. Mitterrand feared that a strong US-German alliance could undermine France's future role in a unified Europe. He therefore obtained a firm commitment from Kohl for European integration.[18]

On December 7, 1988, the situation changed fundamentally with Gorbachev's famous speech at the UN General Assembly, where he declared the Cold War to be over and announced the dawn of a "New World Order." He presented a new vision based on his concept of a common European home.

Within this global concept, socialist and capitalist countries ought to work together and both superpowers should lead the international community through multilateral cooperation into a peaceful, prosperous, and secure future. His speech changed the international narrative, and the Western alliance came under pressure to present their own vision on how to unite Europe and end the Cold War.[19]

"A COMMONWEALTH OF FREE NATIONS"

In January 1989 the new US president had no coherent strategy on how to deal with the changing situation in Europe. Bush was generally recognized as not being creative in what he himself called the "vision thing."[20] For him there was no need for a new world order at that time, as he had already made clear in his inaugural address:

> We know what works: Freedom works. We know what's
> right: Freedom is right. We know how to secure a more just
> and prosperous life for man on earth: through free markets,
> free speech, free elections, and the exercise of free will un-
> hampered by the state. For the first time in this century, for
> the first time in perhaps all history, man does not have to
> invent a system by which to live. We don't have to talk late
> into the night about which form of government is better.
> We don't have to wrest justice from the kings. We only have
> to summon it from within ourselves. We must act on what
> we know.[21]

Nevertheless, Bush knew that Gorbachev had the initiative and was domi-nating the public debate about the future of Europe. Moreover, the new president was worried that the Soviet secretary general could use this advan-tage to pit the Allies against each other, split the alliance, and undermine the American dominance on the Continent. Shortly after moving into the Oval Office, he therefore warned a journalist: "If we don't regain leadership, things are going to fall apart."[22]

The new US administration was in a tight spot to win back the initia-tive within public discourse, and the overall situation was not advantageous. The US economy was still struggling after the 1987 stock market crash, and the fiscal deficit was growing dangerously. Germany and Japan had become serious economic competitors, and on Capitol Hill politicians feared that European integration could lead to a "Fortress Europe,"[23] wherein US companies were forced out of the European single market set to emerge in 1992. Domestically, the decreasing tensions between the Soviet Union and the United State aroused peoples doubts about the US engagement in Europe and the huge military spending on European security. Adding more concerns, West Germany, a vital NATO member, was, from the perspective of some foreign policy experts—including Henry Kissinger and Richard R. Burt—in danger of switching sides and colluding with Gorbachev to achieve reunification. The controversy about the modification of the NATO Short Nuclear Force (SNF) amplified concerns about the transatlantic alliance disintegrating.[24] All these developments increased the fear of an "imperial overstretch"—as it had recently been predicted by Paul Kennedy in his famous book *The Rise and Fall of the Great Powers*.[25] Kennedy's thesis received much criticism.[26] At the same time it catalyzed public debate about the future role of US leadership in a globalized world, and the fear of US decline became a central theme of the presidential election campaign in 1988, which also then shaped the new administration's perspective in 1989.

Initially, in the first three months, the new administration kept a low public profile, in order to carefully assess the situation and to design a strategy to counter the complex and dynamic developments. To this end, the Bush administration also consulted with its closest allies, including the FRG, an important partner.

In early February, Bush and Kohl exchanged letters, sketching out their views on international developments. The chancellor also sent a delegation to Washington to negotiate a solution of the SNF problem. During these exchanges, Kohl and his envoys began advertising the idea of a European peace order. Kohl laid out that the fortieth anniversary of NATO offered an opportunity for presenting a new strategy for the alliance that also included a vision for the future of Europe. He argued that for the last four decades NATO had underwritten freedom, human dignity, human rights, and self-determination in Western Europe and that it would remain the guarantor of common security on the Continent. A new strategy therefore had to combine two elements that had prevailed in the past: security and arms control. Both elements would help to overcome the division of Europe and create a peaceful order for the future.[27]

In mid-February, Baker traveled to Europe to meet with his Allied counterparts. On his stop in Bonn, he talked with Genscher and Kohl, who again promoted their ideas about the future NATO strategy and a European peace order. Beyond that, Genscher pointed out why he saw the EC as important for the future of Europe and why it had to be included in any future concepts. For him, Eastern Europeans saw Europe's integration as the model of freedom that attracted them and motivated their political reforms. Moreover, Genscher said if people in the US asked, "Where do the Germans want to go?" the answer was simple: "Even more into the European Community. Even more into the free world."[28] He described European integration as the most important factor in creating a truly peaceful and stable Europe.

Kohl in contrast underlined that for him there was no substitute for NATO. There was "no 'third way,' no 'walking between the worlds,'" as he made clear.[29] Germany would always be on the US's side. But he also warned Baker that this stance would be up for discussion if the Social Democrats gained a majority in the upcoming elections in 1990. He then referred to the idea of the Harmel Report, that NATO use the arms control issue to ease tensions between East and West and therefore contribute to a peaceful settlement in Europe. Moreover, the chancellor tried to convince Baker to put trust in Gorbachev and his political reforms. Even though Kohl said that no one could know if the Soviet secretary general would be successful, but if he was, "we would experience a true triumph, because communism would be reduced to absurdity after 70 years."[30]

The first meeting between Baker, Genscher, and Kohl illustrates three important aspects: first, the good and intensive exchange between the two sides; second, how the German government tried to implement their ideas of a European peace order into the NATO overall concept; third, how reserved the new US administration acted in early 1989. At no point did Baker express specific ideas about the future of Europe. Instead, he listened to Genscher's and Kohl's remarks attentively and approvingly.

Back in Washington the administration started working on its own vision for the future of Europe. President Bush instructed the National Security Council "to produce a political concept of the future of Europe, incorporating judgments about likely evolution of its division between East and West and a sense of new opportunities for the United States in continuing to assure that our relations with western Europe develop in an environment of stability, prosperity and community." Bush made clear to the NSC that "the central importance of American leadership remains. This leadership must set a positive course for the future . . . in setting the agenda for a reinvigorated Atlantic community." He never questioned US dominance in Europe and was against isolationist demands. But he thereby anticipated the main intention of the future concept: to preserve US leadership in Europe.[31]

Concerning Eastern Europe, he reaffirmed: "Our objectives in that region, to see popular aspirations for liberty, prosperity and self-determination met, are still valid." However, he ruled from the outset that "those aspirations cannot be realized as long as the Soviet occupation of East-Central Europe continues." Accordingly, the people of Eastern Europe could not achieve freedom under Soviet rule, meaning that their countries had to detach themselves from the Soviet zone of influence and that the Soviet Union's dominance in Eastern Europe had to be pushed back. This reveals a major difference from the West German idea of a European peace order. For Bush a peaceful coexistence of socialism and capitalism in Europe was not possible.[32]

On the defense strategy Bush revealed how his experience[33] shaped his perception of the present and influenced his conception of the future: "Throughout the post-war era, we have successfully provided for the security of the United States and for the furtherance of our security interests in the world by following a broad national defense strategy of containment."[34] Containment had been introduced by President Harry S. Truman in response to the expansion of the Soviet sphere of influence after World War II. Although elements of this doctrine were indeed relevant throughout the Cold War, it was an oversimplification to reduce the US grand strategy of the past four decades entirely to the Truman Doctrine of 1947. In doing so, Bush not only omitted President Dwight D. Eisenhower's "roll-back" strategy of the 1950s but also, and more important, the détente policies of the 1960s and 1970s that emphasized cooperation rather than containment.[35] This shows that Bush, unlike his European partners, attached far less importance to the policy of détente for current developments. Accordingly, he concluded: "Our rebuilding of American military strength has served as an essential underpinning to our past success. We must preserve that strength as the underpinning for our future efforts. Changes in Soviet domestic and foreign policies, including some announced but not yet implemented, are hopeful signs. But it would be reckless to dismantle our military strength and the policies that have helped make the world less dangerous, and foolish to assume that all dangers have disappeared or that any apparent diminution is irreversible."[36] Instead of approaching Gorbachev as Kohl and Genscher did, Bush urged caution and to maintain the political pressure on Moscow. He also clearly distanced himself from the policy of his predecessor, who had improved relations with the Soviet Union in a series of summit meetings beginning in 1986.[37] Instead, Bush proceeded from the 1940s policy of military deterrence. He still saw the Soviet Union as the major threat and wanted to regain the upper hand in Europe. For Bush the Cold War was not over in early 1989.

However, he knew that this strategy came at a high price and that the ever-increasing military budget was a major cause of the growing US national debt; he needed to reduce spending on the military without minimizing its potential. Bush therefore instructed the NSC to prepare a proposal for the reduction of troops in Europe and possible disarmament initiatives of conventional weapons without the US losing its military strength.[38]

As the new president had announced in his inaugural address, he did not want to reinvent the world but to adapt the system already established in the West to the new situation and thus preserve it for the future: "I do not expect this review to invent a new defense strategy for a new world. On the contrary. I believe that our fundamental purposes are enduring and that the broad elements of our current strategy—our alliance, our military capabilities—remain sound. This defense review should assess how, with limited resources, we can best maintain our strength, preserve our alliance, and meet our commitments in this changing but still dangerous world."[39] These assumptions in the National Security Reviews formed the basis on which the new administration built its concept of a future order for Europe. Bush was thus presenting an essentially conservative approach aimed at preserving existing structures rather than developing new ones.[40]

The first response to the president's request came a month later from Brent Scowcroft. In a memorandum dated March 20, the security adviser discusses "what vision for the future of Europe" the United States should present to their allies at the NATO summit in May. Scowcroft advised the president to point out a political goal for the year 2000:

> The weakness in Gorbachev's notion of a "common European home" is that its occupancy is defined by geography; also, if the East Europeans could, they would evict the Soviets from

their part of the home. The Americans, on the other hand,
can only be guests in a home so defined. The real glue that
binds the Atlantic Alliance is commonality of <u>values,</u> not geography. This premise suggests that we advocate the existence
of a "Commonwealth of Free Nations." The Atlantic Alliance
forms the core of this group, but it embraces any country
that truly shares its values. Within Europe, the CSCE process
offers guideposts for Eastern movement toward a true sense
of shared ideals. We hope that all the countries of Eastern
Europe will be part of this commonwealth as they, one by
one, rejoin the Western cultural and political tradition that is
part of their heritage.[41]

For Scowcroft, Europe and the United States were united by a common history, culture, demography, values, and security needs. American
power was thereby essential for any stable equilibrium on the Continent:
"In years to come, only we can balance the inherent strength of what is
still, and likely will remain, the dominant military power in the Eurasian
landmass—the Soviet Union. Geopolitical realities will endure. Of course,
Gorbachev is less threatening than his predecessors. So, in its day, was the
Weimar Republic." The United States thus had to remain the dominant
political power in Europe to protect peace and unity on the Continent in
the future.[42]

NATO was essential for preserving American influence in Europe, and
the fidelity of the FRG as a key ally within the alliance was "uniquely in-
dispensable to the success of that policy." That is why, he said, Bush should
do everything he can to support Kohl's domestic position and prevent the
country from getting closer to Moscow. A vision for Europe's future thus
had to include the "German question," Scowcroft noted. Bush should
not promise immediate political reunification but offer some promise of
change, of movement. In dealing with Gorbachev the president should
point out that the US welcomed perestroika to the degree that it humanized
the USSR at home and demilitarized it abroad. The goal had to be that
someday the US would be able to deal with the Soviet Union on the same
normal and equal terms as with other states—maybe by the year 2000.

The main part of Scowcroft's memo then focused on a possible arms control initiative to be presented on the upcoming NATO summit in late May.

This initiative "reiterate[d] the need for a continuation of extended nuclear deterrence as the ultimate guarantor of NATO's strategy of flexible response." It should therefore stress "that the Alliance's military security depends on the maintenance of adequate deterrent and defensive capabilities during this turbulent period." But it should also offer "hope for a less militarized Europe." The president had to point out that the current proposal on conventional force reduction talks, which aimed at getting two sides to parity, "is not the end of the story. Part of Europe's return to normalcy must include a passing of the period when it was necessary to have millions of armed men face each other in Central Europe." Scowcroft's ideas about the future role of NATO were very close to the Harmel Report, though he didn't mention that. Finally, he again brought up the idea of an "Open Skies" agreement, first announced by President Eisenhower in 1955, the idea being to exchange extensive information on military installations with the Soviets by letting both sides do routine aerial overflights: "That idea would also underscore that the Soviets are now acting on what has always been our agenda."[43]

A second memorandum, from Philip Zelikow on April 13, followed the same line. The author adopted the idea of a "Commonwealth of Free Nations," based not on geography but on shared values and common experience.[44] But his additional counsel was to welcome the political role of the EC and to say that the US was eager to develop and intensify the mechanisms of consultation and cooperation as well as manage the transition to a common European single market in 1992. He also provided detail on the conventional arms initiative, proposing moreover a CSCE summit in 1990 to monitor progress made in the implementation of human rights in Eastern Europe. Zelikow's memorandum was a supplement to Scowcroft's concept, adding more details about the future role of NATO, EC, and CSCE. Both papers set the main theme for Bush's vision in 1989.

Another approach was presented by Bruce Gelb, the director of the United States Information Agency. He proposed a public initiative focusing on the Berlin Wall, in reference to Reagan's famous speech in 1987. This idea was rejected by the members of the NSC, because they thought that it was "unlikely to evoke the broad moral pressure it intends, nor will it persuade Moscow that it is 'in its own best interest' to tear down the Wall. While the occasional well-placed speech is a highly useful reminder of the hideous symbol of Europe's division, a sustained campaign might be seen as empty posturing."[45]

However, the State Department outlined their ideas for a Berlin initiative shortly afterward to Baker. This concept was remarkably similar to the West German idea of a European peace order.[46] It focused on three major institutions: first, NATO, to build a new security structure for Europe by reducing its military component and enhancing its political role; second, the EC, to strengthen institutional and consultative ties as well as to encourage its cooperation with the Eastern Europeans; and third, the CSCE, to develop the security basket through new confidence-building measures to reduce the risk of war, to enhance the economic basket by working together on conceptual and practical questions involved in transition from planning economies to free competitive markets, and to build on progress on human rights in general. Although the idea of a Berlin initiative that carried forward Reagan's 1987 approach was rejected, Baker kept its core elements in mind.

The review process was concluded in late April, and after a four-month-long "policy pause," the Bush administration went public to demonstrate that "a coherent world view" had emerged from this process.[47] The campaign to regain the upper hand in the narrative about the future of Europe began on May 12 with a speech at Texas A&M University, in which Bush presented the results of the review on the Soviet Union. Bush acknowledged the ongoing transformation in Eastern Europe and offered Gorbachev the opportunity to "move beyond containment." He declared that the new strategy of his administration was not simply aimed at containing Soviet expansionism but rather at integrating the Soviet Union and the Eastern European countries into the "community of nations" by supporting democratization and market reforms. However, he also urged his listeners still to be cautious and to stay strong, so that the Soviet Union would have no reward in pursuing expansionism again. He formulated five demands Gorbachev should fulfill to prove that he was trustworthy, and he also proposed the Open Skies agreement.[48]

Bush's speech in Texas was not well received. His demands were the same Gorbachev himself had offered earlier in New York. Moreover, the use of the outdated term "containment" irritated West German and Soviet diplomats alike, and while Bonn judged the choice of his words as unfortunate, Moscow received them as aggressive and insulting.[49] The international response was correspondingly critical, and many people within the US were disappointed, as Baker retrospectively admitted.[50] Despite this critique, the first contours of the US government's new concept of European order emerged here. The main goal was to integrate the Soviet Union into the (Western) international system developed after World War II.

In his second speech, in Boston on May 21, Bush presented the results of the review of relations to Western European countries. In the presence of French president Mitterrand, Bush praised the European American community as being held together not only by a common enemy but above all by cultural ties and shared values: "Our ideals are those of the American Bill of Rights and the French Declaration of the Rights of Man."[51] He argued that "it is precisely because the ideals of this community are universal that the world is in ferment today . . . a resurgent western Europe is an economic magnet, drawing eastern Europe closer toward the commonwealth of free nations." The EC was therefore seen as the driving force for political change in Eastern Europe, animating the political progress through its Soft Power. Bush thus concluded that "a strong, united Europe means a strong America."

But beyond that he explained to the American audience why the United States needed to remain engaged in Europe: "We must never forget that twice in this century American blood has shed over conflicts that began in Europe. And we share the fervent desire of Europeans to relegate war forever to the province of distant memory. But that is why the Atlantic Alliance is so central to our foreign policy. And that's why America remains committed to the Alliance and the strategy which has preserved freedom in Europe. We must never forget that to keep the peace in Europe is to keep peace for America." NATO was important because "behind this shield, the nations of western Europe have risen from privation to prosperity, all because of the strength and resolve of free people." In his Boston speech Bush publicly mentioned the idea of a commonwealth of free nations for the first time. Although he did not go into detail and focused on the relations with the EC, this speech shows how the American future concept took shape. It assumed that Europe and the United States were connected by common values and that Eastern European countries could become part of this community by adopting these values.

The climax of the public campaign was the NATO summit on May 30. On his arrival in Brussels, Bush repeated the central idea of his concept in front of the press. NATO had guaranteed peace and freedom in Europe for forty years and would continue to do so in the future. The EC was the center of a free, prosperous, and peaceful Europe, and the Soviet Union and the Eastern European states should be integrated into the community of free nations: "As I've said a number of times, we seek to move beyond containment. We want to see an end to the division of Europe, and we want to see it ended on the basis of western values. We will join western European nations in encouraging the process of change in the Soviet Union, pointing to the day when the Soviet Union will be welcomed as a constructive participant in the community of free nations."[52]

During the following internal meeting of the NATO council, Bush elaborated on his ideas. The transatlantic alliance had made a "long peace"[53] possible. This was the result of shared values and the joint defense of these values by NATO: "Now our success has yielded a chance to enter a new era, one in which we hope the rewards of freedom and prosperity can be shared by all of Europe." Western values should be enforced throughout all of Europe with the help of the EC, NATO, and CSCE. "The West has succeeded in setting today's international agenda. Now we must look ahead on the kind of future we want to build." A strong EC, he said, was in the US interest because it accelerates the enforcement of those values. For that reason, he stated, the EC also remained a "partner in world leadership." NATO too would build up pressure through a disarmament initiative to promote change by creating incentives to adopt Western values: "A major part of NATO's new mission is opening up eastern Europe to western values and freedoms." The CSCE could help to spread those values and to ensure that they were implemented and adhered. It could develop standards for conducting free elections and send election officials to the Eastern European states and the Soviet Union: "Ultimately, it is the responsibility of the east Europeans to bring about change, but our goal must be to encourage it, guide it to the extent we can, and welcome those who wish to join the commonwealth of free nations."[54] Bush's remarks were well received by the participants and contributed significantly to the overall success of the summit. NATO expressed its unity and a willingness to act. On the SNF question a compromise was reached, and the final declaration expressed not only the president's ideas but also the West German government's concept. A closer look at the declaration shows that terms like "Commonwealth of Free Nations" or "containment" are missing in the document. Instead, the references to the West German concept of a European peace order are remarkable: "We want to overcome the painful division of Europe, which we have never accepted. We want to move beyond the post-war period. Based on today's momentum of increased co-operation and tomorrow's common challenges, we seek to shape a new political order of peace in Europe." This order of peace should be based on the recognition of common values: "In keeping with our values, we place primary emphasis on basic freedoms for the people in Eastern Europe. These are also key elements for strengthening the stability and security of all states and for guaranteeing lasting peace on the continent." The declaration directly referred to the Harmel Report and emphasized the interplay between deterrence and détente for NATO's future as a political organization that promotes a peaceful transition in Europe. The declaration thus represents a synthesis of both concepts.[55]

The final act followed on May 31. Bush joined Kohl and Genscher to consolidate the strategically important alliance. In a speech in Mainz, Bush connected all elements of his concept. Its goal therefore was to "move beyond containment" and to integrate the Soviet Union and the Eastern Europe countries into the "commonwealth of free nations, . . . [to] let Europe be whole and free." Concerning the reunification of Germany, he declared: "Just as the barriers are coming down in Hungary, so they must fall throughout all of eastern Europe. Let Berlin be next—let Berlin be next! Nowhere is the division between East and West seen more clearly than in Berlin. And there this brutal wall cuts neighbor from neighbor, brother from brother. And that wall stands as a monument to the failure of communism. It must come down." Moreover, to strengthen the political ties to West Germany, Bush extended an offer to Kohl to become a "partner in leadership."[56] Flattered by the offer, the chancellor knew that it was a win-win situation for both: Kohl needed a strong ally to strengthen his domestic standing and to enforce the international acceptance for his idea of a European peace order; for Bush this partnership offered him prime access to European politics beyond NATO. West Germany had a lot of leverage in Eastern Europe, and as a major economic power and a founding member of the EC, the country was a strategic anchor for US interests in Europe.

The concept of a commonwealth of free nations took up key aspects of the idea of a European peace order. Western values such as democracy, human rights, and a free-market economy should be implemented, while institutions such as the EC, the CSCE, and NATO promoted and guided this process. But in contrast it was built on the notion that the socialist states be integrated into the Western-dominated international system. A peaceful coexistence of different political systems was not intended; instead, it was common values that secured peace and security in the future and preserved America's influence on the Continent. For the US administration the Cold War was still not over, and they wanted to regain the advantage.

NEW ATLANTICISM

The rapid developments in Eastern Europe during the summer of 1989 and, finally, the fall of the Berlin Wall changed the perception in the US administration: an end to the Cold War suddenly seemed possible. But alongside joy over the events, there was growing concern that the situation might get out of control and that the US would lose influence once Europe was united. These concerns accelerated the pressure on the US government to present a new strategy for handling the situation and laying out a more coherent concept for the future of Europe.

During the summer, when the Iron Curtain began to disintegrate in Hungary and the Polish people elected a non-Communist prime minister, there was still great mistrust toward Gorbachev within the Bush administration.[57] The violent crackdown on protests in China reinforced the skepticism within the White House that the path toward a "Europe whole and free" would be smooth. The Soviet secretary general had not condemned the violence in Beijing explicitly (though neither did Bush), and during a visit in Paris he warned that for him it would be "unreal" and "dangerous" if some said they would like "to see the problem of Europe solved by the displacement of socialism."[58] However, just a day later Gorbachev again reaffirmed, in front of the European Council, that he would respect the right of each people to choose their political system. NSC members still kept their "residual doubts" that "stem from the nagging suspicion that somewhere out there, there is a limit to that tolerance," as they pointed out to the president in late June.[59]

Nevertheless, the West Germans tried to convince Bush to intensify cooperation with Gorbachev and to get more engaged. Since May Bush and Kohl had been in close contact and regularly exchanged views about the rapidly changing situation. Kohl and Genscher tried their best to persuade the US president to put trust in Gorbachev. Kohl reported in detail about his meeting with Gorbachev in June and confirmed to Bush that Gorbachev had again committed to the right of self-determination.[60] Bush "listened very carefully" but still did not seem convinced that the "hour of . . . triumph"[61] was near, as Kohl had suggested earlier.[62] When Genscher talked with Bush and Baker during a visit in Washington in late June, he assured them that he had stressed during a meeting with Gorbachev in Bonn that "any discussion about the future of Europe must include the US and Canada as part of this Europe, this 'common European home.'" Genscher speculated now that "Gorbachev feels that US involvement in Europe is in Soviet interests."[63] This was not quite true. During Gorbachev's visit to Bonn from June 12 to 15, the secretary general complained about Bush's reluctance and that his public statements about a sudden withdrawal of Soviet troops from Eastern Europe "would disrupt the process of building trust between the East and the West and destroy everything that has been achieved so far."[64] But with his intimations to Bush that Gorbachev invited the USA to join the "common European home," Genscher wanted to convince the president to take the lead of the rapprochement process between East and West.

Bush's thinking began to change only when he traveled to Poland and Hungary, where he met with their new, reform-minded leaders on July 9 and 10. They convinced him of their willingness to overcome Communist rule and to implement economic, and democratic, reforms. And when Bush spoke in front of cheering and applauding crowds in Gdansk and Budapest, he was "touched by the emotional response he received" and acknowledged that "new and extraordinary possibilities exist. Those very possibilities make it realistic to think in terms of moving toward a Europe whole and free."[65] Bush realized that the political transformation in these countries was irreversible, and that the US was close to missing a historical chance if it did not act immediately.[66]

Thus, during his flight back to Washington, the president decided to write Gorbachev a letter and ask for a personal informal meeting to "sit down and talk . . . to reduce the chance that there could be misunderstanding between us . . . [and] to get our relationship on a more personal basis."[67] Gorbachev accepted the invitation, but negotiations about the meeting site became complicated and long lasting. Meanwhile, starting in September, thousands of East German refugees fled to the West German embassy in Prague, their goal to escape from there to the FRG. In Leipzig every Monday, more and more people took to the streets to demonstrate against the socialist regime of Erich Honecker. And while the situation in the GDR deteriorated further, international and domestic pressure on Bush grew.

On October 11 NATO secretary general Manfred Wörner, in a conversation with the US president, urged him to maintain his "strong leadership during this time of uncertainty." The West German Christian Democrat counseled Bush to "use the alliance for managing East-West relations. . . . We need to identify NATO more as a political alliance dealing with political change. Your leadership during the summit galvanized the alliance. We still live on that. We should follow up on the summit declaration to link NATO with positive values like peace, change and greater freedom." To support his request, Wörner further argued that

> although this is not for the public, the EC role in Poland is good but now there is a pattern of leaving things to Europe. It is in the interest of the U.S. to use NATO as a political platform to coordinate policy, not just on defense, but as an instrument for your leadership and influence. . . . Many groups are now involved with eastern Europe—The EC, the OECD, the World Bank, etc. NATO should not take their place in implementing policy, but we need one place for coordination of common approach. The role of NATO here is equivalent to visible American Leadership. . . . Don't let the Europeans go their own way.

Bush reacted cautiously. After he had to admit that he needed to make cuts in the defense budget that hopefully "will not have too strong . . . effects on our allies in Europe," he cautioned Wörner that "we should just not be imprudent, not push the Soviets beyond that hidden line. . . . You don't handle this with a new initiative every day or call the shots on how fast change will come to all these governments." The president concluded that it was better to "stay on the high ground."[68]

Kohl also appealed to Bush to deliver a public message on NATO and that "changes in the east are only possible if we stand together." He needed Bush's support because he was under severe domestic pressure from the left. More and more people in West Germany doubted the future role of NATO and were thereby criticizing the chancellor's policy. Bush confirmed his endorsement and complained that "we are getting criticism in the Congress from liberal Democrats that we ought to be doing more to foster change, but I am not going to go so fast as to be reckless."[69]

Bush held back and waited for his meeting with Gorbachev before making plans on how to move on. But the fear of losing ground in Europe became imminent even within the US administration. Francis Fukuyama, who had just published his famous article "The End of History?"[70] visited Bonn in late October. At that time Fukuyama was serving as deputy director of the State Department's Policy Planning Staff. During a meeting with his West German counterparts, he expressed great concerns that overcoming the status quo in Europe could diminish the role of the US and that the opening of the EC to Eastern Europe was seen as a critical issue in Washington. If the EC was successful in acting as a magnet for the whole of Europe and gradually created pan-European structures, the question for the Americans was whether there was still a place for them in Europe.[71]

Still, the US administration remained on its high ground to observe the situation. Meanwhile, Soviet and US negotiators agreed on an informal summit meeting in early December in the Mediterranean Sea off the island of Malta. But events escalated fast. On November 7, with the situation in the GDR further deteriorating, a journalist challenged Bush during a press conference: "You have failed to show leadership. You have failed to put the U.S. ahead of the curve on these things that are happening. . . . Why don't you have any new ideas."[72]

The fall of the Berlin Wall on November 9 amplified the fear of losing control of events and changed the US perception of Gorbachev and his policy, not overnight but in its aftermath. When the wall came down everyone was caught by surprise. Helmut Kohl, who was on a state visit in Poland when he received the news, rushed back from Warsaw the next day to deliver an emotional speech in front of a hissing crowd (the conservative politician was not popular in Berlin). He nonetheless went on by thanking the United States and Gorbachev for their support in making this "great historical day" possible. "Unity, law and freedom"—slogans of the West German national anthem—were lying ahead for a "free German Fatherland," he announced.

On the other side of the Atlantic, Bush and Baker, overwhelmed by the events, stumbled into a press conference, where they did not have much to say besides the fact that they were "very pleased with this development."[73] The next day Kohl called Bush from the chancellor's office in Bonn and reported enthusiastically on his impressions. While the chancellor was talking, Bush made handwritten notes that reveal what was really on his mind. "No conflicts. . . . No Tiananmen here," he wrote. This shows that the fear of another massacre like that in Beijing was still dominant. But further notes also reveal Bush's conviction that a continued American presence in Europe had to be a vital component of whatever came next to "keep the West secure."[74]

The Bush administration needed time to assess the new situation, but the chancellor couldn't wait any longer. On November 28 Kohl announced what he called his Ten-Point Program in the Bundestag, proposing a slow and cautious approach to achieve a European peace order. With such an approach, the establishment of "confederate structures" should lead to the unification of Germany and Europe. That would be done within the framework of European integration, supported by enhanced CSCE negotiations and backed by strong transatlantic ties to the United States.[75] The incorporation of the reunification process into an EC, CSCE, and US alliance should assure Germany's neighbors that a reunified Germany would not be a threat to them in future. Kohl intentionally did not mention NATO, because he was aware that NATO membership of a reunified Germany would be the most difficult question in the upcoming negotiations with the Soviet Union.[76]

Although worried that Kohl had not mentioned NATO, Bush in general welcomed the chancellor's initiative. Kohl's approach set the conditions for the president, who, according to historian Jeffrey Engel, "wanted calm in the heart of Europe. But he also saw in Germany's unification an opportunity to cement an American place across the Atlantic for the foreseeable future, no matter what Gorbachev's revolution might ultimately bring."[77]

Besides Kohl, Bush was the only Western leader in November 1989 who welcomed the idea of a reunification of Germany. He had three reasons. First, he did not see Germany as a potential threat, unlike Margaret Thatcher and others. For Bush, democracy had been established on solid ground in the FRG, and the country was a crucial partner within the Atlantic alliance.

The second point was that he did not blame Germany alone for the violent history of Europe. Bush feared that without American oversight European countries would once again fall back into their past belligerent patterns. Organizations like the EC were only possible because the United States had stabilized the democratization and economic recovery after World War II, and for Bush it seemed inevitable that without the US the "European squabbling" would come back and undermine the "Long Peace" established after 1945.[78] He thus made clear that "in a New Europe, the American role may change in form but not in fundamentals. . . . We will remain in Europe."[79]

Third, the fate of Germany was decisive for the US. Already, in August 1989, Scowcroft had pointed out to the president that "managing our relations with Germany is likely to be the most serious geopolitical challenge our country faces over the next decade, unless we have to cope with a disintegrating Soviet Union." Bonn's public repudiation of the alliance position on SNF was unprecedented and threatened the very basis of extended nuclear deterrence, on which the security of NATO, and Europe, rested, the security adviser explained. For Scowcroft, Genscher was the driving force behind these efforts and therefore needed to be stopped: "The immediate challenge for U.S. leadership in Europe is not Gorbachev's 'common European house' but the growing attraction of 'Genscherism,' a vision strong on disarmament and détente, but devoid of a security dimension." That's why the security adviser counseled Bush to support Kohl domestically and weaken Genscher's influence on West German foreign policy. In November 1989 Bush and Scowcroft knew that the chancellor had not informed his foreign minister in advance about his actions and that the two had a tense relationship. The US president now saw a chance to turn them against each other.[80] While Kohl's Ten-Point Plan frightened other European leaders, who feared that a reunified Germany would upset the existing order, Bush recognized the opportunity to secure US influence in Europe and create a stable order for the future.

When Bush met with Gorbachev at Malta on December 2 and 3, 1989, he had already placed himself behind Kohl's concept. After the Soviet leader was reassured that Bush would not "dance on the wall," Gorbachev reaffirmed that he would not interfere. The Brezhnev-Doctrine thereby became history, and Bush accepted the fact that the Cold War was finally over.[81]

At the following NATO summit in Brussels, Bush presented the first ideas for the future shape of "A New Europe" and "A New Atlanticism," as he called them. But it was Baker's job, after the summit, to present the whole strategy to the public. In his speech on December 12 in front of the Berlin Press Club at the Steigenberger Hotel, the secretary of state sketched out the new US vision for the future architecture of a post–Cold War Europe. The core elements of this concept were based on the ideas that were outlined for the Berlin Initiative in April 1989, and the idea of a New Atlanticism followed the same three lines. The first was to transform NATO into a political forum for consultation between Western countries so that it could sustain in future, even without the Soviet threat. Second was to accept that the

European integration would form the framework for a unified Europe and to assure the United States that it would be part of this process; to codify this, Baker demanded a "transatlantic declaration" to secure future consultation and cooperation between the EC and the US. Third was to enforce the CSCE as an instrument to support the rapprochement and transformation in Eastern Europe: "On this basis, a new Atlanticism will flourish, and a new Europe will be born."[82]

The concept of a New Atlanticism combined key aspects of the West German European peace order as well as Bush ideas developed around the concept of a commonwealth of free nations. Its creation reveals how different perceptions influenced each other and thereby illustrates the crucial role of the US–West German partnership in 1989. Furthermore, it shows that the US government was mainly motivated by concerns of losing influence on the Continent when Europe would unite.

* * *

The relations between the United States and Europe were at a crossroads in 1989. Kohl's concept of a European peace order changed in 1990 when he realized that the socialist system in the GDR would collapse, and the idea of peaceful coexistence would thus become obsolete. But the idea of a New Atlanticism prevailed during the following Two-Plus-Four negotiations and shaped the reunification of Germany and Europe.

Years later, participants like Condoleezza Rice, Philip Zelikow, and Robert Hutchings described this as a moment of triumph in the history of US foreign policy. In their view, Baker and Bush had recognized the opportunity to reunite Germany, to win the Cold War, and to establish a post–Cold War order in benefit for the whole of Europe.[83] This triumphalist historical narrative was enhanced during the Donald J. Trump administration, when scholars contrasted the "prudent" and "forward looking" diplomacy of Bush and Baker with Trump's "erratic" and "short-sighted" foreign policy.[84] Vladimir Putin's argument, that the United States exploited the situation to expand NATO and encircle Russia, amplified this triumphalist interpretation of the events of 1989. This chapter shows that the US administration was not led by a spirit of triumph but, rather, by uncertainty and deep concerns in 1989 of losing influence after the Cold War ended. The administration wanted to secure its position to create a stable and peaceful equilibrium in Europe. But the peace order thereby created became history with the Russian invasion of Ukraine. War has returned to the Continent, underlining the importance of a vital Western alliance to reestablish peace in Europe.

NOTES

1. I want to thank Katerina Banks and Friedrich J. Asschenfeldt for digitizing archival documents for me in the USA, when COVID made it impossible for me to visit these archives myself.

2. Kristina Spohr, *Post Wall, Post Square: Rebuilding the Word after 1989* (London: William Collins, 2019), 18.

3. Mary Elise Sarotte, *1989: The Struggle to Create Post–Cold War Order* (Princeton, NJ: Princeton University Press, 2009), 119–49.

4. See, e.g., Mary Elise Sarotte, *Not One Inch: America, Russia, and the Making of Post–Cold War Stalemate* (New Haven, CT: Yale University Press, 2021); Sergey Radchenko, Timothy Andrews Sayle, and Christian Ostermann, eds., "NATO: Contested Histories and Future Directions," special issue, *Journal of Strategic Studies* 43, no. 6–7 (2020).

5. This chapter was written in March 2022, shortly after the Russian invasion of Ukraine.

6. That's not equivalent to the Soviet concept of "peaceful coexistence."

7. Rachèle Raus, "Egon Bahr und das Konzept einer 'europäischen Friedensordnung' (1963–1970)," CVCE, 2006, https://www.cvce.eu/obj/rachele_raus _egon_bahr_und_das_konzept_einer_europaischen_friedensordnung_1963 _1970-de-72b54117-68d2-450a-92aa-8ca668c75d6d.html.

8. Ulrich Lappenküper, *Die Außenpolitik der Bundesrepublik Deutschland 1949–1990* (Munich: Oldenbourg Verlag, 2008), 23–27.

9. Helga Haftendorn, "Entstehung und Bedeutung des Harmel-Berichts der NATO von 1967," *Vierteljahrshefte für Zeitgeschichte* 40, no. 2 (1992): 169–221.

10. "Harmel-Report," NATO, December 12, 1967, https://www.nato.int/cps/en/ natohq/official_texts_26700.htm.

11. Lappenküper, *Außenpolitik*, 33; Phillip Rock, *Macht, Märkte und Moral: Zur Rolle der Menschenrechte in der Außenpolitik der Bundesrepublik Deutschland in den sechziger und siebziger Jahren* (Frankfurt am Main: Peter Lang, 2010), 258–61.

12. Chancellor's report about his trip to Moscow, November 11, 1988, vol. 11/106, Bundestag.

13. Gerhard A. Ritter, "Deutschland und Europa: Grundzüge der Außenpolitik Genschers 1989–1992," in *Hans-Dietrich Genschers Außenpolitik: Akteure der*

Außenpolitik, ed. Kerstin Brauckhoff and Irmgard Schwaetzer (Wiesbaden: Springer, 2015), 209–40; Andreas Wirsching, "Die Charta von Paris, die Vision einer liberalen Weltordnung und die deutsche Außenpolitik 1990–1998," *Jahrbuch zur Liberalismus-Forschung* 33 (2021): 169–90.

14. Hans-Peter Schwarz, *Helmut Kohl: Eine politische Biographie* (Munich: Deutsche Verlags-Anstalt, 2012), 489–534; Andreas Wirsching, *Abschied vom Provisorium: 1982–1990* (Stuttgart: Deutsche Verlags-Anstalt, 2006), 563–72.

15. Remarks from Helmut Kohl, March 18, 1987, vol. 11/4, Bundestag; State of the Nation: Remarks from Helmut Kohl, December 1, 1988, vol. 11/113, Bundestag; Government Statement: Remarks from Helmut Kohl, December 9, 1988, vol. 11/117, Bundestag; Siegmar Schelling, "Wir müssen eine Friedensordnung vom Atlantik bis zum Ural schaffen," *Welt am Sonntag,* March 21, 1989: 25–26; David Marsh, "A Chancellor for All Seasons," *Financial Times,* February 10, 1989, 14.

16. Hermann Wentker, *Die Deutschen und Gorbatschow: Der Gorbatschow Diskurs im doppelten Deutschland* (Berlin: Metropol-Verlag, 2020), 364–69.

17. *Akten zur Auswärtigen Politik der Bundesrepublik Deutschland* (hereafter *AAPD*), vol. 1988, doc. 19.

18. For French skepticism about the "European peace order," see *AAPD,* vol. 1988, doc. 4; *AAPD,* vol. 1988, doc. 306; *AAPD,* vol. 1988, doc. 19; for Mitterrand's standpoint on the reunification of Germany, see Frédéric Bozo, *Mitterrand, the End of the Cold War, and German Unification* (New York: Berghahn Books, 2009), 83–164; Ulrich Lappenküper, *Mitterrand und Deutschland: Die enträtselte Sphinx* (Munich: Oldenbourg Verlag, 2011), 259–302.

19. Forty-Third General Assembly, Provisional Verbatim Record of the Seventy-Second Meeting, December 7, 1988, A/43/PV.72, Official Record of the United Nations.

20. Jeffrey A. Engel, *When the World Seemed New: George H. W. Bush and the End of the Cold War* (Boston: Houghton Mifflin Harcourt, 2017), 8.

21. Inaugural Address, January 20, 1989, Public Papers, George H. W. Bush Presidential Library (hereafter GHWBPL).

22. Engel, *When the World Seemed New,* 72.

23. Steven Greenhouse, "The Growing Fear of Fortress Europe," *New York Times,* October 23, 1988, 1.

24. Henry A, Kissinger, "A Memo to the Next President," *Newsweek,* November 19, 1988; Richard R. Burt, "U.S. Partnership with Western Europe," Speech at the Annual Meeting of the "Atlantic Bridge" in Bonn, June 8, 1988, B136/34320, Bundesarchiv (BArch); Richard M. Nixon, "American Foreign Policy: The Bush Agenda," *Foreign Policy* 68, no. 1 (1988/1989): 199–219.

25. Paul M. Kennedy, *The Rise and Fall of the Great Powers: Economic Change and Military Conflict from 1500 to 2000* (New York: Random House, 1987).

26. Roundtable: Paul M. Kennedy and Walt Whitman Rostow, "Pointers from the Past," *Foreign Affairs* 66, no. 5 (1988): 1108–13; Samuel P. Huntington, "US Decline or Renewal," *Foreign Affairs* 67, no. 2 (1988): 76–96.

27. *AAPD*, vol. 1989, doc. 38.

28. *AAPD*, vol. 1989, doc. 40.

29. *AAPD*, vol. 1989, doc. 41.

30. *AAPD*, vol. 1989, doc. 41: 192.

31. Comprehensive Review of US–West European Relations, February 15, 1989, National Security Review, GHWBPL.

32. Comprehensive Review, 1.

33. For Reinhart Koselleck's concept of "Future Past" and the construction of historical Futures, see Reinhart Koselleck, *Futures Past: On the Semantics of Historical Time,* trans. and with introduction by Keith Tribe (New York: Columbia University Press, 2004).

34. Review of National Defense Strategy, March 3, 1989, National Security Review, GHWBPL.

35. Hal Brands, *What Good Is Grand Strategy: Power and Purpose in American Statecraft from Harry S. Truman to George W. Bush* (Ithaca, NY: Cornell University Press, 2014).

36. Review of National Defense Strategy, March 3, 1989, National Security Review, GHWBPL.

37. Beth A. Fischer, "Visions of Ending the Cold War: Triumphalism and US Soviet Policy in the 1980s," in *Visions of the End of the Cold War in Europe, 1945–1990,* ed. Frédéric Bozo et al. (New York: Berghahn Books, 2012), 294–308.

38. Review of National Defense Strategy, March 3, 1989, National Security Review, GHWBPL.

39. Review of National Defense Strategy, S. 2.

40. Spohr, *Post Wall,* 18; Sarotte, *1989,* 119–49.

41. Memorandum from Brent Scowcroft for the President, March 20, 1989, NATO Summit at Brussels, Belgium (May 29–30, 1989), Case Number 2002–2036-F, GHWBPL.

42. Memorandum from Brent Scowcroft.

43. Memorandum from Brent Scowcroft.

44. Memorandum from Philip Zelikow for Robert Gates, April 13, 1989, NATO Summit at Brussels, Belgium (May 29–30, 1989), Case Number 2002–2036-F, GHWBPL.

45. Memorandum from Robert L. Hutchings for Robert M. Gates, April 17, 1989, NSC, Robert L. Hutchings Files, Country Files, CF001413, no box no., folder 2, GHWBPL.

46. It is not clear if Baker or some State Department employee wrote the document, but it has Baker's handwritten remarks on it: Notes re Berlin Speech Initiatives, April 1989, box 108, folder 4, James A. Baker Papers, Princeton University Library.

47. "Policy Pause," Engel, *When the World Seemed New*; "a coherent world view," Memorandum from Marlin Fitzwater for General Scowcroft, May 1, 1989, NATO Summit at Brussels, Belgium (May 29–30, 1989), Case Number 2002–2036-F, GHWBPL.

48. Remarks at the Texas A&M University Commencement Ceremony in College Station, December 5, 1989, Public Papers, GHWBPL.

49. Telegram from Ambassador Ruhfus (Washington, DC) to Bonn, May 12, 1989, Zwischenarchiv B32, vol. 179537, Politisches Archiv des Auswärtigen Amtes (hereafter PAA); Eberhard Kölsch, Speech from President Bush about U.S.–Soviet relations in Texas, May 12, 1989, Zwischenarchiv B32, vol. 179537, PAA.

50. James Addison Baker, *The Politics of Diplomacy: Revolution, War and Peace, 1989–1992* (New York: Putnam, 1995), 93–94.

51. Remarks at Boston University Commencement Ceremony in Massachusetts, May 21, 1989, Public Papers, GHWBPL.

52. Remarks Upon Arrival at the North Atlantic Treaty Organization Summit Meeting in Brussels, May 28, 1989, Public Papers, GHWBPL.

53. This term refers to the concept developed by John Lewis Gaddis in 1986: John Lewis Gaddis, "The Long Peace: Elements of Stability in the Post War International System," *International Security* 10, no. 4 (1986): 99–142; John Lewis Gaddis, *The Long Peace: Inquiries into the History of the Cold War* (New York: Oxford University Press, 1989).

54. The President's NAC Intervention May 29, 1989, NATO Summit at Brussels, Belgium (May 29–30, 1989), Case Number 2002–2036-F, GHWBPL.

55. Declaration of the Heads of State and Government Participating in the Meeting of the North Atlantic Council, May 29–30, 1989, NATO-Archive, https://www.nato.int/docu/comm/49-95/c890530a.htm.

56. Remarks to the Citizens in Mainz, Federal Republic of Germany, May 31, 1989, Public Papers, GHWBPL.

57. Engel, *When the World Seemed New*, 198–201.

58. James Markham, "Gorbachev Says Change Will Sweep Bloc," *New York Times*, June 6, 1989, 3.

59. Quote from Engel, *When the World Seemed New* 201.

60. Memcon with Helmut Kohl, June 15, 1989, Memcons/Telcons, GHWBPL.

61. Telcon with Helmut Kohl, May 5, 1989, Memcons/Telcons, GHWBPL.

62. Telcon with Helmut Kohl, June 15, 1989, Memcons/Telcons, GHWBPL.

63. Memcon with Hans-Dietrich Genscher, June 21, 1989.

64. Engel, *When the World Seemed New*, 206.

65. White House Press Briefing, July 12, 1989, box 108, file 7, James A. Baker Papers, Princeton University Library.

66. Engel, *When the World Seemed New*, 226.

67. Engel, 228.

68. Memcon with Manfred Wörner, October 11, 1989, Memcons/Telcons, GHWBPL.

69. Telcon with Helmut Kohl, October 23, 1989, Memcons/Telcons, GHWBPL.

70. Francis Fukuyama, "The End of History?," *National Interest* 16 (Summer 1989): 3–18.

71. *AAPD*, vol. 1989, doc. 332, Results of the Chiefs of Staff Meeting with the USA, October 26, 1989.

72. Engel, *When the World Seemed New*, 248.

73. Remarks and a Question-and-Answer Session with Reporters on the Relaxation of East German Border Controls, November 9, 1989, Public Papers, GHWBPL.

74. Quotation and interpretation from Engel, *When the World Seemed New*, 271.

75. Helmut Kohl's Ten-Point Program, November 28, 1989, vol. 11/117, Bundestag.

76. Sarotte, *1989*, 48–87.

77. Engel, *When the World Seemed New*, 274.

78. Engel, 274.

79. Thanksgiving Address to the Nation, November 22, 1989, Public Papers, GHWBPL.

80. Memorandum from Brent Scowcroft for the President, August 8, 1989; Robert L. Hutchings, 2001–1166-F, CF01413–15, GHWBPL.

81. Engel, *When the World Seemed New*, 293–312.

82. James A. Baker, Secretary of State, Remarks on Europe, December 12, 1989, http://aei.pitt.edu/101501/.

83. Philip Zelikow and Condoleezza Rice, *Germany Unified and Europe Transformed: A Study in Statecraft* (Cambridge, MA: Harvard University Press, 1995); Robert L. Hutchings, *American Diplomacy and the End of the Cold War: An Insider's Account of U.S. Policy in Europe, 1989–1992* (Washington, DC: Woodrow Wilson Center Press with Johns Hopkins University Press, 1997).

84. Philip Zelikow and Condoleezza Rice, *To Build a Better World: Choices to End the Cold War and Create a Global Commonwealth* (New York: Twelve, 2019), 409–30; Andrew S. Natsios and Andrew H. Card Jr., eds., *Transforming Our World: President George H. W. Bush and American Foreign Policy* (London: Rowman & Littlefield, 2020), 1–9, illus. 15; President Bush Address in Mainz—Germany Post NATO Speech, May 31, 1989, credit: GHWBPL, 41-AV-P03639-018-05311089.

CHAPTER 10

Performing the Wall after Its Fall

MATT CORNISH

STUPID AND BRUTAL

During the months of November 1989 through October 1990, Berlin transformed from a global symbol of division into a beacon of hope for reconciliation generally and liberalism specifically. But the theater made during and just after this period was fractured, discordant. As journalists eagerly described the *Wende,* or turning point, playwrights and directors questioned what had really changed in German history. As politicians used metaphors of "marriage" and "blooming landscapes," playwrights and directors drew on images of divorce and infertility. As historians reevaluated the role of the nation and nationalism in German history, casting Germany as newly normal, playwrights and directors exposed still-bleeding, self-inflected wounds. And as everyone celebrated *Wiedervereinigung,* or reunification, playwrights

This article was written with the support of a Humboldt Research Fellowship for Experienced Researchers. Parts of some sections were published earlier as "Prelapsarian," in *PAJ: A Journal of Performance and Art* 41.3 (September 2019): 44–51. Republished with permission. Translations are by the author unless otherwise noted.

and directors questioned connections between the Federal Republic present and Prussian myths of the original unification in 1871.[1]

In my book *Performing Unification: History and Nation in German Theater after 1989,* I examined how German theater artists in the 1990s and 2000s drew on the past to challenge the historical understanding and collective identity of Germany. Important artists attacked the myths and historiography of the Wende and Wiedervereinigung with great viciousness—Heiner Müller (1929–94), a playwright and director from the German Democratic Republic; Frank Castorf (1951), a director from the GDR; Botho Strauß (1944), a playwright from the Federal Republic of Germany; Rolf Hochhuth (1931–2020), a playwright from the FRG. Take, for example, this moment, from Castorf's production *Clockwork Orange,* loosely adapted from the Anthony Burgess novel, which premiered at the Volksbühne am Rosa-Luxemburg-Platz, in the former East Berlin, in 1992: "Police in full riot gear stormed the stage and crapped in their pants as Chancellor [Helmut] Kohl spoke on a TV," while other "actors tossed around a life-size headless doll in the image of the chancellor."[2] Kohl, of course, was the celebrated longtime chancellor of Germany who led the reunification process. Later in the same production, the great actress "Silvia Rieger danced around wearing an advertisement sandwich board with 'Rosa-Luxemburg-Platz' on one side and 'Horst-Wessel-Platz' on the other."[3] Rosa Luxemburg was a Marxist revolutionary murdered (martyred) in 1919; Horst Wessel was a Nazi stormtrooper murdered (martyred) by Communists in 1930. Called "Horst-Wessel-Platz" from 1933 until 1945, the square, where the Volksbühne sits, was renamed for Rosa Luxemburg by the GDR in 1947, and the Berlin government considered renaming the square again in the early 1990s.[4] With all of these renamings (and there were many more), exactly how normal is the Berlin Republic? Or take *Rheinische Rebellen* (Rhineland rebels), also adapted by Castorf from the Arnolt Bronnen play for the Volksbühne in 1992: "A man in a bowler hat ate a banana with gusto, licked the peel, dropped it, and then slipped on it, over and over, as he tried to run across the stage to his wife."[5] Bananas had been luxury items in the GDR, and they became a symbol of East German desire to integrate with the West. Castorf satirized everyone. He "attacked the Ossi [Easterner] desire to integrate into the capitalist West, trading their socialist pasts for lives as petit bourgeois. But he also satirized the way the West forced that integration through nomenclature, hoping that if you renamed the streets, you could remake the people. Throughout Germany's history, the powerful have rechristened Berlin's streets after themselves, over and over again, like Rieger spinning in her sandwich board. Castorf stands athwart history here and shouts: 'Stop! We are who we were.'"[6]

For Castorf, as for many other theater artists in the 1990s, there was no Wende with the fall of the Berlin Wall: German history just kept on going, as stupidly and brutally as ever before.

BORDERS AND BELONGING

Borders can be useful. Though arbitrary and artificial, even when demarcated by mountains or bodies of water, borders nonetheless help us make sense of the world, giving us a chart by which we orient ourselves. The borders around a concept aid us in communicating the concept: they outline an idea, allowing it to be more easily imagined. People like borders. They distinguish what is ours from what is our neighbor's and convey how far we can go before reaching someplace unknown. This makes them dangerous. But borders need not just confine or limit, whether the restrictions be to ideas, to forests, or to people. In English, a border can be a garden. We speak of "useful border annuals,"[7] like pansies, alyssum, and twinspur, set in black mulch, marking the edge between yard and forest. Borders can be ornamental, as with the gilded edges of a coat. They are the frame around an object that intensifies the object—while sometimes the border becomes itself an object.

That borders require control, protection, and surveillance is not byproduct but product, the natural quality of the border. Flowers must be protected from weeds, lest the border become fuzzy, rough frontier instead of trimmed edge. Without firm stitching, the coat gives way, becoming mere pieces of fabric. Sometimes the confines of the frame narrow: the distinction between what belongs and what does not can seem natural and unchangeable—and permanently under threat. So the border expands, pushing outward, capturing new space.

Geographically, Germany might appear to have clear borders, the North Sea and the Baltic, the Rhine and the Alps. At the same time, that its borders are overdetermined goes without saying (almost). August Heinrich Hoffmann von Fallersleben's lyrics to "Das Lied der Deutschen" (Song of the Germans, 1841)—which rhapsodize of a Germany stretching from the

Meuse (in Belgium and the Netherlands) to the Neman (Lithuania), and from Adige (Italy) to the Belt (Denmark)—remind us of how often Germany's boundaries have expanded and contracted. Questions of who belongs within these borders, and who does not, have been adjudicated at various times by vernacular dialect, written language, clothing, *Kultur,* gesture, music. Adjudicated, in other words, through performance: and performed again by Castorf and other theater artists after the great border around West Berlin and between the Germanys suddenly, seemingly, disappeared.

DIE MAUER

The Berlin Wall, *die Mauer,* is something of a disembodied soul, its material gone to dust, its absence ever more absent. Walking *(spazieren)* through Prenzlauer Berg, with its conspicuous consumption in the form of baby carriages and shops selling Scandinavian children's clothing, 100 percent bamboo, you might think, This was the West. You would be wrong. It is Castorf's old neighborhood, where he grew up and where he made performances from 1991 until 2017: during those years, giant neon letters reading "O-S-T" (East) dominated the top of the Volksbühne am Rosa-Luxemburg-Platz. Now Prenzlauer Berg is crowded with migrants from Bavaria and America, the apartments (heated by coal into the 1990s) chicly *saniert* and offered on Airbnb. To a newly arrived visitor in Berlin, the former Western districts of Neukölln, still ragged, and Wedding, miles of gray, might feel more like their fantasy of the East than Prenzlberg.

It took a long time for the border between West and East Berlin to get this way, with so little demarcation remaining. In *Performing Unification,* I look at several plays and performances specifically about the Berlin Wall, including *Goldener Oktober* (Golden October) by the Western playwright Elfriede Müller, which premiered in 1991:

> Set in October 1990 (as legal unification took effect) on
> "a drafty stage,"[8] this now mostly forgotten play unfolds
> a history of the Wende in the landscape of the former
> Todesstreifen (death strip) in Berlin, the border zone used
> by GDR police to prevent refugees from fleeing the country.
> Here a collection of forlorn Westerners and Easterners gather
> in a bar, their attempts at romance and dialogue disastrous.

Goldener Oktober presents the commercialization of individuals, bodies, and emotions that followed the introduction of capitalism into the border zone.[9]

In the early 1990s, the *Todesstreifen* was still visible, legacy of the wall that was much more than a wall, with additional fortifications as well as empty space that allowed guards to see (and shoot) people attempting to flee to the West. While West Berlin was inhabited right up against the border, buildings in East Berlin along the wall were razed, bricked up, and abandoned, and the land they stood on was legally contested for many years. Such structures in the former East were taken over by young squatters who became artists, opening theaters, galleries, and coffee shops; later, developers got to work and fixed up apartments, extraordinarily cheap rents rose, more developers moved in, and now, after thirty years, the borderlands *Goldener Oktober* presents as infertile have bloomed with bourgeoisie shopping for bamboo baby clothes.

In the thirty-plus years since November 9, 1989, a generation has grown up without the wall, while the generation that caused it to be built is dying off. The border will pass—is passing—out of living memory. If you ride your bike through Berlin today, as I write in 2022, you may notice lines of bricks running along some streets, like Axel-Springer-Straße (until 1996 Lindenstraße), a quiet memorial to the Berlin Wall. Other than these bricks, the border is invisible—except to careful eyes, which might notice that the buildings in the former Todesstreifen are newer and larger than the buildings most everywhere else.

The Berlin Wall today is a tourist trap. In 2019 the *New York Times* ran an article presenting earnest debates about whether a Hard Rock Hotel should be built next to Checkpoint Charlie.[10] Why were people complaining? Checkpoint Charlie was already all but a Hard Rock Café. Tourists have a list. They go to Checkpoint Charlie and take pictures on each side of East and West, here actually north and south of the guard hut on Friedrichstraße. They go to the East Side Gallery, the longest stretch of the "Berlin Wall" still in existence, with panels painted by graffiti artists in 1990. A symbol of a symbol, the East Side Gallery does not so much represent the wall as represent our ideal mental image of it: tall and imposing concrete blocks covered with graffiti. To get a sense of the border's full, horrible infrastructure, missing at the East Side Gallery, they go also to the Berlin Wall

Memorial, a *Gedenkstätte* (literally "memory place") along Bernauer Straße. There, some of the wall's infrastructure was preserved and then, between 2008 and 2013, partially recreated and ghosted with photographic displays to give the visitor a sense of the original. The especially fit tourists might run the Berlin Wall Race (100 Miles Berlin), which circles the former West. And there's much more to do, including Trabant limousine tours, something even Heiner Müller couldn't dream up for the nightmare in his play *Wolokolamsker Chaussee* ("I woke up and everything was orderly").[11]

BORDERLESS

May Ayim, a Black German poet and activist (1960–96), writes in the conclusion of "borderless and brazen: a poem against the german 'u-not-y,'" from 1990:

> i will go
> yet another step further and another step and
> will return
> when i want
> if i want
> and remain
> borderless and brazen.[12]

When I think of borders, I think of soldiers, of confinement. Of real people suffering because capricious limits are enforced with deadly consequences. But borders can be permeable, even intentionally so, allowing transfer. A border can be a wide-open gate that marks the distance between past and future, like the line that approximates where the Berlin Wall once stood, bricks as memory device instead of fortification. Neither here nor there, borders are margins that often attract the marginal. I am reminded of Ödön von Horvath's *Hin und her* (Here and there, 1934), a play written between the world wars in Austria, a no-longer-empire that had embraced (and held tight) many different traditions, languages, and peoples—now distilled. Ferdinand Havlicek is being deported, expelled from the land where he has always lived into the land where he was born. But he is not a citizen in this new, old country. So he stands on a bridge (which sits on a turntable), negotiating with border guards, flirting, and gazing at the stars.

The play is part farce, part romantic comedy. Borders are often senseless and sad, but they are also places of possibility: bridges and other infrastructure can be repurposed through performance to become festive spaces of in between.[13] It is possible to act borderless within borders.

THE VOLKSBÜHNE AM ROSA-LUXEMBURG-PLATZ

During the 1990s and into the 2000s, Castorf chronicled at the Volksbühne am Rosa-Luxemburg-Platz the creep, the stampede, and finally the total victory of capitalist values in the former East Berlin. Already in his version of Friedrich Schiller's *Die Räuber* (The robbers), which premiered September 1990, we see the desperate grasping of newly possible materialism, and disgust at the grasping. In *Hauptmanns Weber* (1997), an adaptation of Gerhard Hauptmann's *The Weavers,* a bunch of slackers speaking East Berlin slang sit around in their underwear, wearing white T-shirts printed with the logos of aspirational brands, such as Boss and Chanel (see fig. 12). Castorf's adaptations of Bulgakov and Dostoevsky in the early 2000s were staged in designer Bert Neumann's *Neustadt,* a "new city" of wasted, wasteful capitalist desire built out into the Volksbühne's auditorium: the audience sat on risers outside fully realized buildings, inside of which the actors, chased by camera crews for hours at a time, performed. In his version of Tennessee Williams's *Sweet Bird of Youth,* titled *Forever Young,* from 2004, audiences watched an America refracted through Neumann's designs. Martin Wuttke and Kathrin Angerer, two longtime collaborators with Castorf and extraordinary actors, dove into swimming pools, shouted at each other, and looked brilliant amid palm trees. Capitalism was seemingly at the limit of its decadence. By the time Castorf made *Die Brüder Karamasow* (*The Brothers Karamazov*), in 2016, toward the end of his twenty-five-year tenure at the Volksbühne, the gig was up. There wasn't much left of the East.

For *The Brothers Karamazov,* also designed by Neumann, all the seats were removed from the auditorium and the audience lounged on huge beanbags. In the back of the space, built into the balcony, there was a narrow three-story building (blinking sign: *Zimmer frei,* rooms free) and a blindingly neon sign for Koka Kola. Spread around the auditorium and stage were an enclosed sauna in light wood, a small dacha with a pointed roof, and a shallow pool with a gazebo rising out of it. The set was a labyrinth, you never quite knew where the performers were. Everything was covered with red Cyrillic letters. Nobody in the audience had a great view, but the actors were often out of sight anyway, performing inside the three-story building—in one room there was a giant portrait of a young Stalin—or even up on the roof of the Volksbühne. A projection screen behind the pool allowed everyone to watch the cameras racing after the actors.

The production was six and a half hours long. There's something about Dostoevsky's soul that matches Castorf, something almost juvenile, along with the feeling of being at the end of something and not the beginning, while Dostoevsky's characters and Castorf's actors share the same angst and desperation. Castorf's method in *Brothers Karamazov*—endless monologues, babbled and screamed, growing increasingly perilous and mad—matched, even exceeded Dostoevsky's book, which Castorf sometimes interrupted with excerpts from a novel by D. J. Stalingrad, an anarchist, antifascist Russian expat threatened with extradition by Moscow. This wasn't a linear adaptation of the novel, as it jumped back and forth, but Castorf's *Brothers Karamazov* still told the novel's story: всё дозволено, *alles ist erlaubt*, everything is permitted (after the death of God). After intermission, Ivan Karamazov, played by the Christ-thin Alexander Scheer, ran up to the Volksbühne's roof to deliver the Grand Inquisitor monologue, crawling on and over the neon O-S-T letters (see fig. 10). The white froth of his spit landed on the camera that followed him. Can we really tolerate freedom? What is lost and what is gained in belief? This is a life of wonders, of secrets, of suffering, and of submission. The actors became increasingly tired, struggling eventually to climb a fire escape outside the three-story building; the women were running around in high heels, sometimes ridiculously high. The characters shouted their desire to go to America, while the actors threw into the pool a life-size reproduction of Hans Holbein the Younger's "The Body of the Dead Christ in the Tomb." Christ's body in the Holbein painting is decomposing; you can smell the putrefaction. Germany, Heiner Müller wrote in 1989, is two Europes, one of Rome and one of Byzantium.[14] Berlin is less than a hundred kilometers from the Polish border. Polish, Dostoevsky teased in *The Brothers Karamazov*, is basically funny Russian. To whom did Berlin belong in 2016? You can fight Coca-Cola, but that's what they want, *das Volk*.

Early in his career, during the Cold War, Castorf made his art from the restrictions on life in the German Democratic Republic; later, he used the new restrictions on life in the united Federal Republic. We think of ourselves as free. But Castorf insists we are nothing of the sort. Capitalism and liberal democracy shape and control and erect barriers: you can have anything you want, as long as it's on the menu of the Hard Rock Café.

THE *FREIE SZENE*

The *Freie Szene,* or independent performance scene, is generally defined by its not belonging: it presents itself as the negative image of state and city repertory theaters (*Staats-* and *Stadttheater*) like the Volksbühne. State and city theaters—I will refer to them simply as public theaters from now on—are large institutions with many salaried employees, and they receive ongoing funding from public coffers. Hierarchical institutions, public theaters are organized around a visionary artistic leader like Castorf, the *Intendant* or *Intendantin.* In the independent scene, individuals or collectives working (mostly) outside the public theater system apply for short-term grants. As opposed to the ranks and orders of public theaters, the independent scene finds its basic structure in parataxis: all performance elements (design, acting, directing) and all performers are typically meant to be equal, both onstage and in the rehearsal process.[15]

Although it has existed for many years, depending on your definition at least since the 1980s, the Freie Szene began to take a more prominent place in the German theater discourse in the early 2000s. Productions from the Freie Szene provide a nice way of looking at how ideas of unification changed in the German imagination a decade and two decades after 1989. In *Performing Unification,* I looked at several examples from the Freie Szene, for example by Rimini Protokoll, a group of three artists who use historical and archival documents (letters, photographs, speeches, statistics) as well as, often, regular people instead of trained actors, all to revise narratives and help audiences better understand the past. Here's how I described Rimini Protokoll's *50 Aktenkilometer: Ein begehbares Stasi Hörspiel* (50 kilometers of dossiers: A walkable Stasi audio-play, 2013), a performance you experience by smartphone, walking through the former East Berlin:

> For the next three and a half hours I listen to recordings
> of events in 1989 as they happened, large demonstrations
> as well as personal affairs; Stasi officials (Ministry of State
> Security secret police) speak, as do informers, dissidents, and

other GDR citizens. In addition to recordings made in 1989,
Rimini Protokoll includes later recollections, individuals
discussing their experiences twenty years ago. My Android
cell phone uses GPS to track me, and when I arrive at certain
locations, marked by orange circles on the phone's map, the
phone plays a report that lasts between one and ten minutes. Sometimes I pause and listen, following the occasional
instructions, for example: walk into the Radisson Hotel,
formerly the Palasthotel, act like a normal guest, sit down by
the bar, look around inconspicuously. Are you being watched?
A flaneur, I sometimes just walk on, out of one circle and on
toward another.[16]

50 Aktenkilometer does something that no history book, or even a standard theater production, ever could: we write and rewrite history with our
bodies, walking through space and time.

There's also the completely different group She She Pop, seven women
and one man, all graduates of the same university (Gießen, where the Rimini Protokoll members and many other Freie Szene artists trained as well),
who make raucous performances about their own lives. Their production
Schubladen (Drawers) premiered in 2012 and featured a rotating cast of four
members of She She Pop born in the FRG—like everyone in the group—in
conversation with four women who had been born in the GDR. The performance was devised by She She Pop and their guests during rehearsals,
built out of their experiences before and after 1989, and symbolized by the
wheeled boxes (drawers) they had with them onstage, full of photos, records,
and books. As with *50 Aktenkilometer,* in *Schubladen* She She Pop added
personal stories to the archive of the Berlin Wall and, in this case, especially
the stories of East German women, which were often funny and tender, and
not limited to stories of the Stasi, attempted escapes, and protest. It became
clear during the performance that the West and East German women did
not fully understand each other, even twenty-three years after unification,
that their individual pasts, carried in the wheeled boxes, were still influenc-
ing their present lives—and also that they didn't speak different languages,
that the so-called "wall in their heads" was not insurmountable.

Two decades after the fall of the wall, much of the anger we saw in
the 1990s had dissipated, but it wasn't replaced by hope. On the stage, I

watched increasingly sophisticated attempts to understand the lives of people in the GDR, to complicate the stories of historians, and to understand what divisions remained, as well as why those divisions remained.

AN ELEGY AS ORATORIO

For *Oratorium* (Oratorio), which premiered winter 2018 at the Freie Szene theater Hebbel am Ufer and was invited to the prestigious Theatertreffen festival the next spring, She She Pop made an updated *Lehrstück*. As conceptualized by Bertolt Brecht between the world wars, a Lehrstück, or teaching-learning play, has no audience; here, She She Pop cast the audience as actors. The onstage performers were draped with cloth in strange patterns over street clothes, like postmodern medieval priests; there was a small group of She She Pop members and a larger chorus of regular Berliners ("local delegates"[17]), who had been cast from the street (fig. 11). In the auditorium, we looked up at the supertitles, but instead of reading them quietly to ourselves, we spoke our lines out loud, engaging in dialogue with the onstage performers. We were asked to choose which lines to read: do I belong in the chorus of the Well-Offs, the Mothers without Pensions, the Theater Studies Professors? The scenarios (Brechtian *Fabeln*) circled uncomfortable facts of private ownership: an artist's sunny apartment in Prenzlauer Berg will be sold; renters will be, in a quite material way, pushed out, while others with enough money to buy move in. The subtitle of the performance is *Kollektive Andacht zu einem wohlgehüteten Geheimnis* (Collective meditation on a well-kept secret). Waving flags in patterns that echoed the costumes as two musicians played trumpet and vibraphone in a kind of demonstration of music, reminiscent of Hanns Eisler, She She Pop madly and gladly pushed us toward conclusions we didn't want to reach. How can we distribute resources more, shall we say, equitably? (Not equally.) Do we—can we—not only believe in, but also enact, solidarity? This was meant as a rehearsal for our lives, as She She Pop's Chorus of Theater Studies Professors announced toward the end.

She She Pop's oratorio is cacophonous, never quite in harmony. It's an elegy to a lost Berlin, the chaotic city of the 1990s, when squatters could semilegally occupy abandoned buildings, when art was cheap and everywhere. Artists like the members of She She Pop could live, really *live,* in Berlin back then—by 2018 the liminality of borderless Berlin had disappeared, and artists couldn't get by in Prenzlauer Berg, the neighborhood they had made after the fall of the wall. *Oratorium* concluded by bringing onto the stage the Chorus of Inheritors, the people who can afford Prenzlauer Berg because their grandparents and parents will die someday and provide. They weren't onstage to be shamed, just to remind us all, inheritors and not alike, that we're not born equally. One could read this as an attempt to move us toward new forms of collectivity. But what's the conclusion? *Oratorium* got uncomfortably close to the slogan "Berlin for Berliners," which doesn't sound so bad until one widens the scope a bit and begins to chant "Germany for Germans." With the Berlin Wall gone and the borders within the Schengen Zone more ornament than obstacle, even those on the left, it seems, sometimes get nostalgic for keeping people out.

THIRTIETH ANNIVERSARIES

Did anyone care about the thirtieth anniversary of the fall of the Berlin Wall? It was a busy time for anniversaries, here amid Heiner Müller's accumulated wreckage: "I was Hamlet. I stood at the shore and talked with the surf BLABLA, the ruins of Europe in back of me."[18] The year 2018 was the hundred-year anniversary of the November revolution in Berlin, the hundred-year anniversary of the end of World War I, the two-hundred-year anniversary of Karl Marx's birthday. The Tiananmen Square protests had been brutally repressed thirty years before. It was hard to remember to prepare for the thirtieth anniversaries of the fall of the Berlin Wall and German reunification, in 2019 and 2020 respectively.

Horst Seehofer, the federal minister of the interior at the time, forgot. In April 2019 he suddenly realized that the anniversary of reunification was coming up and applied to Minister of Finance Olaf Scholz (now chancellor) for 61 million euros in "unforeseen" funding. On the Süddeutsche Zeitung website, embedded with the article revealing Seehofer's letter, was a survey, with almost 17,000 participants, asking whether this anniversary of German unification is "very important" or has "no great meaning." The average response: right in the middle.[19] That seems about right.

COMRADES

At Hebbel am Ufer Theater (HAU), a festival in spring 2019: "Comrades, I'm Not Ashamed of My Communist Past: Memory Politics 30 Years after the Fall of the Berlin Wall," with reprisals of She She Pop's *Schubladen* and andcompany&Co.'s *little red (play): "herstory"* (premiered 2006). A Freie Szene group like She She Pop, "andcompany&Co. makes performances that crash dada into neoliberalism, remixing Bertolt Brecht and Heiner Müller for our age of capitalistic nonsense."[20] *little red* is an especially fun production, jumping around in great piles of Cold War detritus, from speeches by Ronald Reagan to the uniform of the Young Pioneers, state-sponsored Communist scouts. The protagonist is a reimagined Little Red Riding Hood, a West German commie feminist (like Nikola Nord, who played the role) who gets lost in the forests of time, back and forth between 1961, 1989, and today, skipping through the artists' own histories alongside grand historical narratives.

For "Comrades," HAU commissioned Karsten Krampitz, German author and journalist, born in the former East, to write a short essay reflecting on the circumstances. "Official commemorations have falsely narrated the German Democratic Republic in fundamental ways," Krampitz writes, of the tendency to tell the story of the GDR only through the Stasi, its victims, and its villains. "Very few East Germans see themselves in the postulated historical images of communist despotism. A life that cannot be narrated makes people sick."[21] Telling some stories of that life was the project of She She Pop with *Schubladen,* to talk about growing up in the GDR and during the division of Germany.

We could easily afford this festival too much prominence, given my focus here on theater after the fall of the wall. "Comrades" was only one week in HAU's programming, finding itself amid festivals and projects on, to name just two: Afro-Futurism (in honor of the one hundred fiftieth anniversary of W. E. B. DuBois's birth) and Einar Schleef (to celebrate what would have been Schleef's seventy-fifth birthday).

Autumn 2019, at the actual thirtieth anniversary of November 9, 1989, brought few festivals and performances about the wall. And amid the global coronavirus pandemic, there was no way for artists to bring people together to commemorate, recollect, and repent the thirtieth anniversary of unification in 2020. There were small exceptions. At Zionskirche in Prenzlauer Berg, a church important to the resistance in the GDR, a series of events took place between March and November 2019, experimental music concerts and visual art exhibits, on the theme of *Grenzfälle,* falling borders, plural, not singular.[22] So the anniversary hadn't been totally forgotten. It just wasn't all that extraordinarily important, it seems.

A NEW PALACE IN BERLIN

The new Berliner Schloss, begun in 2013 and built on the rubble of the Palast der Republik, itself built on the rubble of the old Königliches Schloss (royal palace), no longer represents the power of the state itself but instead the imaginary of the Berlin Republic. Self-conscious and self-possessed, looking back at a brutal history and forward toward a future it hopes to define in the image of its values, the building is enormous, with seemingly endless gallery spaces. The long corridors and high ceilings could belong to a conference center or even an airport. Here we find the most recent iteration of Berlin's struggle with its past and future, in the permanent exhibit *Berlin Global,* which opened with the building itself in summer 2021.

In *Performing Unification* I wrote about a "memory boom" in the museums and memorials of Berlin post-1990, and about the increasingly participatory nature of exhibitions in the 2010s.[23] "The mode of representation in memory museums relies upon narratives told through objects, dioramas, and text while requiring that visitors complete the loop of meaning by actively engaging with the exhibits, imaginatively projecting themselves into the stories of characters."[24] While participatory museum exhibits, such as those at the Bernauer Straße Memorial and at the German Historical Museum, advertise their openness in allowing people to engage with the real past in subjective ways, visitors nonetheless follow an exhibit's script. They perform with their bodies the story the curators are telling. And what is that story? "The museums echo post-unification historiography as written by conservative historians [such as Jürgen Kocka and Ernst Nolte], fostering an increased consciousness of national identity by emphasizing the similarities between individual lives in East and West Germany . . . , as well as legitimizing the latter's political and economic structures against those of the East."[25]

Berlin Global is doing something similar, but with a noticeable shift in values that tells us something interesting about the transformations in Berlin during the past thirty years. Here the history of Berlin is told thematically—with sections on revolution, war, fashion, free space, and boundaries—and with a great deal of technology. Visitors are given armbands that allow them to make choices as they walk through the exhibits: do you share free space, or do you make free space on your own? At the end, you are given feedback on your choices, how you prefer to balance the values of freedom, equality, security, and tradition, and you are encouraged by docents and by a space for lounging to talk to other visitors about their responses. While the Berlin Wall and the division of Germany are a part of several thematic sections, shown as having shaped the art scenes in Berlin, for example, it is far from the only division emphasized throughout, including in the "boundaries" section. In fact, the point is less to show past boundaries than to "reveal boundaries in Berlin today," including especially "racist exclusion, inaccessible areas for wheelchair users, and parts of the city where residents can no longer afford to live."[26] Touchscreens attached to surveying levels on tripods allow visitors to choose stories about these kinds of boundaries, told by people who have experienced them, while standing on an abstract map of Berlin's streets and rivers. As throughout *Berlin Global,* there is a strong emphasis on equity, diversity, and inclusion, and on postcolonizing the museum (perhaps in part a response to heavy criticism of the ethnological exhibits elsewhere in the Humboldt Forum).[27]

Although the experience is intended to be highly participatory, as with the Bernauer Straße Memorial and the German Historical Museum, you can move only within the narrative set by *Berlin Global* curators. In that narrative, the Berlin Wall recedes into the background. It does not disappear, but the wall does not have the emphasis it would have been given in the 1990s or even early 2000s. The Cold War is a small part of a larger story of a dynamic and forward-looking city "connected with the world."[28] There's no emphasis on the nation as an imagined community, German or otherwise. Instead we tour, through the exhibit, a "global" Berlin, full of diverse residents and visitors with cosmopolitan, liberal values, eager to talk with one another about their place in the city and the world.

WIR SIND DAS VOLK

It is difficult to overemphasize the anger of performances made in the early 1990s about reunification. Western playwright Rolf Hochhuth's *Wessis in Weimar* (Westerners in Weimar, 1993), a documentary play developed from sources that include newspaper articles and political speeches, was subtitled *Szenen aus einem besetzten Land*—scenes from an occupied country. It features economic exploitation, suicides, and murder, all following from the euphoria and privatization of reunification. While that anger subsided over the decades, and both division and reunification became more of something that was sometimes funny in productions such as *Schubladen* and *little red,* it never totally went away. In *Wir sind das Volk* (We are the people) the rage came roaring back.

Created by Slovenian avant-garde industrial band Laibach with Heiner Müller scholar and dramaturg Anja Quickert, *Wir sind das Volk* put the poetry and dramatic scenarios of Müller to music.[29] Though subtitled *Ein Musical aus Deutschland* (A musical from Germany) the production was more of a cabaret, with a series of songs and recitations connected by theme rather than by story. Laibach singer Milan Fras served as master of ceremonies, his hooded silhouette presiding stiffly over center stage with a microphone stand and a gravel voice that would challenge even Tom Waits. Müller, who had spent his adult life in the German Democratic Republic and never turned against the regime or emigrated, even when his plays were banned, disparaged reunification without expressing any nostalgia for the GDR. Often described as "postmodern,"[30] Müller's writing is elliptical and abstractly allegorical, with often-grotesque imagery (Goebbels giving birth to Hitler's child, a wolf, in *Germania Tod in Berlin* [Germania death in Berlin], 1971–78) and wild associations (between the French Revolution, Caribbean slave rebellions, and Bertolt Brecht in *Der Auftrag* [The mission], 1979–80). Laibach's music, which sounds as if someone found a way to turn barbed wire into sound, fits Müller's dramaturgy perfectly. In *Wir sind das Volk* there are two big barrel drums onstage, a drum set, an electric guitar, a DJ making electronic sounds with his iMac laptop—and, unusual for Laibach, a string quartet. It's loud enough that there were earplugs available in the theater's lobby. Though softened in places by the strings, the music demanded submission, with Fras at one point chanting "Ordnung und Disziplin" (order and discipline).

The stage was equally demanding, dark and serious and often enveloped in fog, with musicians on various levels in a semicircle around Fras, the percussionists high above the others and center stage. Projections wrapped around the stage and the auditorium, enfolding the audience into the performance—there was a map of concentration camps in Eastern Europe, as well as images of mothers and children from neoclassical sculpture and painting. Laibach's music, released in 2022 as an album of the same title, was interspersed by speeches, mostly by Müller, whose words also provided many of the lyrics for the songs. It's difficult to excerpt Müller, but here's an example, from "Seife in Bayreuth" (Soap in Bayreuth, 1993), performed by Agnes Mann late in the ninety-minute production:

> As a child I heard the adults say:
> In the concentration camps Jews were made into soap.
> Since then I cannot
> Stand soap and avoid even its smell.
> Now I am living, because I'm directing TRISTAN,
> In a new apartment building in the city Bayreuth.
> . . . .
> When I opened the window for the first time: soap.
> The building the garden the city Bayreuth smell of soap.[31]

Collectively, the music, the words, and the atmosphere created a mood of fear and wrath. "Ten Germans are dumber than five Germans,"[32] Mann says at one point, a well-known Müller aphorism, and the closest the production gets to humor. If reunification was supposed to normalize Germany back in 1990, Laibach and Quickert work to show the nation's depravity continuing into the 2020s: the exact opposite of the narrative told by the Humboldt Forum, with its celebration of Global Berlin. Curtain calls are normally quite long in Germany, compared to the United States, and mostly unchoreographed, with the performers gradually dropping their masks as they repeatedly bow for the audience; here, the performers refused a curtain call. Instead, Slovenian philosopher and artist Peter Makler walked onstage in a military uniform and delivered a diatribe against Germany and Germans: Your applause is not wanted, you murderers. We are the people, and together we are dumb and dangerous, stupid and brutal.

THE GRASS THAT GROWS OVER THE BORDER

While I have been working on this essay, Russia invaded Ukraine. It feels, living in Berlin, about 1,500 kilometers from Kiev, as if there has been a significant shift in the relationship between Germany and Russia, who have, since the early 1990s, been something like strange, mutually dependent but not totally trustful cousins. Now there are Ukrainian flags everywhere, in front of the state museums and on the facades of public theaters, blue and yellow stripes lighting up the sides of tall buildings. Will the Cold War return? Already, in mid-April, about one and a half months since the invasion began, as I finish editing, it feels unlikely. The relationship will be much less trusting, and much stranger, and perhaps the borders between

Rome and Byzantium will become clearer and move farther east. Wars are full of unknown unknowns. How will this war shape future museums and memorials, future theater productions? We can only be sure that the theater will not want to forget.

I leave you with Heiner Müller, a poem first published in 1958 as "Der Vater" (The father) and performed in *Wir sind das Volk.*

> A dead father would have maybe
> been a better father. The best
> is a father born dead.
> New grass is always growing over the border.
> The grass must be ripped up
> again and again that grows over the border.[33]

NOTES

1. For more on these metaphors and myths, and how they were used by politicians, journalists, and historians, see Matt Cornish, *Performing Unification: History and Nation in German Theater after 1989* (Ann Arbor: University of Michigan Press, 2019), 56–61.
2. Cornish, 131.
3. Cornish, 131.
4. See Moaz Azaryahu, "German Reunification and the Politics of Street Names: The Case of East Berlin," *Political Geography* 16, no. 6 (1997): 479–93.
5. Cornish, *Performing Unification,* 131.
6. Cornish, 132.
7. "border, n.," OED Online, March 2022, Oxford University Press, https://www-oed-com.proxy.library.ohio.edu/view/Entry/21617?rskey=YbTQq9&result=1&isAdvanced=false.
8. *Eine zugige Bühne.* Elfriede Müller, *Goldener Oktober,* in *"Die Bergarbeiterinnen" und "Goldener Oktober"* (Frankfurt am Main: Verlag der Autoren, 1992), 82.
9. Cornish, *Performing Unification,* 65.
10. Melissa Eddy, "At Checkpoint Charlie, Cold War History Confronts Crass Commercialism," *New York Times,* February 4, 2019, https://www.nytimes.com/2019/02/04/world/europe/checkpoint-charlie-berlin-cold-war.html.
11. "Ich wachte auf und alles war in Ordnung." Heiner Müller, *Wolokolamsker Chaussee IV: Kentauren,* in *Gesammelte Werke,* Band 5: Die Stücke 3 (Frankfurt am Main: Suhrkamp, 2002), 23.

12. Maya Ayim, "borderless and brazen: a poem against the German 'u-not-y,'" trans. Maya Ayim, *Affilia: Journal of Women and Social Work* 23, no. 1 (February 2008): 92.

13. See, for example, Elaine A. Peña, "Paso Libre: Border Enactment, Infrastructure, and Crisis Resolution at the Port of Laredo 1954–1957," *TDR: The Drama Review* 61, no. 2 (Summer 2017): 11–31.

14. "Wir sind zwei Europa, das eine von Rom, das andere von Byzanz geprägt." Heiner Müller, "Nachricht aus Moskau," *taz.am Wochenende,* February 25, 1989, 19, https://taz.de/Nachricht-aus-Moskau/!1820876/.

15. See also Matt Cornish, "Introduction," in *Everything and Other Performance Texts from Germany,* ed. Matt Cornish (Calcutta: Seagull Books, 2019), viii, xvi–xvii; and Manfred Brauneck, "Preface," in *Independent Theatre in Contemporary Europe: Structures—Aesthetics—Cultural Policy,* ed. Manfred Brauneck, trans. Rhonda Farr, Rachael McGill, and William Wheeler (Bielefeld: Transcript Verlag, 2017), 13–41.

16. Cornish, *Performing Unification,* 5.

17. She She Pop, "Oratorio," June 2017, https://sheshepop.de/en/oratorio/.

18. Heiner Müller, *Hamletmachine,* in *Hamletmachine and Other Texts for the Stage,* ed. and trans. Carl Weber (New York: PAJ Publications, 1984), 53.

19. Cerstin Gammelin, "Bundesinnenministerium übersieht 30 Jahre deutsche Einheit," *Süddeutsche Zeitung,* April 29, 2019, https://www.sueddeutsche.de/politik/seehofer-scholz-deutsche-einheit-1.4426100.

20. Cornish, "Introduction," xxiii.

21. "Im postulierten Geschichtsbild von der kommunistischen Gewaltherrschaft finden sich nur die allerwenigsten Ostdeutschen wieder. Ein Leben aber, das nicht erzählt werden kann, macht Menschen krank." Karsten Krampitz, "DDR neu erzählen," HAU Hebbel am Ufer, March 2019, https://www.hebbel-am-ufer.de/fileadmin/Hau/festivals_projekte/Comrades/hau_comrades_krampitz.pdf.

22. Zionskirche Berlin, accessed May 1, 2022, http://www.grenzfaelle2019.de (website discontinued).

23. Cornish, *Performing Unification,* 145.

24. Cornish, 149.

25. Cornish, 152.

26. *Berlin Global: Berlin Exhibition at the Humboldt Forum Guide,* brochure in possession of author.

27. For more on the controversies surrounding the Humboldt Forum, see Graham Bowley, "A New Museum Opens Old Wounds in Germany," *New York Times,* October 12, 2018, https://www.nytimes.com/2018/10/12/arts/design/humboldt-forum-germany.html. For more on the museum's response, see Elizabeth Grenier and Sarah Hucal, "Humboldt Forum Tackles Colonial Issue with New

Museums," Deutsche Welle, September 22, 2021, https://www.dw.com/en/
humboldt-forum-tackles-colonial-issue-with-new-museums/a-59249590.

28. *Berlin Global.*

29. At the live performance I attended on March 27, 2022, two of the main performers, Milan Fras (of Laibach) and German actress Agnes Mann, were ill
with coronavirus and could not perform; a recording of Laibach's singing was
played and his figure sometimes appeared as a video projection, while Mann's
lines were taken by another actress in the production. Afterward I met with
Quickert so that I could get a better idea of what the production was meant to
look and feel like had Fras and Mann been available.

30. See, e.g., Jonathon Kalb, *The Theater of Heiner Müller* (New York: Limelight
Editions, 2001), 19.

31. "Als Kind hörte ich die Erwachsenen sagen: / In den Konzentrationslagern
wird aus den Juden Seife gemacht. / Seitdem konnte ich mich mit Seife /
Nicht mehr anfreunden und verabscheute Seifengeruch. / Jetz wohne ich,
weil ich den TRISTAN inszenziere / In einer Neubauwohnung in der Stadt
Bayreuth. / . . . Als ich das Fenster aufmache zum erstenmal: Seifengeruch. /
Das Haus der Garten die Stadt Bayreuth riechen nach Seife." Heiner Müller,
"Seife in Bayreuth," in *Gesammelte Werke 1: Die Gedichte* (Frankfurt am Main:
Suhrkamp, 1998), 245.

32. "Zehn Deutsche sind dümmer als fünf Deutsche." Heiner Müller, "Gespräch
mit Uwe Wittstock," in *Gesammelte Irrtümer 3: Texte und Gespräche,* 2nd ed.
(Frankfurt am Main: Verlag der Autoren, 1996), 148.

33. "Ein toter Vater wäre vielleicht / ein besserer Vater gewesen. Am Besten / ist
ein totgeborner Vater. / Immer neu wächst Gras über die Grenze. / Das Gras
muss ausgerissen werden / wieder und wieder das über die Grenze wächst."
Heiner Müller, "Der Vater," in *Gesammelte Werke 1: Die Gedichte* (Frankfurt
am Main: Suhrkamp, 1998), 41.

CONTRIBUTORS

MATT CORNISH is associate professor of theater history and interdisciplinary arts at Ohio University. In 2021–22 he held a Humboldt Research Fellowship for Experienced Researchers, working at the Freie Universität Berlin. He is the author of *Performing Unification: History and Nation in German Theatre after 1989;* coeditor of a recent issue of *TDR* on contemporary performance in Germany (67, no. 2, summer 2023); editor of *Everything and Other Performance Texts from Germany;* and coeditor of *Postdramatic Theatre and Form.* A contributing editor to the journal *PAJ,* his essays have been published in a range of magazines, academic journals, and books.

SETH GIVENS is a historian at the Marine Corps History Division. He received his PhD in military history from Ohio University, where he wrote a dissertation on Berlin's role in US policy and strategy toward Europe throughout the Cold War. He has published an official history on Marine Corps operations in the Vietnam War, *On Our Terms: U.S. Marines in Operation Dewey Canyon, 22 January to 18 March 1969,* and is working on the history of the Marines in Operation Iraqi Freedom.

HOPE M. HARRISON is professor of history and international affairs at The George Washington University. She is an expert on Germany, Russia, the Cold War, the Berlin Wall, and the politics and culture of memory. She is the author of *After the Berlin Wall: Memory and the Making of the New Germany, 1989 to the Present* (Cambridge University Press, 2019) and the prize-winning *Driving the Soviets Up the Wall: Soviet-East German Relations, 1953–1961* (Princeton University Press, 2003) as well as the audiobook *The Berlin Wall: A World Divided* (Audible / Great Courses, 2021).

STEPHAN KIENINGER is a Global Fellow at the Woodrow Wilson Center for Scholars. His forthcoming book is *NATO and Russia at the Crossroads: Strobe Talbott and the Rise of the Post–Cold War Order* (Columbia University Press, 2025). His previous books include *The Diplomacy of Détente: Cooperative Security Policies from Helmut Schmidt to George Shultz* (Routledge, 2018) and *Dynamic Détente: The United States and Europe 1964–1975* (Rowman & Littlefield, 2016).

ERIN MAHAN is chief historian of the Office of the Secretary of Defense and director of the Pentagon Library. She is also the author of *Kennedy, De Gaulle and Western Europe* (Palgrave, 2002) and, most recently, coauthor with Patrick Garrity of *Averting Doomsday: Arms Control during the Nixon Presidency* (University of Virginia Press, 2021).

SAMUEL MINER is a research associate at the Institut für Zeitgeschichte in Munich, where he is working on the project "The Federal Labor Court between Continuity and New Beginning after 1945." His research areas include recent German history and legal and constitutional history, as well as the history of democracy. Miner is currently revising his dissertation into a book manuscript tentatively called "The Exiles' Return: Emigres, Anti-Nazis, and the Basic Law."

SUSANNE MUHLE is a historian at the Berlin Wall Foundation, where she works on museum displays, public education, and historical research. She is the curator of a new memorial site at the former Checkpoint Charlie. Her book *Auftrag: Menschenraub. Entführungen von Westberlinern und Bundesbürgern durch das Ministerium für Staatssicherheit der DDR* (Mission abduction: Kidnappings of West Berliners and West Germans by the GDR's ministry of state security) appeared in 2015.

CHRISTIAN F. OSTERMANN directs the History and Public Policy Program at the Woodrow Wilson Center for Scholars in Washington, DC. The longtime director of the Cold War International History Project (now part of the History and Public Policy Program), Ostermann is the author of *Uprising in East Germany, 1953* (CEU Press, 2001) and, most recently, *Between Containment and Rollback: The United States and the Cold War in Germany* (Stanford University Press, 2021), winner of the prestigious Richard W. Leopold Prize of 2022 from the Organization of American Historiansand the 2022 Harry S. Truman Book Award from the Truman Library Institute.

PETER RIDDER is head of curatorial at the Cold War Museum Berlin. His book *Konkurrenz um Menschenrechte: Der Kalte Krieg und die Entstehung des UN-Menschenrechtsschutzes, 1965–1993* (Competition over human rights: The Cold War and the emergence of UN human rights protections) appeared in 2022, and Ridder is currently working on a book tentatively titled "The Search for a New World Order: US and West German Envisaged Futures at the End of the Cold War, 1988–1992."

THOMAS SCHWARTZ serves as distinguished professor of history, professor of political science, and professor of European studies at Vanderbilt University. His most recent book is *Henry Kissinger and American Power: A Political Biography* (Hill & Wang, 2020). His previous books include *America's Germany: John J. McCloy and the Federal Republic of Germany* (Harvard University Press, 1991) and *Lyndon Johnson and Europe: In the Shadow of Vietnam* (Harvard University Press, 2003).

INGO TRAUSCHWEIZER is a professor of history at Ohio University and served as director of the Contemporary History Institute until summer 2022. His books include *The Cold War U.S. Army: Building Deterrence for Limited War* (University Press of Kansas, 2008) and *Maxwell Taylor's Cold War: From Berlin to Vietnam* (Kentucky University Press, 2019) as well as several edited volumes in the Baker Series in Peace and Conflict Studies.

INDEX

Numbers in *italics* indicate pages with illustrations.

Ford administration and Gerald R. Ford, *137*, 197

Forrestal, James V., 46

France: Algeria war, 7, 120, 124; Berlin crisis response, 114–15, 116, 118–20, 123–28, 130–31nn21–22, 132n41; deterrent effect of forces in West Berlin, 5, 56, 57; division of Germany and Berlin and occupation zone, 21–22, 27–29, 40–41, 142–43; military policy, 124–28; NATO disenchantment, 123–28; NATO strategy and the Franco-German entente, 126–28; nuclear capabilities and strategy, 124–26, 128, 132n41; occupation and rebuilding of Germany, xii; occupation zone maps, *xv, xvi;* Prussian Rhine Province occupation, 18; Quadripartite Agreement role, 8; Rhineland independence, 19; uprising response, 79; US relationship, 7, 114–15, 116, 123–28, *135;* West Berlin defense, 4–5, 39, 118–20

Frankfurt am Main, 24, 41, 42

Frankfurt Documents, 29–30, 37n34

Fras, Milan, 255, 259n29

freedom and democracy: Berlin Wall as symbol to not take for granted, 7–8, 162–63; fighting for, 163

Freiburg, Johanna, *139*

Freie Szene, 248–50, 252

Friedenau, Theo (Horst Erdmann), 72

Fukuyama, Francis, 2, 231

Gauck, Joachim, 155, 168n59

Genscher, Hans-Dietrich, 9, 214, 215–16, 219, 227, 233

German Democratic Republic (GDR). *See* East Germany / German Democratic Republic (GDR)

Germany: acceptance of postwar division, 4, 15–17, 34–35; acknowledgment of past, importance of, xiv; alignment with Western values, alliance, and institutions, 9–10; allied military, xi; division and occupation zone creation, 20–21, 27–29, 142–43; division during WWII, 16; evolution, xi, xiv; healing the divide between East and West, 7–8, 162; history and confronting and learning from negative aspects of past, 141–42; inner-German relations, 9, 191–99, 201–6, 209n38; international security role, 10; learning lessons

from past, xiv; occupation zones map, *xv;* postwar division, 21–22, 27–33; progress in through international support, xi; rapprochement policy and unification, 33–34, 203–6; rearmament, 55; relationship building with US, xi–xiii, 228–34; resentment toward people and country after WWII, xiii; Russian economic ties, 141; Ukrainian support, 141–42; US soldiers in Germany, xi–xii

Global South, 2

Goebbels, Joseph, 20, 255

Goldener Oktober (Golden October, Müller), 243 44

Gorbachev, Mikhail: Bush meeting with, 228–31, 233; "common European home" concept of, 9, 213–17, 228–29; distrust of policies of, 216, 219, 228–29; influence of, 217; Reagan "Tear Down This Wall" speech and, 2; reforms of and Peaceful Revolution, 155, 158, 160, 204

great power competition, 2

Gromyko, Andrei, 120, 131n22, 146–47, 199

Häftlingsfreikauf (prisoners' ransom), 90

Hallstein Doctrine, 173

Halverson, Gail, xiii

Harmel Report, 214–16, 219, 223, 227

Hauptmann, Gerhard, 140, 246

Hauptmanns Weber (*The Weavers,* Castorf adaptation), *140*, 246

Havlicek, Ferdinand, 245–46

Hebbel am Ufer Theater (HAU), 251–52

Helsinki Summit and Helsinki Final Act, 194, 196, 197–98, 215

Hessen, 25, 38n43

highway projects, 192–93, 198

Hildebrandt, Alexandra, 153

Hildebrandt, Rainer, 71, 72

Hin und her (Here and there, von Horvath), 245–46

history: end of, 2; relevance of guidance from, 1, 2, 10–11

Hitler, Adolf, 20, 255

Hochhuth, Rolf, 241, 254

Hoffmann von Fallersleben, August Heinrich, 242–43

Höher, Wolfgang Paul, 98, 106n32

Holocaust and Holocaust Memorial, 21, 141, 153–54, 156, 157–58, 162–63

Honecker, Erich, 149, 151, 152, 195, 196, 198–99, 200–202, 203–4, 205, 209n38, 229